# SAN FERNANDO, REY DE ESPAÑA

Statue of Padre Junípero Serra and the Indian boy, Juan Evangelista,
in Brand Park, 1978. Sculpture by Sallie James Farnham of New York. *KEP.*

# SAN FERNANDO, REY DE ESPAÑA

## An Illustrated History

By
Kenneth E. Pauley and Carol M. Pauley

Foreword by
Doyce B. Nunis, Jr.

THE ARTHUR H. CLARK COMPANY
Spokane, Washington
2005

ISBN 0-87062-338-9

THE ARTHUR H. CLARK COMPANY
P.O. Box 14707
Spokane, Washington 99214

ON THE TITLE PAGE: The logo of Mission San Fernando, engraved by Anthony Kroll (see Abbreviations). In the mid-1970s Msgr. Francis J. Weber modified the original design, which had previously been used for a 1920s fundraiser for the mission. Artistic license in the current version is apparent, as the sun is shown rising from the north, behind the convento. The logo is used for the mission's letterhead, invitations, book covers, etc. *AK/ACSFM.*

Library of Congress Cataloging-in-Publication Data
Pauley, Kenneth E.
  San Fernando, Rey de España : an illustrated history / by Kenneth E. Pauley and Carol M. Pauley ; foreword by Doyce B. Nunis, Jr.
    p. cm.
  Includes bibliographical references and index.
  ISBN 0-87062-338-9 (hardcover : alk. paper)
  1. San Fernando, Rey de España (Mission : San Fernando, Calif.)—History. 2. San Fernando, Rey de España (Mission : San Fernando, Calif.)—History—Pictorial works. I. Pauley, Carol M. II. Title.
  F869.S26P38 2005
  979.4'93—dc22
                                                    2004025377

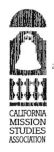

Grants from
the CALIFORNIA MISSION STUDIES ASSOCIATION
and the SAN FERNANDO VALLEY HISTORICAL SOCIETY
in supporting the publication of
*San Fernando, Rey de España: An Illustrated History*
are gratefully acknowledged.

# CONTENTS

# DEDICATION

(*top, left*) Marie Toma Walsh ("The Mission Bells of California") and John Stephen McGroarty ("Mission Play") stand atop the *bóreda cilindrica* (barrel vault) over the sacristy and behind the famous *campanil* at Mission San Gabriel, on September 8, 1931—the 160th anniversary of Mission San Gabriel's founding and the 134th anniversary of Mission San Fernando. *ACSFM.*

(*bottom, left*) Marie Harrington (née Walsh), dressed in Las Damas attire, at a party with her husband, Mark, in 1963. *SFVHS.*

(*top, right*) Norman Neuerburg, age twenty-eight, in 1955, poses in the temporary Mission San Fernando chapel, which is adorned with a portion of the Ezcaray Collection. The chapel was in the large room farthest east on the first floor of the convento. *KEP.*

(*bottom, right*) Dr. Norman Neuerburg on July 13, 1988, at Taix's Restaurant, Los Angeles, California, after he spoke to the Los Angeles Corral of the Western-ers on the subject of Mission San Borja in Baja California. *FQN.*

# FOREWORD

IN 1997 Mission San Fernando, Rey de España, celebrated the bicentennial of its founding on September 8, 1797, by Fr. Fermín Francisco de Lasuén, second president of the Franciscan missions in *Alta California*. To honor this special occasion, a program was presented in the mission church by a group of invited scholars to commemorate that historic event. Papers were subsequently published as a special issue of the *Southern California Quarterly*, the publication of the Historical Society of Southern California, a journal for which I have served as editor since 1962. I had the pleasure of participating in the program, which was included in the publication. At the time, it was hoped that Dr. Kenneth E. (Ken) Pauley would offer a visual presentation, but time and circumstance deterred that prospect. Now it is an added pleasure to comment on the importance and significance of Ken's finished work as reflected in the pages that follow.

First, the reader should know that Ken has spent almost two and one-half decades in the preparation of this volume. He has cast his net wide in locating and identifying appropriate photographs and artistic images for inclusion herein. To that end he had the assistance of Rev. Msgr. Francis J. Weber, director of the mission and archivist/historian for the Archdiocese of Los Angeles, as well as the invaluable input of a mutual friend, the late Dr. Norman Neuerburg, historian of the California missions, with his particular attention to the photographic and art records of the state's missions.

Not long after Ken launched his project, he was joined by his wife, Carol, as author. Between them they have labored to perfect the manuscript. That end has been achieved in this, the finished product of untold hours of dedicated research and textual refinement. Their joint efforts have provided greater accuracy and scholarly enhancement to what can only be heralded as a joint labor of historical love.

Second, this is the first attempt at an all-inclusive illustrated history of Mission San Fernando in Alta California, comparable to the one undertaken some years back by Rev. Maynard J. Geiger, O.F.M., for Mission Santa Barbara. In their endeavor to produce a definitive visual mission history, the Pauleys have left, figuratively speaking, no photo collection unfurrowed. The end result is a comprehensive and fascinating graphic testament of the mission as caught by the camera in decades past as well as the present. Since there is hardly any visual record of the mission prior to the advent of photography, with the exception of a few sketches and lithographs, the visual historical legacy embraces only the last 150 years.

The mission's history is vividly captured in the surviving images, but its past has not always been pretty. In the wake of secularization, 1835–37, San Fernando gradually fell into dreadful decay and disrepair through human negligence. However, at the end of the nineteenth century, the revival of the public's interest in restoring the historical patrimony of the Golden State was spearheaded by the California Landmarks Commission (CLC), a task now enhanced by the recently established California Missions Foundation (CMF)—but with one major exception. The CLC served as a catalytic agent that stimulated private individuals and groups to undertake the restoration of the ruined Franciscan missions. The CMF, on the other hand, is a non-profit corporation whose aim and function is to raise funds to assist the present-day missions with grants for specific restoration projects and/or special maintenance needs.

Mission San Fernando's restoration has been graphically captured in a myriad of photographs, paintings, sketches, lithographs, maps, and architectural drawings. The process itself was long and arduous, but the assiduous efforts of Dr. Mark R. Harrington should not go unnoted in that effort. Once accomplished by the 1950s, nature dealt the establishment two devastating blows. The 1971 Sylmar earthquake destroyed the mission church, requiring its demolition and complete reconstruction, happily an accurate replica of the original. The 1994 Northridge earthquake caused considerable damage to a number of the buildings, though the church came through in good condition. This time the most serious damage was inflicted on the adobe *convento* building, i.e., convent or monastery, the first two-story structure to be built in California. Indeed, it was the original intent of the building and safe-

ty inspectors to red tag the building for demolition. Had it not been for Msgr. Weber, such would have been the end result, but he tenaciously sought to have the structure *yellow-tagged*—which meant it would be preserved through retrofitting and restoration, a project realized by federal grant support from the Federal Emergency Management Agency (FEMA). These two modern-day episodes in the life of the mission, in addition to the long, slow decay from mission times, are also chronicled in the pages that follow.

Today, the mission flourishes. A number of its original buildings are faithfully restored; the grounds are well maintained, and the public, especially groups of school children, are regular visitors—visits made more meaningful by the handsome museum displays and signage as well as the availability of knowledgeable volunteer docents. Thus the mission's history is preserved and at the same time shared. This illustrated volume will only enhance both of these present-day functions, which together give a living presence to Mission San Fernando in this, the twenty-first century.

DOYCE B. NUNIS, JR.
Distinguished Professor Emeritus
of History
University of Southern California
January 24, 2004

# ACKNOWLEDGMENTS

THE MAKING OF *An Illustrated History* has been a labor of love for the past twenty-seven years. During the long journey of collecting images and researching materials for this book, we have been extremely fortunate to have met individuals whose interests centered on history but encompassed photography, art, anthropology, archaeology, and ethnology. Some of them, with whom we had a mere acquaintance in the early days, have become our dear friends over the years. Our book has substantially improved from its initial writing because of their suggestions and advice.

As our collection activities began in the 1970s, some of the individuals we met back then are now deceased and others have since retired. We would like, however, to acknowledge them and the institutions they represented (although some no longer exist as they have merged or been acquired by other institutions) along with those who have assisted us more recently. We are grateful to all of these for sharing their expertise and providing access to their photographic and research archives.

We are pleased to have the Arthur H. Clark Company of Spokane, Washington, as our publisher and grateful that Robert A. Clark, President, was willing to publish our book, replete with illustrations. We are honored to have such a venerable publisher and appreciate the professional assistance of Ariane C. Smith, whose expert text editing and design and layout have greatly enhanced the materials we provided.

Robert Senkewicz and Rose Marie Beebe supported our work by sharing their knowledge with us, providing timely and critical advice to improve our text. They were instrumental in this book's seeing the light of day. As boosters they helped us obtain a grant from the California Mission Studies Association. Also, a grant from the San Fernando Valley Historical Society, obtained through the efforts of James B. Gulbranson, President, and Dr. Richard Doyle, helped support publication.

❁     ❁     ❁

For photographs, images and museum library materials we are grateful to: Susan Snyder, University of California, Berkeley; John Cahoon and William Mason, Seaver Center for Western History Research at the Natural History Museum of Los Angeles County; Jennifer Watts, The Huntington Library; Simon Elliott, Special Collections Research Library, University of California at Los Angeles; Carl S. Dentzel and Ron Kinsey, the Southwest Museum; Kim Walters and Marilyn Kim, Braun Research Library at the Autry National Center/Southwest Museum; Dolorez Nariman, the erstwhile Title Insurance & Trust Company Research Collection; Dace Taube, who oversees the TICOR Collection (now residing at the regional California Historical Society), Doheny Memorial Library at the University of Southern California; Victor Plukas, Security Pacific National Bank Photographic Collection; and

Carolyn Cole, Los Angeles Public Library, which now houses the SPNBC Collection.

We express our thanks to the late Larry Booth, who worked at the Photographic Department of the San Diego Historical Society. At the beginning of our collecting, he generously shared his technical expertise with us on the reproduction and care of rare photographs and documents.

Msgr. Francis J. Weber, Archivist and Director of the Archival Center, allowed the authors to explore, make measurements, and photograph the premises freely. He generously allowed us free rein to select photographs from the Archival Center on numerous occasions. We thank Glenn Farris for his critical reading and suggestions for correcting measurements. We would like to give recognition to the artists who provided original artwork commissioned for this book: Troy Greenwood for graphics and architectural drawings; Russell Ruiz for an oil painting and sketches; Andrew Dagosta for a watercolor painting; and Jim Valtos for pen and ink sketches. Our thanks go to Edan Milton Hughes, who provided a source for biographies of Western artists and photographers, in his *Artists in California 1786–1940.*

Many experts in their specialties have critiqued our text, suggested improvements and steered us in the right direction: Iris H.W. Engstrand, University of San Diego; John R. Johnson, Santa Barbara Museum of Natural History; Gary Kurutz, California State Library; James A. Sandos, Redlands University; friends William Gram, Ph.D., and his wife, Dorothy; John O. Pohlmann, California Polytechnic State University, Pomona; and R. David Weber and Patrick Carey, Los Angeles Harbor College. David Whitley, archaeologist at Cal State Fullerton, and Carol Rock, Santa Clarita Valley Historical Society, reviewed and provided information on *Rancho San Francisco de Xavier.*

To all these individuals, and especially to JoAnn Adams, whose "Lucky Star" inspired us to hold on to our dream, we express our deep appreciation.

# INTRODUCTION

ON THE FRONTIER of Nueva España, the Spanish military and missionaries frequently named places and institutions in honor of patrons and saints. At least three major institutions in this vast region were named for Saint Ferdinand III (A.D. 1198–1252), king of Castile and Leon, who was canonized by Pope Clement X in 1671 for his role in defeating the Moors (Muslims) in southern Spain.

One of these was the Colegio de San Fernando, a missionary establishment built in Mexico City in 1734. It was the daughter college of Santa Cruz de Querétaro, founded in 1683 for the purpose of training missionaries to convert Indians to Christianity, during the time when colonization was spreading outward from the heart of Mexico.

On the overland party of the expedition, or *entrada*, into Alta California in 1769, Don Gaspár de Portolá, captain of the Spanish Army dragoons, and Fray Junípero Serra, O.F.M., the newly appointed *presidente* of the Baja and Alta California missions, traveled on horseback ahead of the cavalcade, with one soldier and two servants. They arrived by nightfall on May 13, 1769, at a northern Baja California site, called Vellikata by the indigenous peoples, that Jesuit priest Wenceslao Linck had discovered three years earlier. The location, not far from today's El Progreso, was renamed Vellacata and finally Velicatá, in deference to Spanish speakers. From 1768 to 1769, Fernando de Rivera y Moncada, veteran Loreto Presidio captain, developed a base of operations there for the two exploration parties passing through on their way to San Diego. On May 14, Serra founded the only Franciscan mission establishment in Baja California, San Fernando de Velicatá, again in honor of King Ferdinand III.

A third establishment bearing Saint Ferdinand's name was the seventeenth mission in the Alta California chain. On September 8, 1797, Fray Fermín Francisco de Lasuén, the second *presidente* of the Alta California missions after Serra, christened it La Misión de San Fernando, Rey de España, the name which New Spain's viceroy, the Marqués de Branciforte, gave it nearly a year earlier. Fray Juan Crespí, one of two missionaries on the expedition of 1769, while establishing a Spanish presence in Alta California, named the broad expanse on which the mission was to be established El Valle de Santa Catalina de Bonónia. The name "de los Encinos" was added later by Francisco Palóu in his version of Crespí's diary in *Noticias de la Nueva California*. It was known under Spanish and Mexican rule as the Valley of the Live Oaks, or Encino Valley, but is known today as the San Fernando Valley.

During the past two centuries, many documents related to Mission San Fernando have been generated: manuscripts and correspondence of the early missionaries; governmental and military documents from Spain and Mexico; Church records of baptisms, marriages, and deaths; journals by adventurers and travelers; newspaper articles; and printed books. We are fortunate that many of these historical documents are extant and have been well preserved.

Images of the mission are also an important part

of its historical record as well. Artists have left us their interpretations in traditional media. Tinted sketches in ink and pencil, lithographs, etchings, and paintings in watercolor and oil were created by famous nineteenth- and early twentieth-century artists such as William P. Blake, Charles P. Koppel, Edward Vischer, Henry Miller, Henry Chapman Ford, Edwin Deakin, Henry ("Harry") Fenn, William Adam, and, in more recent times, Ben Abril and Andrew Dagosta.

The invention of the camera, the development of new photographic processes, and advances in technology over the past 165 years have allowed photographers not only to record but also to interpret people, places, and events through their lens, in ways in which the camera's inventor could not have imagined. Photographers have shown us their world at specific instances in time, allowing us glimpses into a past for which, in many cases, we have no other record. Undoubtedly, photographs have a historical significance but have also gained recognition and are appreciated today for their artistic qualities.

The recording of images, other than through sketches and paintings, began with Louis Jacques Daguerre's invention in 1839. His process involved first coating a copper plate with silver and buffing it to a high polish. Next, iodine was fumed to the mirror-bright surface upon which the silver and iodine combined to form a film of light-sensitive silver iodide. After a long exposure period, a fixer was used to lay bare the non-image portion of the metallic plate. This work was messy and required a great deal of preparation time and materials. A major drawback of the process was that only one image could be produced at a time. Calotypes, ambrotypes, and the wet colloidal negative process, developed in 1851 by Frederick Scott Archer, significantly advanced photography.

James May Ford (1827–77) used the daguerreotype medium to produce the earliest known photographic images of the Alta California missions of San José and Santa Clara. He made the first ambrotypes in California. Carleton E. Watkins was his employee until Watkins started his own studio.

Calotypes, invented almost simultaneously with the daguerreotype, were the earliest paper negatives and are rare today. Many prints could now be made from a single negative, as opposed to a single image with the daguerreotype.

Early photographs of Mission San Fernando in the 1860s through the 1880s were taken by Henry T. Payne, Stephen A. Rendall, Isaiah W. Taber, and William M. Godfrey, all of whom used both the daguerreotype and collodion processes. Unfortunately, no known daguerreotypes of Mission San Fernando exist, as far as the authors can determine. These photographers prepared their albumen prints from collodion negatives, pasted the prints onto cardboard, and marketed them as flat-card mailers (*cartes de visite*) and stereographs. Carleton E. Watkins and Francis Parker also made albumen prints from wet plate collodion negatives. In the 1890s, photographers George Wharton James, Charles B. Waite, William H. Fletcher, Frederick Hamer Maude, Adam Clark Vroman, and Hervé Friend used glass plates whose surfaces were pre-coated with a gelatin emulsion, an innovation that allowed a photographer to skip the arduous process of coating the plate with an emulsion before each exposure.

From the 1870s onward many photographic shops and galleries merged and bought out other photographic businesses. The photographers sold and swapped their collections and renumbered and renamed images, thus clouding the connection of the original photographer to his product and sometimes the link is almost impossible to determine. In the financial panic of the mid-1870s, Carleton E. Watkins lost control of his collection to Isaiah W. Taber. Later, Frank B. Rodolph, an associate of Taber, acquired many of Taber's images and included them in his Rodolph Collection, now housed at the University of California, Berkeley, Library.

From the 1890s to early 1900s mission photographer Charles C. Pierce, the partner of mission photographer James B. Blanchard, took charge of the George Wharton James Collection of Indian images, and Frederick H. Maude bought out the Charles B. Waite photography business in 1895.

One of Mission San Fernando's most important photographers was Charles Fletcher Lummis. He was the mission's champion for restoration, its premier booster, and the founder of the California Landmarks Commission (CLC), also known as the Club, for short. Lummis used an Anthony Patent Duplex Novelette $8 \times 10/5 \times 8$ camera with extra bellows track and J. H. Dallmeyer rapid rectilinear lens. Under the weight of this equipment, plus glass plates and processing materials—all weighing about forty pounds—he captured images of the mission in ruins and disrepair and brought to the public's attention the need for mission restoration and continued preservation. He produced before and after photographs for the mission's centennial celebration on Thursday, September 9, 1897 (one day and one century after the founding date), in order to show CLC members and the public the progress of work and the need for further restoration.

Photographers after the first mission restoration by the CLC were innumerable. Charles C. Pierce, William M. Graham, Warren C. Dickerson, Frank Park, Hugh Pascal Webb, George Brookwell, and Wayne C. "Dick" Whittington were just a few of those who produced exceptional historic images from 1899 through the 1930s.

This book is primarily visual, with images from many artistic media. The images collected by the authors over the past twenty-five-plus years are so numerous and extraordinary that choosing among them was a daunting task. While our aim has been to bring to light unique, distinctive, previously not seen or seldom-seen photographs and art, some familiar works, which are considered vintage, have been included.

The textual history is intended to be complementary to the imagery. Our aim was to be objective and unbiased on some of the disputatious matters regarding the conquest and colonization of Alta California and the treatment of the indigenous inhabitants. On some of these matters the records are quite clear, but we make neither a pro-mission nor anti-mission stand, leaving judgment to you, the reader, and to history.

EXPLANATORY NOTES

Abbreviations used in the captions, notes, and bibliography indicate the institutions and individuals who provided photographs, artwork, and other source material used in *An Illustrated History*. Abbreviations indicate the artists and photographers, and, when information is known, a short biographical sketch is provided in the Abbreviations section at the end of the book. Abbreviations in the captions cross-reference the image of an artist or photographer with the source. Numbers after the biographical sketches and sources are pages on which the images appear for that abbreviation. The words "Courtesy of" are implied in the captions, except in special cases where the source requires credit in a specific format.

Spanish words in the text that are not found in the English *Webster's Third International Dictionary* will be italicized on their first occurrence. Translations are shown in parentheses. (Exceptions are in the Chronology of Events and in instances where the text elucidates the meaning.) Subsequent appearances of these words are neither italicized nor shown with their equivalents.

READER'S NOTE: Fr. is the abbreviation for Franciscan Fray and is synonymous with Padres of the Franciscan Order. The titles for Father, a priest of the regular clergy; Reverend, a title of respect for clergy; and Marqués, a nobleman by birth in Europe, will all be spelled out. Reverend and Marqués will be preceded by the word "the." Use the Abbreviations section when necessary.

The Farnham statue of Father Junípero Serra and the Indian boy, Evangelista, in Brand Park, with the convento in the background, ca. 1945. *CHS/TICOR* (7417).

# CHRONOLOGY OF EVENTS
# IN THE SAN FERNANDO VALLEY

1769   Don Gaspar de Portolá and members of the Spanish Expedition on their trek from San Diego to Monterey discover the San Fernando Valley on August 5.

1797   December 8—Founding and dedication of Mission San Fernando, Rey de España.

1800   Mission wells are dug and filter basin is built.

1804   A building for the mission ranch, Estancia de San Francisco Xavier, is located atop a flat mesa near today's Castaic Junction in the Santa Clara River region.

1806   Building of third church for Mission San Fernando is completed.

Fray Múñoz stops at the San Francisco estancia in October, on the Moraga-Múñoz Expedition of the San Joaquin Valley.

1808   Dam and aqueduct are completed.

1810   Convento, or Long Building, construction begins as reported in Annual Report by Friars Múñoz and Urrestí.

1811   First reservoir and near-circular (sixteen-sided) fountain are built.

1812   Corridor leading from church to east end of convento is added.

Earthquake causes damage to church, requiring the addition of thirty new beams (columns) to support walls.

1813   Nineteen arches (twenty-one including ends) of the convento are completed.

The second fountain (Cordova or Rosette fountain) is built approximately seven hundred feet south of the convento.

1817–18   *Jabonería* is built with two boilers in front of convento.

1819–20   Convento is repaired and remodeled, with second story added.

1820   Second story of convento is raised and roofed.

1822   Workshops are built adjacent to the convento and construction of Mission San Fernando is completed. Fray Francisco González de Ibarra conducts first service in the chapel.

1834–35   Lt. Antonio del Valle is appointed commissioner to secularize the mission.

On May 29, 1835, del Valle becomes the mission's first *mayordomo*, succeeded by Anastasio Carrillo on January 3, 1837.

1842   Gold is discovered by Francisco López in Placerita Canyon, situated on Rancho San Francisco (Francisquito) near mission lands.

1843    Petitions for land grants to Indians of San Fernando Valley are granted by Gov. Manuel Micheltorena.

1845    Gov. Pío Pico leases mission to his brother, Andrés Pico, and Juan Manso for nine years.

1845    Californio-Mexican battle at Cahuenga Pass for Californio "independence" concludes February 20. Micheltorena expelled from California February 22.

1846    Sale of mission lands by Gov. Pío Pico to the Spaniard Eulógio de Célis takes place on June 17. Nine-year lease to Andrés Pico is honored at the time that the land of Ex-Mission Rancho and most of the valley are deeded to de Célis.

   Bear Flag Republic proclaimed in Sonoma and the U.S.-Mexican War begins.

1847    Lt. Col. John Charles Frémont and his battalion enter the Valley of the Live Oaks through the San Fernando Pass, which is renamed after him. American-Mexican war is averted and Gen. Andrés Pico capitulates, signing the Treaty of Cahuenga, which terminates hostilities on January 13.

   Edwin Bryant accompanies Lieutenant Frémont and his troops, visits the mission, and describes it in *What I Saw in California*.

1850    California is officially admitted to the Union.

1851    U.S. Board of Land Commissioners confirms sale of the valley to Eulógio de Célis and also confirms sale of other portions of his ranch properties to individuals.

1852–97  General neglect causes mission to fall into ruin.

1853–54  Lt. Robert Stockton Williamson conducts railroad survey for the U.S. government. The artist on the survey, William Blake, creates a tinted lithograph of the San Fernando Valley and the mission.

   After lease expires, Andrés Pico buys undivided half-interest in Ex-Mission San Fernando lands for $15,000.

   Bishop Joseph Sadoc Alemany files lawsuit to recover mission property that includes church, residence, cemetery, vineyards, and orchards. No resident priests are at the mission from 1853 to 1902. Occasionally, priests from the Plaza Church, Nuestra Señora la Reina de Los Angeles, come out to the mission and officiate.

1856–57  Henry Miller visits the mission and sketches and writes about it.

1857–61  Butterfield Overland Mail Stage uses three rooms in the west end of the convento as a station.

1862    On May 31, President Abraham Lincoln signs the proclamation returning approximately 177 acres and mission buildings to the Church.

1865    Edward Vischer makes two pencil colored sketches (from memory) of the mission and Andrés Pico's family.

1871    Southern half of the valley is sold to San Fernando Farm Homestead Association. Two thousand acres are retained by Andrés Pico as Pico Reserve. I. N. Van Nuys and Isaac Lankershim begin raising sheep.

   Drought kills forty thousand sheep. Van Nuys and Lankershim begin planting wheat and export it to Europe.

1871    Journalist Benjamin Truman describes

Live oak tree in Placerita Canyon under which Francisco Lopez discovered gold in 1842. *KEP.*

the church exterior as "hoary with time and decay."

1874–75 Services are moved from the church to a small chapel in the east room of the convento.

De Célis's son, Eulógio F., sells Ex-Mission Rancho (the northern half of the valley, containing 56,000 acres) to former state senators Charles Maclay and G. K. Porter. Maclay begins subdividing his land interests.

City of San Fernando tract map is filed with Los Angeles County Records.

Henry L. Oak visits the mission and sketches a plan map of the mission complex on March 5, 1874.

1878–99 Edwin Deakin produces three paintings of mission San Fernando: two oils and one watercolor.

A large part of the valley becomes grain fields. Los Angeles Farm and Milling Company (LAFMC) purchases southern part of valley from the Los Angeles Suburban Homes Company. LAFMC exports more than fifty thousand bushels of wheat, oats, and barley.

1881 Writer Helen Hunt Jackson of *Ramona* fame visits the mission.

Porter Land and Water Company is formed. Extensive irrigation program proceeds despite community objections because of growth of land subdivisions.

1882    Carleton E. Watkins photographs four views of the mission.

1883    First valley newspaper, *The San Fernando Comet*, is founded. Henry Chapman Ford visits, paints, and sketches mission and describes use of the convento by the Porter Land and Water Company.

1890    Adam Clark Vroman photographs the mission.

1895–97    Charles F. Lummis spearheads the California Landmarks Club (CLC) and begins campaign to restore the mission.

1897    From June to September protective roofs are placed on the church and convento by the CLC. Lummis takes photographs of buildings pre- and post-restoration and of crowd in front of convento at mission centennial celebration on Thursday, September 9.

1904    Leslie C. Brand forms the San Fernando Land Company.

C. C. Pierce photographs the mission. Southern Pacific Railroad tunnel is blasted through Santa Susana Mountains.

1909–10    El Camino Real bell designed by Mrs. A. S. C. Forbes is placed in front of the convento. Towns of Marian (Reseda) and Zelzah (Northridge) are laid out by the L.A. Suburban Homes Company.

1911    Cities of San Fernando and Burbank are incorporated and the city of Van Nuys is founded.

1912    Archbishop of Oaxaca Eulógio Gillow y Zavalza raises funds to restore some rooms in the convento, which he proposes to use as an agricultural training school for boys and men.

These palms and olive trees were planted south of the convento by the Franciscan friars. Adobe ruins behind the central palm were those of a long structure that housed the tannery, olive storeroom, and soap factory. Charles C. Pierce, ca. 1895. *CCP/CHS/TICOR (176) & SWM-P19077.*

Beneath the shadow of the convento. Charles C. Pierce, ca. 1883, took this photograph of the west wing of the quadrangle, with Porter Land and Water Company farm equipment in front. *CCP/CHS/TICOR* (8997).

| | |
|---|---|
| 1916 | On August 6, Candle Day celebration raises $6,000 from donations of $1 per candle. Proceeds are used to repair roof and strengthen walls of the church. At the top of Zelzah Avenue, the valley's first oil well is sunk. |
| 1920 | Brand donates strip of land in front of the mission to Los Angeles, which becomes Brand Park (also known as Memory Garden). |
| 1922 | Brand has Rosette fountain moved five hundred feet closer to the convento at the west end of Brand Park. |
| 1923 | Priests of the Oblates of Mary Immaculate administer mission until 1953. |
| 1924 | Sallie James Farnham statue of Fray Junípero Serra and Indian boy, Juan Evangelista, is dedicated in Brand Park. |
| 1937 | The second Candle Day fundraiser takes place at the mission to obtain more funding for restoration. |
| 1938 | Three-year restoration plan begins under supervision of Father Charles Burns, O.M.I., and Dr. Mark R. Harrington, consultant on the project. |
| 1940 | Sepulveda Dam is built. |
| 1941 | Restored third church is rededicated on September 8. |
| 1945–46 | Church bell tower is rebuilt after WWII and dedicated by Right Rev. Martin Cody Keating on April 28. "The Three-year Plan" takes eight years to execute, due to interruption by WWII. |
| 1949–50 | Reconstruction of the west wing and the shops and quarters of the south wing is funded partially through the |

Fray Junípero Serra & Old Well. Mission San Fernando—434.
Brookwell photo. *Made by Los Angeles Post Card Co. KEP.*

William Randolph Hearst Foundation. Arthur Ballin is the supervisor. Jasper Schad takes many photographs during restoration. In 1949 the California Historical Landmarks Advisory Committee designated Mission San Fernando, Rey de España, as California Historical Site No. 157.

1952    "Big Red Cars" of the Pacific Electric discontinue operation in the San Fernando Valley.

1956    Valley campus of Los Angeles State College (now California State University, Northridge) is founded.

1963    New roof tiles are placed on the convento and restoration work is performed.

1964    On January 1, the section of the 405 Freeway through the San Fernando Valley opens.

1971    On February 9, Sylmar earthquake breaks bond-beam of the church roof. Church is razed and accurate facsimile is built *in situ.*

1974    On November 4, Cardinal Timothy Manning dedicates the convento and reconstructed fourth church. Belgian carillon bells are placed in the tower.

1981    On September 13, Cardinal Manning dedicates the new Archival Center, built in the west garden of the mission.

1982    Simi Valley Freeway is completed.

1986    New Serra Chapel, located in south wing of the quadrangle, is dedicated by Cardinal Manning on March 2.

1987    Pope John Paul II visits mission on September 16 and is presented with Ben Abril's oil painting depicting the Farnham statue in Brand Park in front of the convento.

1991    Ezcaray collection is sent to Mission San Carlos (Carmel) de Borromeo for cleaning. It is returned to San Fernando and assembled in the church by Richard Menn (protégé of Sir Harry Downie of the Carmel Mission).

1994    On January 17, Northridge earthquake severely damages convento and other buildings.

1996–97  Convento is restored by the California Water Proofing and Restoration Company: O'Leary & Teresawa Architect Consultants. Repairs are funded by a federal grant support from FEMA.

Facsimile guard's or corporal bell tower is placed in original spot atop the west end of the convento.

1997    *Bicentennial Salute, 1797–1997—A Symposium* is held in church on Saturday, September 6 (two days shy of the official founding bicentennial date). Larry Underhill photographs crowd in front of convento.

2001    Belgian Carillon Bell collection is removed from tower on February 8, sent to Philadelphia for cleaning and tuning, then returned to Los Angeles for installation in the new Cathedral of Our Lady of the Angels. An electronic Schulmerich digital auto-bell carillon is installed in the bell tower, along with the original 1809 bell and two Ezcaray bells.

# PART I

# THE EARLY YEARS

Ink sketch made by Russell Ruiz in 1978 of the Indian ranchería "Mispu" near Goleta, California
(near girls' dormitory at the University of California, Santa Barbara, today). The view shows circular *jacales* made of tule,
not unlike those found by the Spaniards when they first entered the Encino Valley in 1769. *RR/KEP.*

## CHAPTER I
# EARLY INHABITANTS

*Only recently have ethnohistoric sources become available that allow us to reconstruct the complex Native American history of Mission San Fernando.*
—John R. Johnson, "The Indians of Mission San Fernando"

THOUSANDS OF YEARS before the Spaniards set foot on California soil, the inhabitants of the San Fernando Valley lived the simple, peaceful life of hunters and gatherers in clustered villages. The early inhabitants have been traced to their Shoshonean roots through their Takic languages. They were members of a larger family, the Uto-Aztecans, a group of linguistically allied tribes whose wide territory extended from Idaho and Montana in North America to Panama in Central America.[1]

The Shoshonean people who migrated to southern California came to occupy a large area, a triangular expanse of land which included virtually everything between a 600-mile-long span along today's California–Nevada border and a 100-mile-long strip of southern California shoreline. In their movement west, they did not stop at the ocean but crossed the channel to the islands of San Nicolas, Santa Catalina, and San Clemente.

By A.D. 1200 tribes had already formed and taken on their distinct and separate linguistic, social, political, and religious identities. Ethnohistorians relate that life was occasionally disrupted with internecine disputes and skirmishes among tribes of different linguistic identities. They settled in and around the San Fernando Valley, a vast area about 8 miles wide by 21 miles long, bounded by the San Gabriel and Santa Susana mountains on the north and northwest, the Simi Hills on the west, the Santa Monica Mountains on the south, and the Verdugo Mountains on the east. The valley is a region with rich soil that rises slowly from an altitude of 500 feet above sea level in the southeast, at the entrance to the San Gabriel Valley, to 1,000 feet above sea level in the northwest at the foot of the Santa Susana Mountains. It has a moderate climate known as Mediterranean dry-summer or, as it is more commonly known, sub-tropical.[2]

Classification of California Indians into branches, divisions, and groups is based on their speech patterns. In the southern California region there were three language families (Takic, Chumash, and Yuman).[3] One Takic linguistic division, Gabrielino,

---

[1]   Alfred L. Kroeber, *Handbook of the Indians of California*, Smithsonian Institute Bureau of American Ethnology Bulletin 78 (Washington, D.C., 1925), 575.

[2]   William McCawley, *The First Angelinos: The Gabrielino Indians of Los Angeles* (Banning, Calif.: Malki Museum Press/Ballena Press, 1996), 35.

[3]   Kroeber, *Handbook of the Indians*, 577. A discrepancy exists between Kroeber's and later ethnographers' linguistic names for groups surrounding the mission. See Johnson, "The Indians of Mission San Fernando," 250. An *(continued)*

Archaeological site near Mission San Fernando during 1938–1945 excavations. *SWM.*

was further divided into three dialects: Gabrielino proper, Fernandeño, and Island Gabrielino. After Mission San Fernando was founded, the padres called the natives nearby San Fernandeños, or simply Fernandeños.

In this area, there were four groups of natives who would later be attached to Mission San Fernando. Three groups—the Fernandeños, the Tataviam, and the Vanyume—spoke Takic languages. The fourth group, the Ventureño, who resided in the nearby Simi Valley and the Santa Monica Mountains, were speakers of a Chumash language, unrelated to the Uto-Aztecan group.[4]

———

extensive database of mission register information assembled by many collaborators allowed Johnson to connect individuals to their relatives and cross-reference them by marriages and burials.

4   John R. Johnson, "The Indians of Mission San Fernando," *Southern California Quarterly* 79, 3 (1997): 252–53. From mission records at the time of mission founding and up to 1814, there were three major Takic-speaking groups at

Around the mission, and mostly in the valley, there were at least 130 *rancherías* (Indian settlements) at the time of the mission's founding.[5] The Fernandeños had complex commercial and social interactions

———

Mission San Fernando: the Gabrielino/Tongva, known as Fernandeños after mission founding, were 40 percent; Tataviam, 25 percent; and Vanyume, 9 percent of the total Indian population. Members of one non-Takic speaking group, the Ventureño/Chumash, who lived in the Simi Valley and Santa Monica Mountains region, were 24 percent.

5   Johnson, "The Indians of Mission San Fernando," 254. Johnson establishes this number from C. Hart Merriam, "Village Names in Twelve California Mission Records," in *University of California Archaeological Survey* Report 74 (Berkeley, Calif.: 1968): 93–102. A significantly higher number of 194 rancherías "supplying converts in the district [San Fernando]" were reported by Fray Zephyrin Engelhardt, O.F.M., *San Fernando Rey—The Mission of the Valley* (Chicago: Franciscan Herald Press, 1927), 142–43. However, seven of these rancherías were also supplying converts to Mission San Gabriel. See Fr. Zephyrin Engelhardt, O.F.M., *San Gabriel Mission—and the Beginnings of Los Angeles* (Chicago: Franciscan Herald Press, 1927), 356; McCawley, *The First Angelinos*, 35.

within their own tribe and with neighboring tribes. They traded with the coastal Chumash for fresh fish and shell bead money and with the Gabrielinos for steatite (soapstone) bowls brought from Santa Catalina Island. They also traded arrowheads and dart points made from chert or other suitable materials such as obsidian with Indians from the Owens Valley. Artifacts found in Bowers Cave near Newhall and Piru suggest major similarities in rituals between the Fernandeños and their northern Tataviam neighbors.[6]

Correspondence between officials of the Spanish government and mission administrators is revealing of the cultural bias toward the Indians and their languages. The Spanish government sent out *interrogatorios* (questionnaires) to missionaries at all of the missions in existence in 1812. Pedro Múñoz and Joaquín Pascual Nuez, both resident friars at Mission San Fernando at the time, gave the following response to *pregunta* (question) 3 regarding language in their *respuesta* (answer) of February 3, 1814: "The *gente de razón* speak Spanish, the Indians speak three distinct idioms; but many Indians understand Spanish although they speak it imperfectly."[7] The dom-

Metates found on the Christin-Porter Ranch about one league (2.6 miles) northeast of the mission during 1936–45 excavations. *SWM.*

inant languages and the place of origin of Indians baptized at the mission were Fernandeño proper (the dialect of the Gabrielino or Tongva language), from the east and south; Ventureño Chumash, from the west; Tataviam, from the north; and by 1814 Vanyume, from the Antelope Valley.[8]

At Fernandeño archaeological sites throughout the valley, *metates*, *morteros*, and *manos*—food preparation items of stoneware—were unearthed in the twentieth century. Some of these sites were near the mission wells and at the filtering basin, and at the nearby Los Angeles Reservoir and Dam in present-day Mission Hills. Others were farther away at Lakeview Terrace near Big Tujunga Wash, the Cienega area of Sylmar, and at Chatsworth at the extreme western end of the valley. These archaeological finds indicate that the Fernandeños inhabited a vast area.[9]

The Fernandeños' enigmatic expressions in pictographs, preserved in caves of the Santa Susana

---

[6]  Robert O. Gibson, *Indians of North America—The Chumash* (New York: Chelsea House Publishers, 1991), 44. In prehistory there was evidence of steatite trading between the Chumash and Gabrielino Indians and obsidian trading between the Chumash and tribes living some 400 miles away in the upper desert at Owens Valley. The Fernandeños are presumed to have had similar commercial interactions with their neighbors.

[7]  Maynard Geiger, O.F.M. and Clement W. Meighan, *As the Padres Saw Them* (Santa Barbara, Calif.: SBMAL, 1976), 20, and Maynard Geiger, O.F.M., *Franciscan Missionaries in Hispanic California: 1769–1848* (San Marino, Calif.: The Huntington Library, 1969), 296. All thirty-six questions (*preguntas*) and the responses (*respuestas*) have been translated into English. Responses regarding the culture and lifestyles of the Indians at their missions were requested by Secretary of the Department of Overseas Colonies *Don* Ciríaco González Carvajal of all the resident missionaries in his famous October 6, 1812, *interrogatorio*. Some historians have used the phrase *gente de razón* to mean people who are Spanish or of mixed blood and therefore not Indian, but the literal translation of the phrase is "people of reason."

[8]  Johnson, "The Indians of Mission San Fernando," 252.

[9]  Edwin Francis Walker, "A Metate Site at San Fernando," in *Five Prehistoric Archeological Sites in Los Angeles, California*. Publications of the Frederick Webb Hodge Anniversary Publication Fund, vol. 6 (Los Angeles: Southwest Museum, 1951), 15–26.

(*above*) Metates, morteros, and manos found at a stoneware burial and ceremonial site in San Fernando. *SWM.*

(*left*) Indian stone dishes found near the wells (filtering basin). Intake (*DWP*) Magazine, *May 1949.*

game, gathered seeds and acorns locally, and traveled to the nearby mountains for pine nuts, their staple food, and *chía.*[10]

The California Indians wore little clothing. They did not use and seemingly did not need European cloth-type materials. The men, boys, and young girls generally went *au naturel*, but the women usually wore a simple apron-type skirt made of either deerskin or the inner bark of willow or cottonwood trees. Occasionally they wore animal hides, such as deer-

Mountains near Chatsworth, and petroglyphs reflect vivid imaginations. The men were skilled in working with stone, wood, bone, and shell. The women excelled in weaving; some of their historic baskets are extant and are displayed in the museum of Mission San Fernando.

These Indians were hunters and gatherers. They hunted deer, antelope, rabbits, and other small

---

[10] Acorns from the California Coast Live Oak (*Quercus agrifolia*) were used in *pinole*. Grasses (*zacates*) harvested as grain likely included alkali sacaton (*Sporobolus airoides*), deer grass (*Muhlenbergi rigens*), and various species of needle grass (*Stipa pulchra, S. lepida*). Also important as a grain was *chía*, the Aztec Nahuatl name of several sage plants (*Salvia*) found in the southwestern U.S. and Mexico, specifically *S. columbariae* found in the San Fernando Valley. Seeds of the *chía* were also used by early natives in the region to make a beverage.

Artifacts made of stone were found near the ruins of the west wing of the quadrangle
and the church. View shows huge stone pots among the ruins.
Frederick H. Maude, ca. 1895. *FHM/SWM P—18964.*

skin and rabbit fur or bird skins (with feathers intact), for warmth in inclement and colder weather.[11]

They had simple needs for shelter. They lived outdoors much of the time and slept in domed, circular *jacales* made of tule, with a hole placed on top for light, ventilation, and smoke exhaust. Insect-infested habitations were burned to the ground and simply rebuilt.[12]

It is believed that the Fernandeños, like their Gabrielino neighbors, were part of an extensive southern California cult that held in esteem a creator deity named Qua-o-ar (Kwawar or kʷáʔuwar in the Luiseño-Juaneño language found farther south

---

[11] Lowell J. Bean and Charles R. Smith, "Gabrielino," in *Handbook of North American Indians—California*, vol. 8 (Washington, D.C.: Smithsonian Institution, 1978), 547.

[12] Ibid., 542. Other structures found within the ranchería consisted of sweathouses for the men, menstrual huts for the women, and a ceremonial, oval, open-air sacred enclosure

---

called the *yovaar* (*yuva'r*) placed near the religious chieftain's (*tomyaar*) or shaman's house. Botanical names for the New World bulrushes or tules used in the construction of *jacales* by the Gabrielino/Fernandeño were most likely *Scirpus acutus* or *S. americanus* (also known as *S. olneyi*). See also Juan Bandini, "1880—A Secularization-Oriented Proposal for Alta California," in Rose Marie Beebe and Robert Senkewicz, eds., *Lands of Promise and Despair: Chronicles of Early California, 1535–1846* (Santa Clara, Calif.: Santa Clara University; Berkeley, Calif.: Heyday Books, 2001), 379.

A stone pot among the ruins of the west wing, ca. 1893.
*Hooker Collection, Archive Center at San Fernando Mission. UNK/ACSFM.*

near San Juan Capistrano).[13] The cult, called Chinig-chinich, may have originated with the Gabrielinos on Santa Catalina Island and then spread to the mainland. When the Spanish arrived, the cult was using *toloache* (see note 15 on page 31) and had extended its influence to other non-Gabrielino groups, primarily those to the south.

During mission times, in the San Gabriel and San Fernando valleys there was evidence that an earlier cult, termed the "northern complex" by Kroeber, recognized a pantheon of deities, which the friars mentioned in the February 3, 1814, respuesta.[14] This group

of deities included no less than five gods—Ukat (Veat or Wewyoot), Tamur (Jaimar or Taamet), Chukit (Chuhuit or Chuuxoyt), Pichurut (Piichorot) and Iuichepet (Quichepet or Kwiichepet)—and one goddess, Manisar (Maniishar), the wife of Iuichepet, provider of corn or seeds for the Indians. (The

---

[13] Kroeber, *Handbook of the Indians*, 622; see also Bean and Smith, "Gabrielino," 548. Details of the cult are found in the classic work by Fr. Gerónimo Boscana, *Chinigchinich, Historical Account of the Belief, Usage, Customs and Extravagancies of the Indians of this Mission of San Juan Capistrano Called the Acagchemen Tribe*, trans. by Alfred Robinson, anno. by John P. Harrington (Banning, Calif.: Malki Museum Press, 1978).

[14] Geiger, *As the Padres Saw Them*, 57–58. Question 12 of the *interrogatorio* reads: "Is there still noticeable among them [the mission Indians] any tendency toward idolatry? Explain the nature of the idolatry and unfurl the means that can be employed to root it out." Fr. Pedro Múñoz and Fr. Joaquin Pascual Nuez, resident missionaries at San Fernando at the time, responded to this question with the five gods listed. In addition, they noted: "The Indians are inclined to idolatry for it is observed that in their race-courses they make large circles in the center of which they raise a pole covered with bundles of feathers from the crow and which is adorned with beads. As many as pass the pole pay homage to it and returning round about blow to the four winds thus asking relief of their necessities." See Kroeber, *Handbook of the Indians*, 622–23.

Spanish spellings and Indian variants are given here. Corn had been introduced by the Spanish by 1795.) Religious rites honoring these gods were associated with the use of *manit* or jimsonweed.[15]

The neighboring Ventureño Chumash peoples believed that Sky Coyote (not to be confused with the terrestrial coyote) and other Sky People divided into two opposing teams and played a perpetual gambling game of *peón* that affected life and death in this world. Rituals were important to everyday life, integrating social behavior and spiritual beliefs to keep in balance the celestial forces impinging upon Mother Earth.[16]

Friendly, gentle, spiritual, and nature-revering—these were the inhabitants who greeted the strangers wandering into their valley.

---

[15] *Datura*, a member of the *Solanaceae* or nightshade family of plants, is used in folk rites for its narcotic and hallucinogenic properties. It was known by the Spanish Californians as "Indian whiskey."

*Manit* (*maanet* or *Mah´-neet*, literally "the grass that talks") is the Gabrielino/Fernandeño name for the jimsonweed plant. Manit was used in religious ceremonies for the five gods and one goddess in the "northern complex." McCawley, *The First Angelinos*, 96 and 144, provides the variant spellings.

*Toloache* is the Nahuatl (the language spoken by the Aztecs) name for the jimsonweed plant, and it was involved with the complex Chinigchinich cult. Toloache was used primarily in the male puberty rite, which was not the most significant of the many rites in the Chinigchinich macroculture. There was no general use of toloache.

The terms *manit* and *toloache*, as used by Spanish Californians and Gabrielino/Fernandeño Indians during mission times, would refer to the species of Datura found in the Los Angeles region, which would be *Datura wrightii* (also known as *Datura meteloides* in earlier works).

---

[16] Bean and Smith, "Gabrielino," 512. The guessing game of *peón* was a favorite gambling game played with graduated sticks, which were hidden and then revealed after wagers were made. Other Chumash games included a wagering game using shell money played by the men, and a dice game, played by the women, in which dice were snail or walnut shells filled with asphaltum. A team game *shinny*, similar to field-hockey, was played with a small ball made of hard wood covered with an animal skin. Upon completion of shinny, the entire team retired to the sweat lodge, the equivalent of our showers. Played by all were variations of the hoop and pole game in which a small hoop made of tied rushes or bark was rolled along the ground and contestants tried to throw a long pole through the rolling hoop.

Some information in this chapter and in the above notes was supplied by Dr. Steven Boyd, curator of the Herbarium, Rancho Santa Ana Botanic Garden, Claremont, California; Dr. James A. Sandos, professor of History at the University of Redlands; and Dr. John R. Johnson, curator of Anthropology at the Santa Barbara Museum of Natural History (SBMNH).

The Old Spanish and Mexican Ranchos of Los Angeles County.
Title Insurance and Trust Company—Research (TICOR) Photo Collection,
Los Angeles, copyright 1919. *Courtesy of the southern division of the California Historical Society. CHS/TICOR.*

# CHAPTER 2
# THE EXPEDITION JOURNALS

*Diary of the journey by land made to the north of California by order of his Excellency the Marqués de Croix, Viceroy, Governor and Captain-General of New Spain, . . . etc.; by instruction of the Most Illustrious Don Joseph de Gálvez, of the Council and Court of His Majesty in the Supreme Council of the Indies, Inspector-General of all the tribunals, Royal Exchequers, and Departments of Finance of His Majesty in the same kingdom and intendant of the King's Army, . . . etc.; performed by the troops detailed for this purpose under the command of the Governor of the Peninsula of California, Don Gaspár de Portolá, Captain in the Dragones de España Regiment.*

—Miguel Costansó,
Introduction to his *Diary* in
*The Portolá Expedition of 1769–1770*

SATURDAY, AUGUST 5, 1769. On the first *entrada* into Alta California, the Spaniards entered the San Fernando Valley, the halfway point on their journey northward to Monterey Bay from San Diego.[1] The party consisted of approximately seventy Spanish soldiers, accompanied by fifteen Christianized Indians who served as laborers and interpreters. On the expedition were Capt. Gaspár de Portolá; the lieutenant of the Catalonian Volunteers, Don Pedro Fages; engineer Miguel Costansó; and Fray Juan Crespí, who have, in their diaries, provided us vivid impressions of the journey and their encounter with the inhabitants.[2]

SATURDAY, AUGUST 5

Captain Portolá:

The 5th, we proceeded for four hours over hills [near Sepúlveda Pass in the Santa Monica Mountains], as the mountain range obstructed our progress by the sea. In this place we found an Indian village of about sixty inhabitants; they made us a present of much grain. Here we rested [for one day] and over two hundred natives came [to our camp] with much grain; they are very docile and generous and we made them a suitable return.[3]

Lieutenant Fages:

From this place a northwesterly route was chosen, toward the point where there appears to be an

---

[1] Frederick J. Teggart, ed., "The Portolá Expedition of 1769–1771: Diary of Miguel Costansó," in *Publications of the Academy of Pacific Coast History*, vol. 2, no. 4 (Berkeley: University of California Press, 1911), 164–327 (hereafter referred to as the Costansó *Diary*). Engineer Miguel Costansó wrote his journal on the 1769 Spanish Expedition, which started on July 14, 1769, and ended back in San Diego on February 7, 1770.

[2] Journal entries of the four diarists for the days before, during, and after leaving the Valley of the Live Oaks are included in their entirety except where they are repetitious or nonexistent for the day.

[3] Donald E. Smith and Frederick J. Teggart, eds., "Diary of Gaspar de Portolá during the California Expedition of 1769–1770," in *Publications of the Academy of Pacific Coast History*, vol. 1, no. 3 (Berkeley: University of California Press, 1911), 53 and 55 (hereafter referred to as the Portolá *Diary*).

opening in the range; this is entered through a canyon between sheer hillsides which, finally becoming more accessible, make it possible to take the slope and ascend to the summit. From this, a spacious pleasant valley is discovered; descending into it, one encounters a very large pool, capable of providing water in abundance. Near it there is a populous Indian village, the inhabitants of which, even to the children, are remarkably affable and peaceable. This valley must be about three leagues wide, its length extending to more than eight; it is entirely surrounded by a chain of mountains; to it the name Valle de Santa Catalina was given.[4]

Engineer Costansó:

Saturday, August 5.—The scouts who had set out to examine the coast and the road along the beach returned shortly afterwards with the news of having reached a high, steep cliff, terminating in the sea where the mountains end, absolutely cutting off the passage along the shore. This forced us to seek a way through the mountains, and we found it, although it was rough and difficult.

We then set out from the Ojos [de Agua] del Berrendo in the afternoon, and, directing our course to the northwest towards the point where there appeared to be an opening in the range, we entered the mountains through a canyon formed by steep hills on both sides. At the end of the canyon, however, the hills were somewhat more accessible and permitted us to take the slope and, with much labor, to ascend to the summit, whence we discerned a very large and pleasant Valley. We descended to it and halted near the watering-place, which consisted of a very large pool. Near this was a populous Indian village, [and the inhabitants were] very good-natured and peaceful. They offered us their seeds in trays or baskets of rushes, and came to the camp in such numbers that, had they been armed, they might have caused us apprehension, as we counted as many as two hundred and five, including men, women, and children. All of them offered us something to eat, and we, in turn, gave them our glass beads and rib-

bons. We made three leagues on this day's journey. To the Valley we gave the name of Santa Catalina; it is about three leagues in width and more than eight in length, and is entirely surrounded by hills.[5]

Fray Crespí:

August 5th. We set out at a little past two o'clock in the afternoon from here at the level and two springs of Saint Rogerius [Ojos de Aqua del Berrendo, according to Costansó], taking a northward course through the mountains, which about half a league after setting out we began to go up to, entering them through a narrow little hollow that led us into the mountains in this direction [the Sepúlveda Cañon]. These are quite high and rather steep; however, very grown over on all sides with a great deal of grass (I have seen none better anywhere), and the hollow which we were following [was] much lined with large sycamores, live oaks, and white oaks and also with a great many small walnut trees laden with quantities of small round nuts with very good meat, only their shells are quite thick and hard to crack; and a great many rose bushes. We went over a high pass, and thence down to a very large valley all burnt off by the heathens, so that from the height it all looked to have been fallowed. At a full three hours, in which we could not have failed to make three leagues, we set up camp beneath a large live oak upon the south side of the valley here, close to a very large pool of very pure water at the foot of

---

[4] Don Pedro Fages, Soldier of Spain, *A Historical, Political and Natural Description of California*, trans. and ed. by Herbert Ingram Priestley (Berkeley: University of California Press, 1937), 16 (hereafter referred to as the Fages *Diary*).

[5] Costansó *Diary*, 181 and 183. On the previous two days Costansó describes the location to which they had traveled. They went west of the Los Angeles River and passed the large swamps of pitch-like material (La Brea Tar Pits) to a place where they wounded and eventually caught a deer-like animal (antelope). At this place issued a spring of water. On the morning of the 5th, scouts set out to examine the coast and the road along the beach and found at the seacoast that a steep cliff cut off their access along the shore. They left the area they called Ojos de Agua del Berrendo and traveled northwest in order to enter the mountains (today called the Sepulveda Pass). According to Raymund Wood in "Juan Crespí: Southern California's First Chronicler," in *Spanish California's Spanish Heritage*, edited by Doyce B. Nunis, Jr. (Los Angeles: HSSC, 1992), 53–54, Ojos de Agua del Berrendo was situated in the vicinity of the Veterans Home at Sawtelle near Westwood. Costansó *Diary*, 183 and 185, contains the entry for August 5.

the mountain range on this side; where we came upon two large villages of very fine, well-behaved, and very friendly heathens who must have amounted to about two hundred souls, men, women, and children. They all stood waiting with their bowls full of gruel and sage refreshment ready to present to us, and were told to bring it to the camp that we were on our way to set up under the shade of a very large white oak. And so they did, bringing us a vast number of basketsful of servings of very good, well flavored gruel, and sage, which our Governor and our Captain received from them, giving the usual beads to all of them, and they sat down with us till told to go, and on leaving said that if we wished they would come back in the morning; they were told yes, and so they did indeed.

This is a large valley that must be not less than six leagues in length from east to west; its width from north to south is not under three leagues; all of it [is] very good, [and has] very grass-grown soil, though most of it had been burnt off, many patches however had not been, where grass still showed. There are the following watering places; upon the south of the spot, the pool I spoke of [yesterday]— a large one, with turtles in it, and a great deal of tule-rush patches and swamps surrounding it; it is of hot water, very good and pure, however, once it is cooled. For about three hundred yards' distance, there is about a *naranja* [an orange-sized flow] of water running out of the aforesaid pool, and by what I could see of the swamp, I thought only little toil might be needed for a good deal greater flow. Another watering place is around about three leagues to eastward, a swamp in a hollow belonging to this valley, where a village was seen. About three leagues off, on the northwest of this valley at the foot of the mountains, on commencing to go up them, there is about a *naranja* of running water in a small stream with a good many sycamores, willows, and live oaks. Another, lying to northward, I shall speak of in the next day's march. A great many walnut trees are along the skirts of the southern mountain range belonging to this place; trees are seen in some spots in the valley here. There are prickly pear patches not very far from the southern pond, and sage from which they make very good gruel, and very good it is for drinking, abounds here.

[It is] a very grand spot for a very good-sized mission with many heathen folk, who are very well-behaved, tractable, and friendly. I called it the Valley of *Santa Catalina de Bononia* [de los Encinos], Saint Catherine of Bologna [of the Valley of the Live Oaks], trusting that in time it shall become such, and belong to this glorious saint. I took the north latitude, and observed this spot as lying in 34 degrees, 37 minutes latitude.[6]

### Sunday, August 6

On the Sabbath, only engineer Miguel Costansó and Fr. Juan Crespí made entries in their journals.

Engineer Costansó:

We rested today, and received innumerable visits from natives who came from various parts to see us. They had information of the appearance of the packets on the coast of the *Canal de Sánta Barbara*. They drew on the ground the outline or map of the channel and its islands, tracing the course of our ships. They also told us that, in former times, there had come to their country bearded people, dressed and armed like ourselves, indicating that they had come from the east. One of the natives

6  Juan Crespí, *A Description of Distant Roads: Original Journals of the First Expedition into California, 1769–1770*, trans. and ed. by Alan K. Brown (Calexico, Calif.: San Diego State University Press, 2001), 345–67 (hereafter referred to as the Crespí *Diary*); Herbert E. Bolton, *Fray Juan Crespí: Missionary Explorer on the Pacific Coast, 1769–1774* (Berkeley: University of California Press, 1927), 150–51. Alan K. Brown demonstrated that Crespí's diary, as published by Francisco Palóu in his *Noticias de la Nueva California* and found in the Bolton reference, was drastically edited; much material relating to the Indians and their surroundings was deleted and some sections of Miguel Costansó's diary were added. Palóu took so many liberties with Crespí's diary that the Palóu version is not very useful. As an example, Palóu—and others quoting him—most often have attached *de los Encinos* to Crespí's original naming of the valley. Interestingly, the Encino Valley has stuck, whereas Saint Catherine of Bologna is seldom seen and even less used. See also the book review of Alan Brown's work by Robert Senkewicz in *Boletín: The Journal of the California Mission Studies Association*, vol. 19, no. 2, Fall 2002, 45–46. Alan K. Brown in a note cites the correct latitude, actually 34°09½'.

related that he had been as far as their lands, and had seen places or towns composed of large houses, and that each family occupied one of its own. He added further, that at the distance of a few days' marches—about seven or eight—to the north we would arrive at a large river which flowed between rugged mountains and could not be forded; and that farther on we would see the ocean which would hinder us from continuing our journey in that direction. However, we left the verification of the information of these geographers to the test of our own eyes.[7]

Fray Crespí:

. . . [on] Transfiguration Sunday, the two of us said Mass [Fr. Francisco Gómez was the other cleric on this journey], and by the time I finished the first Mass they [the Indians] were already back with a great many bowls of gruel and sage, just as on yesterday afternoon. They set it down for us to take, asking nothing in return, and in order not to grieve them we took all of it and gave them whatever we could, although they had asked for nothing.[8]

August 6th. We lay by resting here, while they are out scouting; and the chiefs of these villages here took great measures and sent four heathens with the scouts to show them the watering place they spoke of and the way by which we might get out of this valley; for it is all fenced in by high mountains, and there is no way along the seashore, as I said previously; while the scouts said they had seen countless heathen folk along the shore. We began to meet with regular houses here at this spot, and they have some underground ones that are very large, being like a sort of porticoes within and with a small doorway like a chimney hole through which they go in and out, to protect themselves from the cold. Their lives are governed a bit, there being at all of the villages three or four chiefs, with one chief who is head of all the others and gives them orders, as they do to the rest of the people, and are very readily obeyed, or so we understood. Here also we began to see very well carven wooden flutes that they play on. We understand from these heathens that they each

have only a single wife with the exception of two of their chiefs, who have two.

Now that we have spent all of today with them, to our astonishment they have repeatedly brought us a vast number of basketsful of gruels and sage, at morning, noon, and at evenfall. They asked us whether we had come to stay with them, and we told them we were going onward but would come back and stay if they wished, and they said yes, well pleased with this. They told us that upcountry—pointing northeastward—there were people like us—pointing to the soldiers—with guns, swords, and horses—pointing to our mounts—and there were three Fathers like ourselves (pointing to our habits); that two or three of themselves had been there; that it was reached in thirteen days' travel from sunrise to sunset, and there was a sea close by, and many large animals, which, from their commentary and gestures, we thought must have been buffaloes; and that a great many people from there had come on horseback to their country, and had returned. Whether this is New Mexico or not, who can say.[9] Indeed these heathen folk here have pleased us a great deal, having been, as they have, spending the whole day sitting with us, entirely without weapons or fear, as though they had been dealing with us forever. We saw a great many little children with very red or fair hair, and among them all my heart went out to one little girl, daughter of the head chief, some six years old, who had this sort of hair, and was very well turned out, in their own style: she wore skirts of very fine handsome deerskin reaching from waist to ankles, with a big flounce made of the same deerskin all about beneath, and at the waist, above her little skirts, a kind of a belt some eight fingers broad made of very small shell beads, very close-woven and many-colored, that became her greatly.[10]

---

[7] Costansó Diary, 184–85, in both Spanish and English.

[8] This paragraph, written by Fr. Crespí for Sunday, August 6, was actually placed in his first revision of field notes for the previous day, August 5, 1769; see Crespí Diary, 353–55.

[9] One possible explanation for Costansó's and Crespí's statements about the natives having seen white people like them, with armament and horses, is that such as story may have been passed along by natives who had come earlier from the Colorado River, where they had met and received this communication from Adelantado Don Juan de Oñate and his companions, in 1604. See David J. Weber, The Spanish Frontier in North America (New Haven, Conn.: Yale University Press, 1992), 82.

[10] Crespí Diary, 355–59, in both Spanish and English.

The next day, the party proceeded north across the valley, then camped at the foothills of the Santa Susana Mountains.

### Monday, August 7

Captain Portolá:

The 7th, we proceeded for three hours, crossing a canyon. We halted at the foot of some hills where there was sufficient water and pasture.[11]

Lieutenant Fages:

Passing through this valley, which was named also the *Valle de los Encinos*, one goes a matter of the three leagues of its width in order to reach the foot of the range. Here there was water in abundance for the people, but very little for the animals.[12]

Engineer Costansó:

We crossed the Valle de Santa Catalina, which is nearly three leagues wide, and pitched our camp at the foot of the mountains that we had to enter on the following day. There was, among rushes and reeds, more than enough water for the people, but very little for the animals.[13]

Fray Crespí:

August 7th. We set out a little before three o'clock in the afternoon from the large valley and pool of Saint Catherine of Bologna here, course due north, in order to get to a watering place found by the scouts. On this course, we crossed the plain here, which was all burnt off but has very good soil. Across this level we went for three full hours, in which we must have made three leagues, and came to a hollow upon the north of this valley, about half a league before the mountains that lie beyond it. This is a vastly lush hollow, having a great deal of swamp, very green with reed-grass, tule-rushes, and many other kinds of plants, where we saw a good-sized channel with very good water with a bit of a flow, there among the many weeds. There is a great deal of very dark, friable soil for cropland, and water enough for a town; as we were only passing through, I was unable to be sure whether it can be irrigated,

but judged that it might, if once worked upon, as the greenness of the spot evidences there being a good amount of water. (And so let this watering place be kept in mind for a more thorough survey of the location, showing whereabouts is best suited for a town, whether at the pool, or here, whenever it comes time for laying out a town.)

There are a good many large live oaks, white oaks, sycamores, some cottonwoods, and willows at this hollow; and the mountains lying next to here show some pine trees upon their summits.[14]

On the following morning, the party experienced difficulty ascending the steep Santa Susana Mountains and descending from the mountain's precipitous east end.[15] The band continued on past the headwaters of the Santa Clara River and traveled down along the riverbed, arriving at a populous village known as Chaguayabit. On this day, the journalists describe their journey.

### Tuesday, August 8

Captain Portolá:

The 8th, we proceeded for six hours over one of the highest and steepest mountains and halted in a gully where there was much water and pasture. Some natives appeared and begged us to go to their village which was near; there we found eight villages

---

[11] Portolá *Diary*, 25.

[12] Fages *Diary*, 16.

[13] Costansó *Diary*, 185.

[14] Crespí *Diary*, 358–61.

[15] This would be the San Fernando Pass, later designated Frémont's Pass, honoring Lt. Col. John C. Frémont and his battalion, who arrived in the Encino Valley on January 11, 1847. When buckboard and stagecoach traffic increased between the mission and its *estancia*, San Francisco de Xavier, a vertical slice was made into the steepest portion of the pass to ease passage. This deep cut can still be seen today just off Highway 5 and is called "Beale's Cut." It gets its name from Lt. Edward Fitzgerald Beale, who created and deepened it in the 1850s and 1860s. Lieutenant Beale, noted for his command at Fort Tejón, may have created the cut for his short-lived camel train between Fort Defiance in Albuquerque and Fort Tejón. Beginning in 1858, the Camel Corps was used for freight transportation between the forts until Beale was recalled to serve in the East in the Civil War. See Andrew Rolle, *California, A History*, 4th ed. (Arlington Heights, Ill.: Harlan Davidson, Inc., 1987), 224.

"Beale's Cut" or Frémont's Pass, as it was also known, was a path sliced through the tall San Fernando mountains by Lt. Edward Fitzgerald Beale, commander at Fort Tejon (thirty-four miles north of the mission), and his U.S. Corps of Engineers between 1850 and 1860. *Unknown photographer, ca. 1884. LAA.*

erate width running amid numerous willows and poplars. This place was called Ranchería del Corral [near today's Castaic Junction].[17]

Engineer Costansó:

We entered the mountain range, the road having been already marked out by the pioneers who had been sent ahead very early in the morning. Part of the way we traveled through a narrow canyon, and part over very high hills of barren soil, the ascent and descent of which were exceedingly difficult for the animals. We descended afterwards to a little valley where there was an Indian village; the inhabitants had sent us messengers to the Valle de Santa Catalina, and guides to show us the best trail and pass through the range. These poor fellows had prepared refreshments for our reception, and, as they saw that it was our intention to move on so as not to interrupt the day's march, they made the most earnest entreaties to induce us to visit their village, which was off the road. We had to comply with their requests so as not to disappoint them. We enjoyed their hospitality and bounty, which consisted of seeds, acorns, and nuts. Furthermore, they furnished us other guides to take us to the watering-place about which they gave us information. We reached it quite late. The day's march was four leagues.

The country from the village to the watering-place is pleasing and picturesque on the plain, although the surrounding mountains are bare and rugged. On the plain we saw many groves of poplars and white oaks, which were very tall and large. The

together—which must have numbered more than three hundred inhabitants—with a great supply of grain. We rested [for one day] where there was a village of about fifty natives.[16]

Lieutenant Fages:

Four leagues after entering the mountains, passing in part through a narrow canyon [the San Fernando Pass] and in part along very high barren hills, the ascent of which is very difficult for beasts of burden, one reaches a small valley; it extends into a pleasant sightly field, on the level expanse of which are seen many poplars and oaks of great size. There is a copious supply of water in a stream of mod-

---

[16] Portolá *Diary*, 55.

[17] Fages *Diary*, 17.

AUGUST 8TH. We set out before a half past six in the morning from this pleasant lush hollow, course north-northwestward. A heathen man had accompanied us to here from the last spot, and this morning another one, sent by his chiefs, appeared here from the place that we are going to. We continued, then, upon our way, and on going about half a league beyond the aforesaid hollow, by various windings about along the foot of the mountains, we went up by a ridge to a very high pass in the range, which was not rocky, instead mere whitish soil, clad with dry grass wherever it had not been burnt.

It was necessary, once having climbed this high pass, to get down a long descent, which we had to do on foot, it being so steep a one as it was. Once down this, we came into another hollow of considerable extent with very good soil, very grass-grown, and very much grown over with large live oaks, white oaks, sycamores, and white cottonwoods. Shortly after coming into this hollow we were met by three more heathens, sent by their chief from the village to which the man belonged who had been accompanying us from the place we set out from. Soon we caught sight of the whole village, awaiting us while encamped in the shade of some trees. (The scouts had come here yesterday, when the heathens of this village presented them with a great deal of seeds, gruel, and very well flavored small raisins.) One of their chiefs, at our own arrival, was making a long speech. We found about a hundred souls seated there, men, women, and children, having 23 quite large baskets set out in front of them for us, prepared with gruel and sage, others with a kind of very small little raisins, and others with water—they making signs to us to take some of this, that they were giving it to us. Our people took what they wished, we stayed a while with them, and our officers made them a present of beads with which they were well pleased. They all are very well-behaved, tractable Indians. There were two old women who were making two very large rushwork—wicker-weave baskets like very large hampers, very finely done, made out of some large grasses which they harvest in this country and which I thought were rushes but proved not to be—and so close woven that they fill them with water and not a drop escapes. There was what we understood to be a bride, here at this village: she was seated in their midst, wearing a great deal of paint and very much decked out in their fashion with all different sorts of their usual shell beads, and this spot became referred to as The Bride's Village, *La ranchería de la Novia*. This hollow, here, some days' march in length, starts here at this village, and was referred to as the Beginning of the Hollow of Saint Clare, *la Cañada de Santa Clara*, lying among the mountains of the holy martyrs *San Largo y Esmaragdo*, Saints Largus and Smaragdus, for so I called the one and the other of them. [These names were given to ranges on either side of the Santa Clara Valley. *The Santa Clara* hollow begins here at Bride's Village.] After a while we pursued our way down the hollow, which has a great deal of very good grass-grown soil. Shortly we came upon a large level, all grown over with very large cottonwoods, large live oaks, white oaks, sycamores, and willows. At a knoll close to this grove, we came upon another large village [Chaguayabit] where there seemed to be running water at a nearby large, lush patch; however, we still passed onward down the hollow and on going about four hours and a half, almost the whole way except the distance over the pass being over level land, we set up camp close to a very large tableland, the whole of it one large vineyard of very lush grapevines with countless rose bushes. There are two large streams of running water, one to one side of the aforesaid tableland and the other to the other; all this also very much grown over with the sorts of trees before mentioned. A grand spot—well provided with very good soil and streams for irrigating it, and with five large villages of heathens and a great deal of timber—for a very large plenteous mission. Trusting that with time it shall become one such, I called it *Santa Rosa de Viterbo*, Saint Rose of Viterbo [Costansó's diary for this day tells us that this place was called *Ranchería del Corral* by the soldiers], belonging to this glorious saint, in the Santa Clara Hollow. Four leagues' march.

At once after camp was made, the whole nearest village, belonging to this spot came over, bringing us a good-sized present of five or six large packets of what first appeared to be a very sweet sort of crushed honeycomb, but then we all thought instead it must be honeydew they had scraped from reed-grasses, as this sort of honeydew is so commonly yielded from reed-grass patches in California [i.e., Lower, or Baja, California]. According to my understanding, it comes from dew falling on those patches, and it is as great a purgative as any honeydew. They accepted it; I warned them however not to eat any unless they wished to perish of diarrhea. Our officers presented them with beads, and they were well pleased. They also made a present of a great many baskets of gruel, sage, and raisins of the sort before mentioned, which are very well flavored: this is a very tiny fruit, yielded by some trees that are very plentiful in this hollow; many of them that I saw were laden with this little fruit, which is like so many grape seeds, very small, and turning black when ripe. I took the north latitude at this spot, and observed it as lying in 34 degrees 47 minutes.*

---

*  Crespí *Diary*, 360–67. [Alan K. Brown notes that the correct latitude is 34°25′.]

The toll gate house on the Newhall side of Beale's Cut (Frémont's Pass), ca. 1884. *By unknown photographer. LAA.*

watering-place consisted of a stream, containing much water that flowed in a moderately wide canyon where there were many willows and poplars. Near the place in which we camped there was a populous Indian village [Chaguayabit]; the inhabitants lived without other protection than a light shelter of branches in the form of an enclosure; for this reason the soldiers gave to the whole place the name of the Ranchería del Corral.[18]

Father Juan Crespí's diary for August 8 is, by far, the most expressive and lengthy on details of the exhausting climb up and out of the San Fernando Valley and descent from the Santa Susana mountain ridge down to the Santa Clara River region. Cres-

[18] Costansó *Diary*, 185 and 187.

pí's description of the villages, the numerous indigenous peoples they encountered, and communications with them through sign language, the lush surroundings and the variety of fruits, including one laxative, warrants its inclusion as a sidebar (previous page).[19]

All four diaries describe both the Encino and Santa Clara river regions as possessing the characteristics favorable for the establishment of a mission: water, seemingly fertile soil, lumber from nearby mountains or timberland, and numerous cooperative Indians.[20] The two areas appeared to be ideal locations. But, time and again development was postponed.[21]

[19] Crespí *Diary*, 360–67.

[20] See Edith Buckland Webb, "Steps Leading up to the Founding of a Mission," in *Indian Life at the Old Missions* (Los Angeles: Warren F. Lewis, 1952), 20–24, which is perhaps the best description available on the specific requirements for mission selection by the missionaries.

[21] It is believed that the long delay in establishing Mission San Fernando was because of Fray Junípero Serra's failing health and his eventual death on August 28, 1784. When Fray Fermín Francisco de Lasuén became the second mission president, he seemed to be more interested in overseeing building expansions of already established missions. Serra's master plan for mission establishment was to alternate between northern and southern locations and to fill in major gaps. Nine missions were founded in eight years under Fray Serra, with six founded personally by him. However, during the next fifteen years under Fray Lasuén, only four were founded, until he began in earnest founding four new ones during 1797–98.

# CHAPTER 3
# EL RANCHO ENCINO

*Encino was considered among the possible sites for San Fernando Mission. When Fray Fermín Francisco de Lasuén visited the site, in 1797, he felt the water supply was inadequate for the envisioned agricultural needs. With the selection of a site some miles north for the mission, Francisco Reyes, the alcalde for El Pueblo de Nuestra Señora [la Reina] de Los Angeles, moved to [el Rancho] Encino and assumed title of the adjoining acreage.*

— Msgr. Francis J. Weber, *Memories of an Old Mission*

ALTA CALIFORNIA'S *asesor* (legal advisor), Pedro Galindo Navarro, began issuing land grants to California settlers as early as 1784.[1] Spanish land grants did not provide title to land but were usufructuary. They were *permisiones* (authorizations) to raise cattle and grow grain under certain restricted conditions of commonality. In almost all cases, they were provisional concessions—favors to *soldados de cuero* (leather-jacketed soliders) who had served either in the Portolá Expedition of 1769 or subsequently under Gov. Pedro Fages' command.[2]

In 1795 there were five ranchos in private possession which were held under Spanish land grants. One of the five early grants in the southern central region went to Juan Francisco Reyes, whose authorization for Rancho Encino was reviewed and confirmed by Fages' superior officer, Gen. Jacobo Ugarte y Loyola, in 1786.[3] Reyes was a thirteen-year veteran of the Royal Spanish Army who had joined the Monterey garrison in 1771 and served out his term at La Misión de San Antonio de Padua, the third Alta Cal-

---

[1] Hubert H. Bancroft, *History of California*, 7 vols. (San Francisco: A.L. Bancroft & Company, 1884), 1: 323 and 609.

[2] Crisostomo N. Perez, in *Land Grants in Alta California* (Rancho Cordova, Calif.: Landmark Enterprises, 1996), 28, wrote: "When the presidios and pueblos were being established, the Commandants of the presidios and the Alcaldes of the pueblos were authorized to grant lots of lands within their jurisdiction. From these first presidual [*sic*, presidial] and pueblo lots, evolved the granting of lands outside of these jurisdictions. These grants of lands were known as Rancho Grants and were granted in order to encourage agriculture and industry, to reward soldiers and to provide land

---

to settlers, who had come to Alta California to colonize the land." See also Bancroft, *History of California*, 1: 609–12 and 662–63, where the conditions, authorization, and granting of these early provisional grants are discussed.

[3] Bancroft, *History of California*, 1: 460–61; see also Francis J. Weber, "Roots of San Fernando Mission—1769," in *Memories of an Old Mission: San Fernando, Rey de España* (Mission Hills, Calif.: Saint Francis Historical Society, 1997), 1–2, where Weber briefly describes Rancho Encino, which ultimately was granted to mission Indians known as Ramón, Francisco, and Roque. It was sold in 1845 to Vicente de la Osa, who had acquired Rancho Providencia in 1843. The ranchos became Rancho Encino y Providencia located south and southeast of the valley.

The majestic oak (*quercus agrifolia*) dotted the Encino Valley at the time Spanish soldiers and missionaries arrived in California. *Photo courtesy of Bruce Pottoroff, Claremont, California.*

ifornia mission. After his retirement from the army, Reyes settled his family in the Valley of the Live Oaks and built an adobe at Rancho Encino, where he kept his livestock as well as that of Cornélio Ávila and others.[4]

Reyes had a presence in the valley, but official records list him as one of twenty new settlers in El Pueblo de Nuestra Señora la Reina de Los Angeles de Porciúncula in 1786. From 1793 to 1795 he was alcalde of the pueblo, whose name was shortened to Los Angeles in 1850. Some historians have claimed that Reyes had established prior ownership of the valley but the historical record does not support such an interpretation.[5]

———

[4] Bancroft, *History of California*, 1: 663, where he describes Reyes taking up residency at Rancho Encino and the transitory tenure of his grant.

[5] Ibid., 1: 461, 561–62, 609–12, and 2: 172. Although *permisiones* needed a written document and an endorsement for these "temporary occupations," in no case was title ever granted in the Reyes authorization. No legal documents were ever given him in place of the temporary grant. For

In 1795 the valley remained, as it had for centuries, inhabited mostly by indigenous peoples. Except at Rancho Encino, it was virtually free from settlement by outsiders.

Meanwhile, preparations were being made at Mission San Buenaventura that would bring a dramatic change to the Valley of the Live Oaks.

———

Reyes there is no apparent evidence of hostility toward the Franciscans, even after they confiscated his home and land for Mission San Fernando. Several facts, however, were recorded by the friars. Reyes held the land for around a dozen years, employing the Indians to herd his livestock, till and harvest his land for the production of corn, beans, and melons, and make a kiln. See Engelhardt, *San Fernando Rey*, 5 and 12. Reyes also acted as sponsor (godfather) to the first ten children baptized on the day of the mission's founding. In 1801 the missionaries found Reyes another plot (simply called the Reyes Rancho) farther north near La Purísima, where he grew wheat, which he traded with the ships plying between San Blas and Monterey. In 1810 the Franciscans acquired his assigned land, but this time purchased it from him, to extend the grazing lands of Mission La Purísima de Concepción.

Sketch depicting Fr. Vicente de Santa María, Sergeant José María Ortega, and
Ensign Don Pablo Cota on the afternoon of August 19, 1795, made by Russell Ruiz, 1978.
Santa María wrote in his journal: "We went to explore the place where the alcalde of
pueblo Los Angeles, Francisco Reyes, has his rancho." *RR/KEP.*

## CHAPTER 4
# THE FOUNDING

*Thus was possession taken of this site dedicated to the glorious St. Ferdinand, King of Spain, and thus was begun the mission with this holy title in accordance with the superior orders of His Excellency the Marqués de Branciforte, Viceroy of New Spain, and of Your Lordship.*

—Fray Fermín Francisco de Lasuén,
Letter to Fray Pedro Callejas, September 8, 1797

FATHER JUNÍPERO SERRA left a legacy of nine missions in Alta California. After his death in 1784, his successor, Fr. Fermín Francisco de Lasuén, added seven more missions to the chain, during the period 1786 to the summer of 1797.[1]

On August 16, 1795, a small band headed south from San Buenaventura to find a suitable site for a mission to be located between the San Buenaventura and San Gabriel missions. The troop consisted of Sgt. Don José María Ortega, Ensign Don Pablo Cota, and four Spanish soldiers. The religious participant was Fray Vicente de Santa María, the cleric whom Fr. Lasuén had selected.[2]

They surveyed several potential sites. The first stop on their journey was at Cayeguez, an Indian ranchería. They continued on, arriving in the late afternoon at Parage (pasillo) del Conejo. The second day they headed east and reached a valley called Simi, but did not find the area suitable, as this narrow corridor did not have sufficient water and had saliferous soil. On the next day, the group rode south and surveyed El Triunfo, situated in today's Agoura Hills near Reyes Adobe Road, not far from where the new El Camino Real was located. Here they found a disappointingly small pool of water, and even if there had been more water, there was little irrigable land. Later, at four o'clock in the afternoon, they traveled along the camino real, going more or less eastward. At half past six in the evening, they arrived at Calabazas, situated at the west end of the Enci-

---

[1] Francis F. Guest, O.F.M., *Fermín Francisco de Lasuén (1736–1803): A Biography* (Washington, D.C.: Academy of American Franciscan History, 1973); Geiger, *Franciscan Missionaries*, 136–42. The biography of missionaries who served during the mission period through secularization is found here. This includes second president Fray Fermín Francisco de Lasuén. An encapsulated biography of Fr. Lasuén may be found in Appendix B.

[2] Engelhardt, *San Fernando Rey*, 3. This is the last classic essay on the seventeenth mission in the Alta California chain.

Franciscan historian Fr. Zephyrin Engelhardt had at his disposal the great wealth of original official documents and correspondence that are in the Archive-Library of Mission Santa Barbara. His work, naturally, has a Roman Catholic point of view.

+ 274

Misson del Serafico Dor S. Buenava. Febe 3 de 1795

Viva Jhs.

Mi mas Venerado. y Estimado Pe Presidte. en cum
plimiento ā lo resuelto por el Sor Pral. de qe. se haga un un registro
despacio, con la maior exactitud, y a toda satisfaccion, a fin de descu
brir el mejor parage, qe. haiga entre esta Misson. y la de S. Gabriel, pa
proceder con acierto, en caso, qe. se conceda la fundacion de otra, entre es
ta, y aquella, y de qe. quiere S. S. qe. corra esta diligencia un Missionero,
y del encargo qe. J. R. me hace confiado en qe. lo he de desempeñar perfectamte.

Digo qe. el dia 16 de Agosto sali de esta Misson. acompañado del Sor
Alferez Dn. Pablo Cota, del Sargto. Dn. Jose Ma. Ortega, y cuatro Soldados
a las doce del dia, y llegamos a la Ranchera. de Cayeguel, distante del camino
Rl. como dos leguas pa. el Norte, y pararla del Parage del Conejo, a las cuatro
de la tarde en donde dormimos. Dia 17 salimos de dho Parage ā las seis, y
media de la mañana, y caminando por el Rumbo del Leste muy poco ā poco,
llegamos ā un Balle, qe. se llama Simi ā las nueve de la mañana, en la media
nia de este Valle encontramos un Pozito de agua en un Arroyo Seco qe. cruza por
medio de este Balle, en donde paramos ā las diez. A las tres de la tarde sa
limos el Alferez, Sargto. dos Soldados, y io, ā registrar un Parage qe. decia el Sol
dado Jose Antº. Lugo haver visto, y qe. tenia Agua, y tierra, y caminando pa.
el Rumbo del Norte de dha Ra. a buen paso llegamos al Parage a las cuatro, y me
dia, y despues de haverlo registrado todo, hallamos ser el agua muy poca, la
cañada sumamente estrecha, y muy lobrega, la tierra salitrosa, y por con
siguiente inservible, nos volvimos al Rl. el qe. caminando al galope llegamos
ā las seis, y media de la tarde. Dia 18 salimos de este Balle ā las seis de
la mañana, y caminando pa. el Sur, fuimos ā registrar el Parage del Triun
fo, ā donde llegamos ā las nueve de la mañana, y haviendo registradolo
hallamos ser inservible no solo pa. una Misson. pero ni aun pa. un infeliz Rancho
por faltarle lo principal como es el agua corriente, pues no encontramos
mas qe. una Poza grande, muy acantilada, de cuya Poza no sale mas qe.
un hilito de agua el qe. ā muy corto trecho se corta, ā mas, qe. aunqe. saliese

The first page of Fray Vicente de Santa María's diary, describing his exploration
of the territory between missions San Buenaventura and San Gabriel.
Written February 3, 1795. *Fr. Santa María/SBMAL.*

46

no valley, and camped overnight. They proceeded eastward the next morning and arrived in the afternoon at Rancho Encino, two leagues north of the camino real, where Reyes joined the party.[3]

Fray Santa María, in a letter dated September 3, 1795, wrote to Fr. Lasuén about the journey. On August 19, 1795, he describes the site near Reyes' rancho in favorable terms:

> In the afternoon, the ensign, the sergeant, the soldier José Antonio Lugo, the alcalde Reyes (who had reached his rancho in the same morning a little after us), and I set out to investigate. We found the place quite suitable for a mission, because it has much water, much humid land, and also limestone; for we came upon a party of gentiles who were finishing a kiln for burning lime which they had already heaped up. Stone for the foundation of the buildings is near by. There is pine timber in the direction of west-northwest of said locality, not very far away; also pastures are to be found and patches very suitable for cattle; but there is a lack of firewood; for the place has no more than is found in the arroyo, which is about one league long. There we found willows, poplars, alders, and a few live-oaks, at a distance of a quarter or a half league from the mission, if it should be founded there. In this place we came to a ranchería [Achooykomenga] near the dwelling of said Reyes—with enough Indians. They take care of the field of corn, beans, and melons, belonging to said Reyes, which with that of the Indians could be covered with two *fanegas* [1 fanega equals 1.6 (Spanish) bushels] of wheat. These Indians are the cowherds, cattlemen, irrigators, bird-catchers, foremen, horsemen, etc. To this locality belong, and they acknowledge it, the gentiles of other rancherías, such as the Taapa, Tacuyama, Tucuenga, Juyunga, Mapipinga, and others, who have not affiliated with Mission San Gabriel.[4]

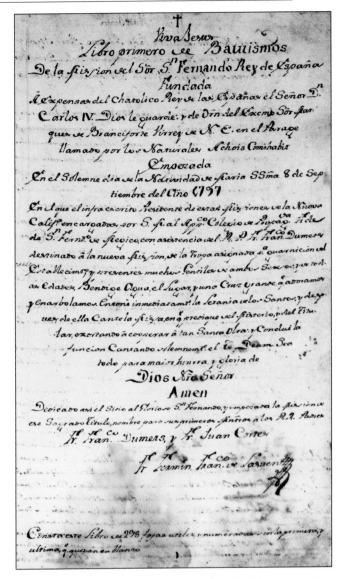

Front page of original San Fernando Mission record: The First Book of Baptismals (*Libro primero de Bautismos*). Lasuén/ACSFM.

---

[3] Ibid., 4–5.

[4] Ibid. Rose Marie Beebe and Robert M. Senkewicz, eds., *Land of Promise and Despair: Chronicles of Early California, 1535–1846* (Berkeley, Calif.: Heyday Books, 2001), 118, where the missionaries' distinction between "neophytes" (baptized Indians) and "gentiles" (unconverted Indians) is described. Recently James A. Sandos has shed consider-able light on these perplexing identities in his "Converting California: Indians and Franciscans in the Mission, 1769–1836," *Boletín: The Journal of the California Mission Studies Association*, vol. 20, no. 1, 2003, 5–10. It has been greatly expanded in *Converting California: Indians and Franciscans in the Mission, 1769–1836* (New Haven and London: Yale University Press, 2004).

Front page of original mission records: The First Book of the Dead (*Libro primero de Difuntos*). *Lasuén/ACSFM.*

(*opposite*) The second page of the Bautismos records the first ten baptisms performed by second *misión presidente* Fr. Fermín Francisco de Lasuén on the day the mission was founded. *Lasuén/ACSFM.*

and, not tarrying, headed for Mission San Gabriel, where they stayed for Mass and a layover. On the fifth day, August 24, they reached the Pueblo of Los Angeles. They continued their journey and arrived at six in the evening at Portezulo, the ranch of the former Los Angeles alcalde, Mariano Verdugo. The next morning they returned to Reyes' Encino ranch. At three in the afternoon the next day, the party began their return to San Buenaventura via the old El Camino Real through the San Fernando Pass.

On August 26, Fr. Santa María wrote that he found the source of the Santa Clara River and saw numerous Indian villages nearby. He weighed the factors which Fr. Crespí and Captain Portolá had considered favorable at an earlier time, but found two reasons for rejecting the site located at the head-waters of the Santa Clara River:

> This zanja is very easy of access, so that with its water some land can be irrigated; but in said district we found no place suitable for establishing a mission. It is six leagues distant from the camino reál to the north and it has the additional draw-back of the pass through the sierra.[5]

---

[5] Engelhardt translated in *San Fernando Rey,* 3–9 (esp. 8), Fr. Santa María's diary written on September 3, 1795, and addressed to Fr. Lasuén. The original diary of Fray Vicente de Santa María in which he writes about the exploration of the territory between San Buenaventura and San Gabriel (4 pp.) is at the Santa Barbara Mission (continued, page 50)

During the next several days, the survey party traveled through more passes and evaluated the suitability of the rancherías along the route to Mission San Gabriel. They left Reyes' ranch, headed north to the foothills of the San Fernando Mountains where they found there was a scarcity of timber, and returned to the ranch for lunch. They then went to Cpl. José María Verdugo's ranch in the Zanja Pass

En el Nombre de Dios todo Poderoso, Padre, Hijo, y Espiri=
tu Santo, tres Personas distintas, y un solo Dios verdadero,
à quien sea Honrra, y Gloria por infinitos siglos de los si=
glos. Amen.

El mismo dia 6 de Sept.e el año 1797, acabada la religiosa funcion
q.e se dice al principio de esta foja, y con la q.e comenzó esta fiesta, con
el Noviso S.n Fernd.o Rey de España, los Gentiles, q.e concurrieron, ofre=
cieron espontaneam.te y con buen afecto diez hijos suios parvulos
cinco de cada sexo, para q.e se Christianasen, Gracias à Dios; y al punto
en la Enrramada misma, en q.e celebrè el S.to Sacrificio de la Misa
bendice la Agua Bautismal, y bauticè solemnemente.

| | |
|---|---|
| 1 Fernd.o Mª Parv.o de Achoicominga | A Fernando Mª como de 1 año llamado de Gentil Coyohua es hijo de Mayo, y de Chemeyo de la Ranchería de Achoicominga. Fue su Padrino Fran.co Perez, el mismo q.e se havia establecido en ese parage. |
| 2 Mariano Fernd.o Parv.o de Yndio | A Mariano Fernando de 2 à 3 años llamado Paqui, hijo de Vaa= mar, y de Vulina de la misma Rancheria. Fue su Padrino Santiago Pico, q.e se arranchado en el parage de Simi. |
| 3 Miguel Maria Parv.o de Yndio | A Miguel Mª de año, y medio, llamado Curur, hijo de Achiango, y de Vahui= hicainan de la misma Rancheria. Fue su Padrino Anastasio Felix Sol= dado de los Ynvalidos, y casado en el Presidio de S.ta Barbara. |
| 4 Gabriel Maria Parv.o de Yndio | A Gabriel Mª de año, y medio llamado Serahgan hijo de Mayo, y de Chemeyo herm.o de Fernd.o Mª de la misma Ranch.a Fue su Padrino Mariano Verdugo casado Sargento retirado arranchado en Cahuenga. |
| 5 Raphael Maria Parv.o de Yndio | A Raphael Mª de 5 à 6 meses, llamado Aquinamohihuaron, hijo de Cacache, y de Lapomihahue de la misma Rancheria. Fue su Padrino Ygnacio Rivera casa= do con Marcela Felix Sarg.to de la Comp.a de S.n Barb.a y Encargado de esta Escolta. |
| 6 Fernando Maria Parv.o de Yndio | A Fernando Mª como de 6 à 7 a.s llamado Huiarraguiña hijo de Pirimabit, y de Suroy de la misma Ranch.a Fue su Padrino Felipe Cortez Soldado de esta Escolta. |
| 7 Maria Fernanda Parv.o de Yndio | A Maria Fernanda de 6 meses llamada Chihuan hija de Mayo, y de Chemeyo hermana de Fernd.o Mª y de Gabl. Mª Fue su Padrino Ant.o Reyes, hijo del dho Fran.co Reyes. |
| 8 Michaela Mª Parv.o de Yndio | A Michaela Mª de 2 à 3 años llamada Huarimon, hija de el Gentil Difunto, y de Si= junamohu de la misma Ranch.a Fue su Padrino el Sobredho Santiago Pico. |
| 9 Gabriela Maria Parv.o de Yndio | A Gabriela Mª de 3 à 4 años llamada Cuinuhya, hija de Chaabe, y de Pebihua, de la misma Ranch.a Fue su Padrino Mari.o Machado, hijo de Juan Machado. |
| 10 Michaela Maria Parv.o de Achoicominga | A Raphaela Mª de 3 à 4 meses llamada Chiauya hija de Pirimabit, y de Huiray herm.a de Fernd.o Mª Fue su Padrino Patricio Pico, à q.e como à el q.e mas adverti el Parentesco Espiri= tual, y el q.e mas Miraciones, y q.e quanto le firme. = ___ |

Fr. Fermin Fran.co de Lasuen

At last, a site was selected. At the end of August 1797, Fr. Lasuén left Mission Santa Barbara with Sgt. Ignacio Olivera and five soldiers in order to establish the new mission. The previous year, on November 12, 1796, Viceroy the Marqués de Branciforte had chosen the name La Misión de San Fernando, Rey de España. After a brief stay at Mission San Buenaventura, Fray Francisco Dumetz, who was appointed the new resident missionary, joined them. The band headed south to Reyes' ranch.[6]

The area adjoining the mission-to-be was called Achooykomenga by the Indians and Achois Comihavit or Achoicominga by the Spaniards, who recorded both spellings in mission documents.[7] Fray

Lasuén blessed the site and named the mission San Fernando, Rey de España, in honor of King Ferdinand III of Spain, the thirteenth-century figure who was canonized in 1671 for his role in defeating the Moors in southern Spain.

On Friday, September 8, 1797, Fr. Lasuén wrote to both his superior, Fr. Pedro Callejas, in Mexico City, and to Gov. Don Diego de Borica. He wrote the following to Diego de Borica:

> It affords me great pleasure to Your Lordship that today, the solemn feast of the Nativity of Most Holy Mary, I blessed water, the grounds, and a large cross which we venerated and erected in a beautiful region known as *Achois Comihabit* by the natives, and located between the Missions of San Buenaventura and San Gabriel. I was assisted by Reverend Father Fray Francisco Dumetz who has been assigned to this mission, and by the troops assigned to guard it, in the presence of many pagans of both sexes and of all ages who showed themselves much pleased and satisfied. I immediately intoned the Litany of All Saints, and following this I sang the Mass, preached a sermon during it, and brought the function to an end by solemnly singing the *Te Deum*.
>
> When breakfast was over, the pagans offered ten of their children, five of each sex, to be baptized, and in the little *enramada*, in the very place where the holy sacrifice of the Mass had been celebrated, I blessed the baptismal font and baptized them solemnly. Thanks be to God. . . .[8]

---

6   Ibid., 10.

7   *Achooykomenga* is the ethnographic spelling proposed by Dr. Pamela Munro, professor of linguistics, UCLA, who specializes in the Gabrielino language. This spelling has been used by William McCawley, *The First Angelinos: The Gabrielino Indians of Los Angeles*, 38–39 (see map on page 36); and John R. Johnson, "The Indians of Mission San Fernando," 252. The variant *Achois Comihavit* is the Spanish spelling attributed to Fray Crespí and used by Engelhardt, *San Fernando Rey*, 10, in the slightly modified form *Achois Comihabit*. See also Bancroft, *History of California*, 1: 561, and Elliott Coues, *On the Trail of a Spanish Pioneer: The Diary and Itinerary of Francisco Garcés, 1775–76*, 2 vols. (New York: Francis P. Harper, 1900), 1: 206. *Achoicominga* is the spelling used in the mission baptismal records for people affiliated with this village.

---

8   Finbar Kenneally, O.F.M., trans. and ed., *Writings of Fermín Francisco de Lasuén*, 2 vols. (Washington, D.C.: Academy of American Franciscan History, 1965), 2: 44, in which the modified spelling of the ranchería *Achois Comihabit* was also used and the translation of "*Gentile*" was given as "pagan." Fr. Lasuén concludes (see epigraph):

May God Our Lord, etc.

*Incipient Mission of San Fernando,*
September 8, 1797.

---

(continued) Archive-Library (SBMAL), catalogued under *Diaries No. 274*. A copy of the title page of this diary is shown herein. By 1795 it was found that traveling north out of the San Fernando Valley toward Mission San Buenaventura was easier via the Conejo Corridor (Rabbit's Pass), the new El Camino Real. Fr. Santa María wrote that the new El Camino Real was six leagues (about 15½ miles) south of both Castaic Junction and the old road. This path is longer but is considerably flatter. It is virtually along the same route that Highway 101 takes today.

# PART II

# LIFE AND WORK

Two Indian women, mother and daughter, are seated in front of their adobe home.
Photograph by G. G. Johnson, ca. 1890. *GGJ/CHS/TICOR* (7156).

# CHAPTER 5
# CULTURE AND LIFE AT THE MISSION

*The Indians as well as the missionaries rise with the sun, go to prayers and mass, which last an hour, and during this time there is cooked in the middle of the square, in three large kettles, barley meal, the grain of which has been roasted previous to being ground; this species of boiled food, which the Indians call* atole, *and of which they are very fond, is seasoned neither with salt or butter, and to us would prove a very insipid mess. . . . The meal continues three quarters of an hour, after which they all return to their labors; in a word everyone is employed in different domestic occupations, and always under the superintendence of one or two of the religious.*

—Jean François Galaup de La Pérouse,
*The First French Expedition to California*

T HE SPANISH MISSIONARIES brought many cultural changes to the indigenous peoples' way of life—in food, clothing, housing, work and recreation. These changes, along with a new religion and its concomitants, had a major impact on the well-being and future of the inhabitants in the valley.[1]

What attracted the natives to live in the mission and what caused them to accept or reject such an intrusion on their lives are questions that are intensely debated today.[2] There is no consensus of thought

---

[1] Webb, "The Tragic Fate of the Mission Indians," in *Indian Life at the Old Missions*, 282–309. For La Pérouse's description while he was at Mission San Carlos in 1786, see Francis Rand Smith, *The Architectural History of Mission San Carlos Borromeo* (Berkeley, Calif.: California Historical Survey Commission, 1921), 22–23; and Jean François Galaup de La Pérouse, *Monterey in 1786: The Journals of Jean François de La Pérouse* (Berkeley, Calif.: Heyday Books, 1989).

[2] Mission critics, to name just a few, include: Robert F. Heizer, ed., *The Destruction of the California Indians* (Santa Barbara, Calif.: Peregrine Smith, Inc., 1974), v–ix; and Sherburne F. Cook, *The Conflict between the California Indian and White Civilization* (Berkeley, Calif.: University of California Press, 1976), Part I—The Indian Versus the Spanish Mission (originally published as Ibero-Americana Volume 21, 1943), 76–84. A treatise critical of the mission system was written by Robert H. Jackson and Edward Castillo, *Indians, Franciscans, and Spanish Colonization—The Impact of the Mission System on California Indians* (Albuquerque: University of New Mexico Press, 1995). A strongly anti-mission posture is taken by Rupert and Jeannette Costo, eds., in *The Missions of California: A Legacy of Genocide* (San Francisco: Indian Historian Press, 1987). Perhaps no defender of the pro-Franciscan cause has been more adamant and prolific than Francis F. Guest, O.F.M., "An Examination of the Thesis of S.F. Cook on the Forced Conversion of Indians in the California Missions," *Southern California Quarterly* (continued)

Indian worker on a ladder harvesting prickly pear fruit (*tuna*) at Mission San Fernando. Drawn by Charles Koppel in 1853, the sketch was subsequently etched and produced by J. W. Orr, Schenectady, N.Y. *CK/JBG.*

among anthropologists, linguists, clerics, and historians, but the theories put forth run the gamut. Two of them are polarizing. At one end of the spectrum is the idealistic, pro-Franciscan view, termed "Christophilic Triumphalism" by history professor David J. Weber.[3] According to this view, the missionaries were self-sacrificing religious men who were benevolent and provided for the spiritual well-being of their charges, as well as their basic needs of food, shelter, and clothing. In short, it was a blissful lifestyle that the natives welcomed and enjoyed in bucolic surroundings. The tranquil life in old Cal-

ifornia mission days was a popular, beloved theme used in romantic stories and mission histories of the early twentieth century.[4]

At the other extreme is the anti-Franciscan view that the natives were victims and that missionization destroyed their culture. Today, "Christophilic Nihilism," alternately known as "Christophobic Nihilism," terms coined by history professor James A. Sandos, is the antithesis of "Triumphalism."[5] The

---

(*continued*) 61 (Spring, 1979): 1–77, and "Cultural Perspectives on California Mission Life," *Southern California Quarterly* 65 (Spring, 1983): 1–65, and "An Inquiry Into the Role of the Discipline in California Mission Life," *Southern California Quarterly* 71 (Spring, 1989): 1–68.

[3] David J. Weber, "Blood of Martyrs, Blood of Indians: Toward a More Balanced View of Spanish Missions in Seventeenth Century North America," in *Columbian Consequences*, David Hurst Thomas, ed., 3 vols. (Washington, D.C.: Smithsonian Institute Press, 1989–91), 2: 429–48.

[4] The myth of the tranquil life in bucolic surroundings was promoted by Helen Hunt Jackson, *Ramona—A Story* (Boston: Cambridge University Press, 1894), and Maria Antonia Fields, *Chimes of Mission Bells* (San Francisco: The Philopolis Press, 1914). Engelhardt's *San Fernando Rey—The Mission of the Valley*, written in the 1920s, is one of a series on the Alta California missions. It is pro-Franciscan, anti-military, and anti-Spanish/Mexican government.

[5] James A. Sandos, "Between Crucifix and Lance: Indian-White Relations in California, 1769–1848," in *Contested Eden: California Before the Gold Rush*, Ramón Gutiérrez and Richard Orsi, eds., *The Magazine of the California Historical Society* 76, 2–3 (Berkeley: University of California Press, 1997): 196–229, esp. 222, and Sandos, "Converting California," 5–10.

indigenous peoples' entire culture is said to have been completely turned upside down. They were dragged against their will to the mission. They had to submit to a "forced conversion" to Christianity or face punishment and were coerced to live in a concentration-camp–like atmosphere.[6] Punishment by flogging was to be expected if they wandered away or escaped from the mission. By submitting to baptism they became *neófitos* (their acceptance of Christianity and true conversion, however, are questionable).[7] Neófitos were subjected to severe physical punishments and acts of humiliation if they regressed. By the act of baptism, they were regarded as having joined the mission community "voluntarily" and were not permitted to change their minds.[8]

Any reader seriously interested in these and other disputatious matters, including the impact of diseases and rebellious native attacks, should consult the readings listed in the notes.[9] Space and pertinence to this illustrated history do not permit their discussion here. Suffice it to say, some of the early inhabitants approached the newcomers and the mission establishment with curiosity; enticed by the prospect of abundant food, shelter, and the warmth and protection of the strangers, they were intrigued by the vestments, rituals, colors, and sounds of the newcomers' religion. Many remained voluntarily. But others took flight, finding mission life unacceptable and the friars' treatment of them cruel.[10] They may have had just cause, as there is ample historic documentation that coercion, threats of death without eternal hope, torture, or punishment for disobeying the rules did take place.

One needs to be cautious about taking either extreme view of mission life, as each is an incomplete and inadequate explanation of mission history and has its own myths. Sandos, who recognizes the polarization in contemporary writings, mentions that he detects "the beginning of a 'new school' of historiography, one that, at least nominally, seeks to move beyond the old pro- and anti-mission dichotomy."[11] One can only assume that the friars were not absolute tyrants and monsters and that the indigenous peoples must have had some measure of satisfaction with mission life at Mission San Fernando, since, at the time of its population peak in 1811, they far outnumbered the friars and soldiers and could have easily escaped if they wished. In that year, there were 1,081 natives, 2 resident friars, and 6 soldiers.[12]

⊛    ⊛    ⊛

The friars transformed the Indians' means of subsistence from hunting and gathering to husbandry. They taught them how to grow corn, wheat, and beans and to raise domestic animals for food. Agriculture provided a steady supply of food and eventually a surplus. In time, the herds at the mission thrived and meat production far outpaced daily consumption. Surplus meat was sun-dried to become *carne seca* (beef jerky).[13] But even with preservation,

---

[6]  Cook, *Conflict*, 73.

[7]  James A. Sandos, "Converting California," 5–10, and "Christianization Among the Chumash: An Ethnohistoric Approach," *American Indian Quarterly* 15 (1991): 65–89.

[8]  Sandos, "Between Crucifix and Lance," 205.

[9]  Refer to those mentioned above. Heizer, Cook, Jackson and Castillo, and Costo and Costo are critical of the mission institution. See also John O. Pohlmann, "California's Mission Myth," Ph.D. diss., University of California Los Angeles, 1974, and Alejandro Murguía, *The Medicine of Memory: A Mexica Clan in California* (Austin: University of Texas Press, 2002). In the chapter "The 'Good Old Mission Days' Never Existed," Murguía is very critical of the mission system. Those more interested in the view of Christophilic triumphalism should refer to the works written by Engelhardt, Geiger, Guest, and Francis J. Weber listed in the Bibliography.

[10]  Jackson and Castillo, *Impact of the Mission System*, 108.

[11]  Sandos, "Between Crucifix and Lance," 222.

[12]  Engelhardt, *San Fernando Rey*, 91.

[13]  Webb, *Indian Life at the Old Missions*, 198–99.

*(above)* Two young children stand in front of what remains of the Indian barracks, ca. 1883.
The old adobe house is an earlier picture of the one below.
*Robert B. Honeyman Jr. Collection, Bancroft Library. D45—IWT/UCB (1905.17160:48).*

*(below)* An elderly Indian woman, who reportedly married nine times, is shown
sweeping outside her adobe home. *D20—USC/TICOR (12072).*

The old adobe structure was home to the gardener, ca. 1885. *USC/TICOR (344)*.

there was such an abundance that meat was left to rot in the sun or was hauled off, placed into piles, and burned.

Agriculture created new livelihoods and skills. The Indians became *granjeros* (farmers) and *arrieros* (muleteers). They also learned the skills of herding, blacksmithing, and tanning that went along with becoming *vaqueros* (cowboys).

Prior to the Spaniards' arrival in the valley, Indian clothing was simple and minimal. In August 1795, Fray Santa María, on the expedition to find a site for a new mission in the Valley of the Live Oaks, penned in his journal that he saw Indian muleteers wearing sombreros, blankets, and shoes. At this early date, the natives' clothing reflected Spanish influence, the result of contact with inhabitants from the nearby Pueblo de Los Angeles and the ranchos of Mariano Verdugo and Francisco Reyes.[14]

In response to question 36 of the 1812 *Interrogatorio* sent to the missions, Friars Pedro Múñoz and Joaquín Pasqual Nuez described the clothing worn by the mission natives:

The clothing the Indians have worn until now are the following: The men wear a shirt of wool called *cotón*, a strip of woolen cloth with which instead of pants they cover themselves and which is called *taparabo* [loincloth], and a blanket. The women wear the same kind of shirt or *cotón*, a petticoat and a blanket. All go barefoot. The means that could be employed to have the Indians clothed would be the encouragement and promotion of commerce. All dress themselves from the products of the mission. Mission San Fernando Rey, February 3, 1814.

—Fr. Pedro Múñoz, Fr. Joaquin Pasqual Nuez.[15]

By 1814, the manufacture of clothing at the mission was well underway. The Indians were able to produce articles of clothing not only for themselves but also for others. Surplus production promoted commerce and mission self-sufficiency.

The friars brought with them strange concepts of design and construction for housing. The buildings were rectangular, not circular like the Indians' individual huts. Adobe, a mixture of clay soil, crushed straw, and water, was their material of choice and supplanted the natural fibers of tule, which the Indians had used for thatching the huts.

---

[14] Engelhardt, *San Fernando Rey*, 9; Bancroft, *History of California*, 1: 662–63.

[15] Geiger, *As the Padres Saw Them*, 148.

The last remnant of Indian housing was located southwest of the mission, ca. 1945. *KEP.*

The Spanish believed that dwellings, as well as other types of buildings, should be permanent. They considered wasteful and inefficient the Indian custom of burning down their huts and rebuilding them nearby to take care of insect and vermin infestations. But it is believed today that this practice provided clean and healthful housing and that the changeover to adobe housing, coupled with different sanitation methods, may have been a factor contributing to the eventual decline in the Indian population.[16]

The friars imposed changes on the Indians' habitation customs. Communal living, with an extended family in a single hut, was no longer permitted. In their living quarters, unmarried members, both young and old, were segregated; the females were separated and locked up at night in their own quarters to protect them from the Spanish soldiers, who were wont to take liberties with the local women,

as there was a dearth of women in the early colonization period.[17] Married couples were allowed to live together in small adobe houses with a community kitchen for food preparation.

[16] Jackson and Castillo, *Impact of the Mission System,* 43–44 and 49.

[17] David J. Weber, *Spanish Frontier,* 247–51, describes the Indians' attitudinal transition from "cautious but friendly curiosity of the Spaniards to soon their contempt." He quotes Fr. Junípero Serra's lament on the Spanish soldiers' lust and rape of the indigenous woman: "It is as though a plague of immorality had broken out." Weber continues, "The soldiers' sexual violence toward Indian woman, either more excessive than on earlier frontiers or better documented, hardened Franciscan resistance to integrating non-Indians into the new mission communities." Other reasons the Franciscans continued to distrust the *gente de razón* and to rebel against integrating them onto mission lands will be discussed in Chapters 11: The Outpost and 14: Secularization and Political Intrigue. Hispanic women did not accompany their husbands to Alta California until the expeditions of Rivera y Moncada (which traveled up Baja California) and Juan Bautista de Anza (which traveled over the Sonora Desert). Both occurred in 1774.

Rogério Rocha, the last San Fernando Mission Indian, poses
in front of an adobe wall, ca. 1900. *SWM-N22126.*

The missionaries brought Roman Catholicism, its colorful trappings, rites, and music to the Indians. They introduced spiritual beliefs and practices that were far different from anything the Indians had known prior to contact with Europeans. They indoctrinated the natives, with the intention of making them neophytes.

On the Portolá expedition to Alta California in 1769, the friars and military used as interpreters a number of Christianized Indians brought from the missions of Baja California. Eventually, the friars and new missionary recruits were supposed to learn the local dialects and a few did, most notably Friars Buenaventura Sitjar and Miguel Pieras, founders of Mission San Antonio de Padua, but none became fluent in the Indian dialects in the San Fernando Valley.[18]

To promote communication, the padres at Mission San Fernando adopted a practical solution. Rather than attempting the nearly impossible task of learning the multitude of dialects spoken in the valley, they taught the indigenous peoples one language—Spanish. But language remained a hurdle, and over the next seventeen years Spanish language fluency among the Indians was still limited, according to the friars' *respuesta* to question 3 of the 1812 *Interrogatorio*.

The number of the baptized Indians grew rapidly at first, from 56 in 1797 to 985 in 1804, but dropped to 963 by 1810. By 1811 the official record jumped to 1,081, but that number was never exceeded. The census numbers remained above 1,000 from 1811 through 1822, after which there was a slow decline. In 1827 the count was 900 neophytes. In the 1835 inventory of property and population, there were 541 neophytes. In 1842, the last year of a regular census, the number had dwindled to 400.[19]

The missionaries brought with them large, hollow metal objects with a metal tongue on the inside. When struck, they created a loud, clanging sound. Bells have been, from time immemorial, an integral part of European religious life, but were unfamiliar to the indigenous peoples. Early on, mission bells served as a time clock, clanging out the time of day for prayers and other activities. They regulated the missionaries' and their wards' lives. Soon the sounding of bells would disrupt the relatively peaceful, quiet lives of the inhabitants.

A normal day at the mission would begin at dawn with the ringing of the *Angelus*, which was rung three times a day—in the morning, at noon, and in the evening—to announce the time of the Angelus, a devotion commemorating the Incarnation. The Angelus called the Indians to prayer in the church. This was followed by a short instruction. Another bell announced breakfast, and then another sent them off to their various assigned tasks. From noon to two o'clock the Indians had lunch, then a siesta, and returned to work until about five o'clock. At six o'clock the Angelus announced evening prayers and devotions, after which supper was served. Neophytes were allowed free time for games and other activities until the Poor Souls' bell rang at eight o'clock. This was the daily routine.

On Sundays and traditional Christian holidays, no work was done. Fiestas and some original Indian ceremonies were occasionally permitted. As a change from the daily routine, excursions to the local mountains to gather seeds, acorns, pine nuts, and berries were also permitted. These outings were more common early in the mission era when food supplies were meager. They were a concession to the Indians' former lifestyle so that neophytes would not feel the need to join their non-mission brethren.[20]

[18] Geiger, O.F.M., *Franciscan Missionaries*, 45–47.

[19] Engelhardt, *San Fernando Rey*, 51–63.

[20] Webb, *Indian Life at the Old Missions*, 40–41 and 57–58, for a very readable account of the Indians' lifestyle as it transi-

Romanticized stories of the missions, most notably Helen Hunt Jackson's *Ramona*, written in 1874, have an enduring power that leaves readers with the impression that mission life was the perfect and tranquil existence. In fact, it was the contrary. In the neighboring Santa Barbara, Santa Inés, and La Purísima missions, the Chumash revolt of 1824 is an example of the growing dissatisfaction that some indigenous peoples had toward the missions and their leaders. The situation led to open rebellion. More serious than most, this revolt caused many Indians to resist and flee from the missions.[21] At San Fernando, rebels joined other gentiles and sometimes assisted in occasional raids on livestock and other mission property.[22]

Upon their capture and return to the mission, Indians who ran away and especially those who did so repeatedly, oftentimes faced severe punishments, including placement in stocks, imprisonment in chains, and lashings. Some mission critics have accused the missionaries of brutality and starvation of the Indians, a few even going so far as to accuse the missionaries of genocide.[23] No doubt, the friars approved of the punishments, which were mandat-

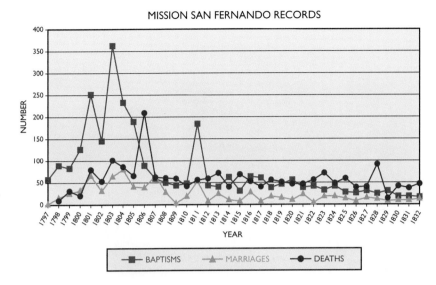

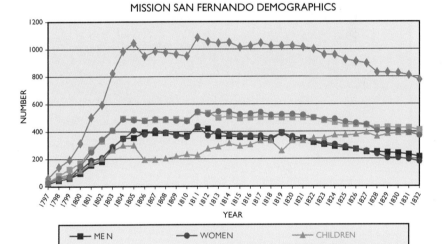

*Courtesy of Troy Greenwood.*

ed by the government. Some critics have suggested that harsh discipline contributed to the decline in the Indian population.[24] Although the punishments are considered "cruel and unusual" by today's standards, mission defenders point out that such punishments were considered appropriate and acceptable in their day.[25]

---

tioned into the mission period. The term *neófitos* (novices or beginners) was used since the eighteenth century by the Spanish clergy to indicate baptized or "Christianized" Indians. For insight into this subject, refer to the writings of James A. Sandos, esp. *Converting California*.

[21] Sandos, "Levantamiento!: The 1824 Chumash Uprising Reconsidered," *Southern California Quarterly* 67, 2 (Summer, 1985): 311–29.

[22] Engelhardt, *San Fernando Rey*, 57.

[23] Rupert and Jeannette Costo, eds., *A Legacy of Genocide*.

---

[24] Cook, *Conflict*, 113–34.

[25] Guest, "Cultural Perspectives on California Mission Life," 1–65.

Ruins of San Fernando Mission, Calif., 1886.
*HL—photPF 6260.*

Amid the controversy two things are evident. First, the Indian population in all California missions (except for Mission San Luis Rey, whose birth rate up to 1825 exceeded the death rate)[26] suffered declines due to disease, homicide, and malnutrition, both before and after secularization.[27] Second, the missionaries did not intend to hasten the demise of the

Indian population, as this outcome was obviously not in their own and the Indians' best interests. The friars' main purpose was to increase the number of Indian converts, thus growing the missions spiritually and economically, and it was much to their dismay that the Indian population diminished.

While Mission San Fernando, along with most of the other Alta California missions, was experiencing a declining Indian population, a policy was about to be put in place which exacerbated the situation: The Mexican government was planning to remove mission administration and lands from Franciscan control. The lives of the Indians were soon to be changed once again.

[26] Zephyrin Engelhardt, O.F.M., *San Luis Rey—The King of the Missions* (San Francisco: The James H. Barry Company, 1921), 220. His data was plotted in Robert H. Jackson, *Indian Population Decline: The Missions of Northwestern New Spain, 1687–1840* (Albuquerque: University of New Mexico Press, 1994), 89–90.

[27] Heizer, *Destruction*, vi.

THE MISSION WAS A HOME AND A WORKING RANCH.
Californio ranch hands pose in front of the door leading to the sala.
Antonio Bandini is seated (*center*) on the bench, ca. 1890. *CHS/TICOR* (*4277*).

(*opposite, top*) Wooden bench in covento arcade, ca. 1895. *UCLA.*

(*opposite, bottom*) Transients with knapsacks walk through the arcade of the convento, ca. 1900. *UCLA.*

(*this page, top*) Families on buckboards are shown in front of the convento's west end, ca. 1900. *CHS/TICOR (7764) and SWM-P19006.*

(*this page, bottom*) Man at the west end of the convento, ca. 1906. *Marie Walsh Harrington Collection. D40—Elson/ACSFM.*

The San Fernando Mission luncheon party preparations are in place. The tables set the arcade is graced with palm fronds, May 30, 1905. On this date, Charles Fletcher Lummis wrote in his diary: "I arise at 6 [A.M.]. I shave, I leave at 7 [A.M.] and take the train at 8:30 [A.M.] to San Fernando. About 160 [people] go [to San Fernando]. People meet us at station and drive to Mission. Find things not so bad there. Photo various things and the meal in the portals of the convent [convento]. They feed us well. Hubbard takes me to his adobe incubator chicken-ranch. See ball game in which the San Fernando boys beat a L.A. crowd—18 to 0. Much completed for me. We leave at 4:30 [P.M.], [I] arrive at 5 [P.M.]." Translated from the part Spanish/part English diary of C. F. Lummis for May 30, 1905. *CFL/SWM-N744/P19102.*

(*right*) The luncheon at San Fernando Mission on May 30, 1905. The party guests are seated at long tables located at the east end of the convento corridor; they are about to eat, with food on their plates. Photo by C. F. Lummis. *CFL/SWM-N750/P19101.*

(*below*) San Fernando Mission (209). Views of Los Angeles and Vicinity in Mid-Winter. By J. B. Blanchard, 569 No. Main Street, Los Angeles, ca. 1895. *JBB/HL—photPF 480.*

209  SAN FERNANDO MISSION

(*above*) Lucretia del Valle, the great-grand-daughter of Antonio del Valle, poses in the corridor of the convento, ca. 1916. She was famous in her own right, making her debut as an actress in John Steven McGroarty's outdoor pageant "The Mission Play" and starring in 850 performances. *SWM-P19104.*

(*left*) Two ladies in festive attire in the convento's portico. Photo by W. C. Dickerson, ca. 1922. *WCD/SWM-N1487.*

A beautiful visitor stands in front of the new wall of Brand Park. In the background
the convento and the commemorative El Camino Real bell can be seen, ca. 1927. *ACSFM.*

(*left*) Two of the mission's 1938–41 restorers are shown in this group picture. When Sergeant Jean C. L'Empereur, who had an active part in restoring the mission, left in 1944, he was honored with a farewell party at the mission. Standing in the back row (*second from the left to the right*): Dr. Mark R. Harrington, Jean C. L'Empereur, Father Charles Burns, O.M.I., Dr. Malcolm McKenzie, and Frank Gutierrez. Entertainers standing at each end and the woman seated in the middle are not known. *ACSFM.*

(*below*) Two ladies in festive Mexican attire converse outside the workshop ruins and the church, which is retained by a buttress, ca. 1944. *KEP.*

As automobile travel became more popular, many motorists frequented the mission. Tourists are seen in their automobile in the north orchard. The adobe wall and church are in the background. Most likely, this was a promotional, i.e., a bogus, postcard, which was a popular way to encourage automotive and aeroplane support and production in the early 1900s. Ca. 1917. *KEP.*

(*left*) Motorists pass each other near the intersection of what became Columbus Avenue and San Fernando Mission Boulevard, ca. 1919. *UCLA.*

(*below*) Three gentlemen stop their touring car and pose on the circular fountain in front of the convento, ca. 1920. *ACSFM.*

(*opposite, top*) Ford Model Ts parked at curb and traveling down the dusty San Fernando Mission Road, ca. 1924. *LAA.*

(*opposite, bottom*) Visitors park their cars on San Fernando Mission Boulevard in front of the convento, ca. 1960. *SPNBPC/LAPL.*

Sketch of "M. of San Fernando," made in 1856. Drawn for his journal, artist Henry Miller
shows the mission's vast surroundings, building complex, herded horses, roaming cattle, three walled-in arches,
and a lean-to at the west end of the convento. *Courtesy of the Bancroft Library, University of California, Berkeley, California. HM/UCB.*

# CHAPTER 6
# AGRICULTURE AND COMMERCE

*The mission of San Fernando is situated at the head of an extensive and very fertile
plain, judging from the luxuriance of the grass and other vegetation now springing up.
I noticed in the granary from which our horses were supplied with food, many thousand bushels of corn. The ear is smaller than that of the corn of the Southern States. It
resembles the maize cultivated in the Northern States, the kernel being hard and polished.
Large herds of cattle and sheep were grazing upon the plain in sight of the mission.*
—Edwin Bryant, *What I Saw in California*

FINANCIAL SUPPORT for Mission San Fernando, and similarly for other California missions, came from the Pious Fund, a sum of
money created by gifts and donations of wealthy
private individuals and religious societies for carrying on missionary work among the natives. The
fund was established and administered by the Jesuits
in 1697 until their expulsion from Mexico in 1767.
The Crown then took control over the fund, hold-
ing its properties in trust for the benefit and support of the missions. A Royal Commission managed it until Mexican independence, when it passed
into the hands of the new government. It remained
under the control and management of Mexico
until 1836. After the Californias were erected into a
diocese, the administration and control of the fund
went to Bishop Francisco García Diego, remaining
with him until 1842, when General Santa Ana issued
decrees stating that the Mexican government would
resume control of the fund and incorporate its prop-

erties into the National Treasury of the Mexican
Republic.[1]

Each Alta California mission was allotted 1,000
pesos for expenses. The money did not go directly
to the mission for which it was intended, but rather
to the Apostolic College of San Fernando in Mexico City, which purchased farm implements, church
and household goods, and other necessities. The
400-peso annual stipend for the missionaries was
sent to them in the form of goods and materials
they requested.

Fledgling missions were largely dependent on the
older, established ones for their initial supply of
food and livestock. Mission San Fernando received
its initial supply of livestock from the four nearby
missions. Second mission *presidente* Fray Fermín

---

[1] Jackson H. Ralston, "Pious Fund of the Californias," in
*Foreign Relations of the United States—1902: United States vs. Mex-
ico* (Washington, D.C.: Government Printing Office, 1903),
Part II, 21–29.

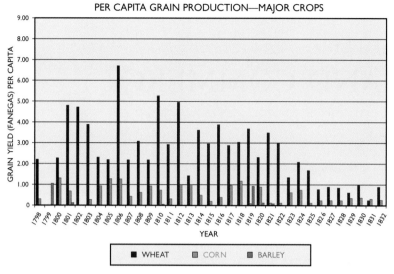

PER CAPITA GRAIN PRODUCTION—MAJOR CROPS

■ WHEAT   ■ CORN   ■ BARLEY

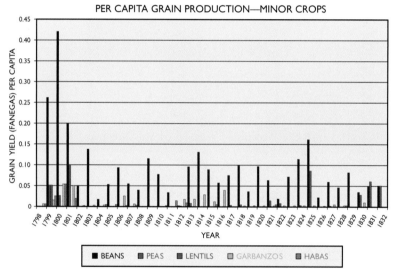

PER CAPITA GRAIN PRODUCTION—MINOR CROPS

■ BEANS   ■ PEAS   ■ LENTILS   ■ GARBANZOS   ■ HABAS

*All graphs courtesy of Troy Greenwood.*

Santa Barbara, San Buenaventura, and San Gabriel.[2]

Contributions from Mission San Juan Capistrano soon arrived. By the end of the month, inventory numbers grew to 18 mules, 46 horses, 16 yoke of oxen, 310 cattle, and 508 sheep.[3]

One year after the mission's founding, 75 bushels of planted crops, including wheat, corn, beans, peas, lentils, and garbanzos, yielded a total harvest of 578 bushels. By 1804, the yield nearly doubled. Two hundred and forty-five bushels of planted crops yielded a harvest of 4,707 bushels of grain. Wheat led the crops, followed by corn, beans, and garbanzos. The cultivation of *habas* (horse or broad beans) in small vegetable patches was attempted in only three years—1801, 1806, and 1813. Likewise, barley was planted in only three years—1799 (having the largest yield), 1801, and 1810. Crops sown and harvest yields for the period 1769–1832 are shown in graphs on pages 76–77.[4]

Livestock was the backbone of the mission economy. Among the livestock, cattle were the most important, providing an array of goods—meat, hides, tallow and other by-products. Cowhides, called *pesos de cuero* (leather dollars), crude rawhide bags filled with tallow, grain, otter skins, hemp, and jerked beef were regularly traded. After 1810 these goods became valuable on the black market, when supplies

Francisco de Lasuén wrote a letter on September 8, 1797, to Fr. Pedro Callejas, the Reverend Fray, Guardian of the College of San Fernando of Mexico. In this letter he enumerated the livestock donated to San Fernando:

> The following have been supplied to the new mission: nine tame mules, ten tame horses, twelve mares with the stallion (stud), eight yoke of oxen, one hundred and twenty cows, three bulls, thirty-two heifers (young bulls), two hundred lambs, four service rams and fifty altered (castrated) ones; and all of these have been donated by the Missions of

2   Fermín Lasuén, "To Fray Pedro Callejas," September 8, 1797, Kenneally, trans. and ed., *Writings of Fermín Francisco de Lasuén*, vol. 2, 44–45; Francis J. Weber, *The Mission in the Valley* (Hong Kong: Libra Press Limited, 1975), 2.

3   Engelhardt, *San Fernando Rey*, 14.

4   Ibid., 97–98.

# MAJOR CROPS
## WHEAT, CORN & BARLEY PRODUCTION
### · MISSION SAN FERNANDO

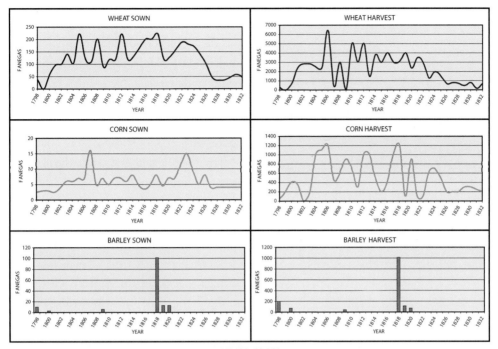

# MINOR CROPS
## BEANS, PEAS, LENTILS, GARBANZOS & HABAS PRODUCTION
### MISSION SAN FERNANDO

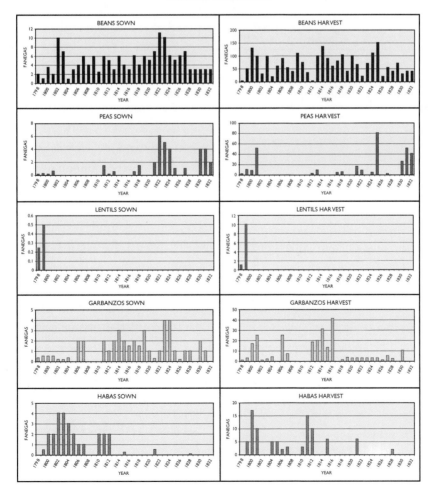

77

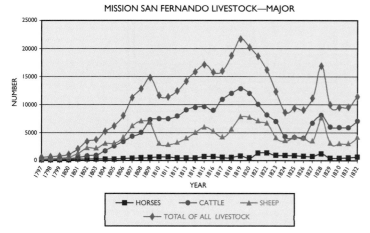

MISSION SAN FERNANDO LIVESTOCK—MAJOR

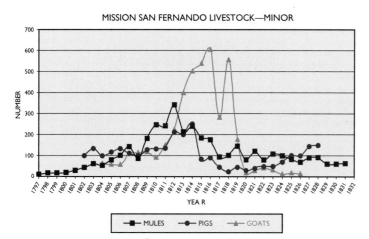

MISSION SAN FERNANDO LIVESTOCK—MINOR

ity. Under Spanish law, trading with foreign ships was illegal but continued nonetheless, until Mexico gained its independence from Spain in 1821 and could trade freely.[7]

In 1819 the herds at Mission San Fernando reached a peak, with 21,745 head in the tally. Cattle led the count with 12,800; sheep, 7,800; goats, 176; horses, 780; mules, 144; and pigs, 45. In the 1820s, their numbers fell considerably.

The Santa Barbara presidio had for a decade depended on Mission San Fernando for agricultural products and manufactured goods, but during the Mexican period, from independence onward, the military's demand for consumables increased and strained the mission's resources. Fray Francisco González de Ibarra constantly complained of the military's demands and the worthless Mexican government drafts used as payment by presidio soldiers.[8] All recorded livestock production for the period 1769–1832 is shown in the graphs on this page.[9]

In 1821 the mission and its outpost, Rancho San Francisco de Xavier, suffered crop damage from insects and varmints. *Chapulines* (locusts) and *orugas* (caterpillars) were common marauding pests. That year, Fr. Ibarra, in one of many letters to Capt. José de la Guerra y Noriega at Santa Barbara, bemoaned the fact that caterpillars consumed the habas and locusts covered the wheat fields.[10] In his letter of September 17, 1821, to the captain, Fr. Ibarra wrote:

> I just came from Rancho de San Francisco. Things are as I said. There are only sixty or seventy fanegas [of corn]. Rabbits and hares and worms have

from Mexico to the mission were interrupted by Mexico's war for independence from Spain.[5]

The time became ripe for illicit commerce.[6] The mission's prized commodities were sold to trading ships off the California coast in exchange for sorely needed supplies. The secluded coves along the coast provided opportune sites for clandestine activ-

5   *California Missions: A Pictorial History* (Menlo Park, Calif.: Sunset Books, 1974), 41–42.

6   William J. Barger, "Furs, Hides, and a Little Larceny" *Southern California Quarterly* 85, 4 (Winter 2003): 382–412.

7   Ibid., 34.

8   Engelhardt, *San Fernando Rey*, 25; John A. Berger, *The Franciscan Missions of California* (New York: G.P. Putnam's Sons, 1941), 172–73.

9   Engelhardt, *San Fernando Rey*; see his table on page 102.

10  Ibid., 38.

(*above*) Horsemen ride in front of the arcade at the west end of the convento. Photo by C. C. Pierce, ca. 1904. *CCP/KEP.*

(*right*) Two horsemen, buckboard and driver in front of the convento and two completed Porter Land and Water Company buildings, ca. 1880. *CHS/TICOR (8998) and SWM-P19005.*

Horses pass in front of convento.
Photo by George Wharton James, ca. 1900. *GWJ/SWM-P19090.*

done damage to the crop. In effect, on Monday I shall order twenty-nine fanegas to be husked, which will be taken as far as San Buenaventura.[11]

In 1827 Fr. Ibarra sent a report to Gov. José de Echeandía explaining the mission's dwindling agricultural output:

*Lands Irrigated.*—In this mission wheat is sown, producing, as a rule, what is necessary for the inhabitants. Neither of corn nor of beans can more than one fanega be planted on account of lack of water; and even this fanega must be sown outside the reg-

ular time, otherwise the *chapulines* will devour them. At Cahuenga and San Francisco are lands quite sufficient for beans and corn; but in the years 1825 and 1826, on account of the great floods that made wide ravines in some places and in others covered the soil with sand, land was very scarce for the necessary corn and beans.[12]

In the same year, Fr. Ibarra wrote in his annual report that there were 6,000 head of cattle and 7,000 sheep. Five years later, the numbers diverged: the inventory of cattle increased by 1,000 but sheep decreased by 3,000. In the ensuing years, the number of livestock declined appreciably.

In June 1838, under Antonio del Valle's administration, the inventory for resources was valued at $156,915, with livestock at $53,854. By 1842, there were 1,500 head of cattle (Engelhardt mistakenly cited

---

[11] Fr. Ibarra's protestations about mistreatment by the military, in his correspondence to Capt. José de la Guerra, commandant of the Santa Barbara presidio between 1821 and 1825, are presented here in English translation. See Engelhardt, *San Fernando Rey,* 38 and 40–44, where the Ibarra translations were made by Fr. Engelhardt, using the original *De la Guerra Papers* found at the Santa Barbara Mission Archive-Library. Englehardt consistently and mistakenly added an accent to fanega in his translations.

[12] Ibid., 47.

Sheep graze on mission grounds north of the complex.
Photo by Harold A. Parker, ca. 1898. *HAP/SWM-P19089.*

7,500), about 2,000 sheep, and 400 horses. In the January 1, 1846, inventory, there was a drastic decline in the herds—to a mere 74 head of cattle, 375 sheep, and 9 yoke of oxen. There was an increase, however, to 726 of unbroken and tame horses.[13]

An unfortunate outcome of secularization (see Chapter 14) was the rapid decline in the number of livestock at the missions. At all the missions, several thousand head of cattle were slaughtered in a relatively short period of time to reap quick profits in hides. The natives, the padres and, egregiously, the officials and commissioners who entered the region after secularization—all had a hand in exacerbating a bad situation.

The slaughter of cattle occurred at all the missions, with Mission San Fernando contributing only a small part to the total massacre. Heavy slaugh-

tering was taking place at Missions San Luis Rey, San Gabriel and La Purísima de Concepción, where individuals not under mission authority were contracted to execute massive kills.[14]

The Mexican governor, the padres, mission administrators, and government officials were also responsible for the slaughter of mission herds. Juan Bandini, a local settler and the administrator of Mission San Gabriel (1838–1840), wrote that over 2,000 head were killed in a day at one mission. The last Mexican governor, Pío Pico, wrote about extensive contracts to kill cattle and says that he himself had a contract to kill over 5,000 cattle at San Gabriel. The padres, under orders from their prelates to convert mission wealth quickly, contributed to the annihilation of the herds; the proceeds of the sales were distributed among the neophytes. Under

[13] Ibid., 65–67.

[14] Bancroft, *History of California,* 3: 348–49.

Mission San Fernando—looking southeast from the Santa Susana Mountains.
Haze hides the Santa Monica Mountains toward Cahuenga Pass, ca. 1930. *CHS/TICOR* (12637).

administrator Domingo Carrillo, a huge slaughter took place at La Purísima de Concepción. Government officials, too, brought ruin to the herds to pay off debts. They employed contractors, vaqueros, and Indians for the express purpose of slaughtering cattle for their hides. In their single-mindedness, they discarded the usual consumable and usable products for which cattle were raised. They left meat in huge piles to rot and pollute the region and discarded the fat, which could have been used to make soap.[15]

William E. P. Hartnell, visitador general of the Alta California missions, while on his inspection tour in 1839 and at Mission San Fernando to take inventory between June 17 and 20, granted license to the administrator of Mission San Gabriel (Juan Bandini) to kill one hundred head of cattle, "mainly for the purpose of making soap." During his visit, he also granted other authorizations to slaughter cows and bulls at Missions Santa Inés and Purísima.[16]

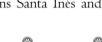

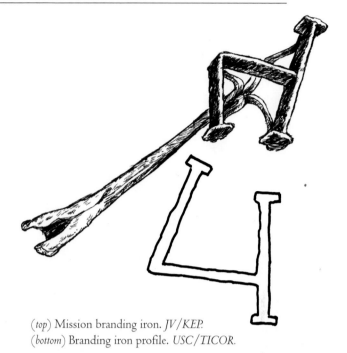

(*top*) Mission branding iron. *JV/KEP.*
(*bottom*) Branding iron profile. *USC/TICOR.*

The vineyards, started from humble grape cuttings brought by Fr. Serra and his companions from Baja California, flourished. By 1832, there were 32,000 grapevines and shoots listed in inventory.[17] The reddish-black grape, the so-called "mission grape," was the only species grown in Alta California until 1833.[18] It produced wine of a pleasant claret type, according to visitors to the mission, and the brandy was also said to be good.

Three individuals spoke of the quality of the wine

at Mission San Fernando post-secularization. Author Edwin Bryant wrote: "The season of the grapes has passed, but there are extensive vineyards at this mission. I drank, soon after my arrival, a glass of red wine manufactured here, and of good quality."[19] Lt. Robert Stockton Williamson, the topographer who came from Gila, Arizona, in 1853 to find a practical route for a railroad to San Francisco, purchased a wine which he described as "a quantity of very pleasant red wine similar to claret."[20] Artist Henry Miller, who came to the mission in 1856, wrote:

> The proprietor and his family being absent, I went to a Frenchman who attends to one of the large orchards and vineyards, for which he shares the prof-

[15] Engelhardt, *San Fernando Rey*, 51.

[16] William E. P. Hartnell, *The Diary and Copybook of William E. P. Hartnell: Visitador General of the Missions of Alta California in 1839 and 1840* (Spokane, Wash.: The Arthur H. Clark Company; Santa Clara, Calif.: CMSA, 2004), 43.

[17] Fr. Francisco González de Ibarra's Annual Report, December 31, 1832, SBMAL.

[18] Webb, *Indian Life at the Old Missions*, 221–22.

[19] Edwin Bryant, *What I Saw in California* (New York: D. Appleton & Company, 1848), 391.

[20] Robert Stockton Williamson, *Report of Explorations in California for Railroad Routes, Explorations and Surveys for a Railroad Route to the Pacific*, vol. 5 (Washington, D.C.: Government Printing Office, 1853): 73–75.

The Encino Ranch at the southern border of the San Fernando Valley.
Members of the Frank L. Millen & Bros. Harvesting Company are shown, 1895. *KEP.*

its of the sales of the fruit, wine and brandy, with the proprietor. I took dinner with the gardener and tasted some of the wine grown here, which was excellent.[21]

In the convento today are visible reminders of wine production at the mission: the wine cellar, the oak kegs, a large boiling kettle, and the water vat where the Indians washed their feet prior to stomping on the mounds of grapes.

_____

[21] Henry Miller, *Account of a Tour of the California Missions, 1856—The Journal and Drawings of Henry Miller* (San Francisco: The Book Club of California, 1952), 42.

The vineyards continued to be productive and were cultivated until September 12, 1874, when the Porter Land and Water Company, owned by former state senators George K. Porter and Charles Maclay, purchased the northern 56,000 acres of the valley, which included the 2,000-acre Pico Reservation. The vines were soon removed and barley was planted in their place.[22]

_____

[22] W. W. Robinson, *The Story of San Fernando Valley* (Los Angeles: Title Insurance and Trust Co., 1964), 24.

(*above*) Piles of barley are stacked in front of the convento by the Porter Land and Water Company, ca. 1883. *IWT/UCB (1905.17160:22).*

(*right*) Bales of hay (Porter Land and Water Company harvest) are stacked up in the chapel of Mission San Fernando. A postcard by the Pillsbury Picture Co., No. 171, ca. 1883. *Pillsbury Picture Co. JBG.*

(*above*) Porter Land and Water Company field is stacked with hay,
ready for baling, ca. 1887. *CHS/TICOR* (*7527*).

(*below*) From the north olive orchard, looking toward the adobe wall and church.
Photo by G. E. Moore, ca. 1900. *GEM/CHS/TICOR* (*7748*) *and SWM-P19072.*

(*right*) The gigantic cactus species *Opuntia tribuloide* was grown as a protective barrier around orchards and vineyards at Mission San Fernando. Unknown photographer, ca. 1900. *LAA.*

(*below*) The olive mill at Mission San Fernando. Photo attributed to C. C. Pierce, ca. 1904. *CCP/CHS/TICOR (536) and SMW-P19071.*

(*above*) Olive trees and ruins of storerooms and workshops south of the mission complex.
This photo was a *carte-de-visite* by William H. Fletcher, 1892. *WHF/LAA.*

(*below*) The view from the southern orchard shows the newly roofed church, whitewash
on the convento, and Porter Land and Water Company buildings. Unknown photographer, ca. 1900. *KEP.*

(*right*) Boiler found in the wine cellar.
*KEP, 1979.*

(*below*) Mechanical wine vat and barrels
stored in the wine cellar. *KEP, 1979.*

View from the south orchards toward the Santa Susana Mountains.
A. C. Vroman, ca. 1897. *ACV/SCWHR (V-1452).*

# PART III

# THE LAND, BUILDINGS, AND ADORNMENTS

View from the south toward the convento, with the Santa Susana Mountains in the distance.
A. C. Vroman, ca. 1897. *ACV/SCWHR (V-1452)*.

## CHAPTER 7

# THE MISSION LANDSCAPE

*The actual site chosen for the mission was on a rancho, owned with dubious legality by Don Francisco Reyes, alcalde of the Pueblo of Los Angeles. As the property actually belonged to Mission San Gabriel, the padres had little trouble ousting Reyes, and they used his small ranch house as living quarters while the mission buildings were rising.*
*—The California Missions: A Pictorial History*

THE PROPERTY on which the mission stood was vast, extending over most of the San Fernando Valley. It was estimated to be 121,542⅓ acres at the time of sale by Pío Pico, the last Mexican governor of Alta California, to Eulógio de Célis.[1]

On the mission grounds were vineyards, gardens, and a nearby stock-ranch. The flourishing fruit and nut trees, growing north and south of the buildings, were noteworthy. In the 1832 inventory, there was a multitude of fruit trees of assorted types, numbered at 1,600.[2] From the 1840s onward, visitors to the mission have described the landscape in prose and pictures.

In 1847, Edwin Bryant, an eastern newspaperman visiting California, accompanied Lt. Col. John C. Frémont and his battalion of American soldiers, who were heading south to engage the Mexican enemy. Of his trip he wrote:

January 11, 1847 . . . We found the pass narrow, and easily to be defended by brave and determined men against a greatly superior force; but when we had mounted the summit of the ridge there was no enemy, nor the sign of one, in sight. Descending into a *cañada* [the San Fernando Pass] on the other side, we halted until the main body came up to us, and then the whole force was again reunited, and the march continued. . . .

Continuing our march, we entered the mission of San Fernando at one o'clock, and in about two hours the main body arrived, and the whole battalion encamped in the mission buildings. . . .

The buildings and gardens belonging to this mission are in better condition than those of any of these establishments I have seen. There are two extensive gardens, surrounded by high walls; and a stroll through them afforded a most delightful contrast from the usually uncultivated landscape we have been traveling through for so long a time. Here were brought together most of the fruits and many of the plants of the temperate and tropical climates. Although not the season of flowers, still the roses were in bloom. Oranges, lemons, figs, and olives hung upon the trees, and the blood-red tuna, or prickly-pear [fruit], looked very tempting. Among the plants I noticed the American aloe (*argave* [*sic*] *Americana*) which is otherwise called *maguey*. From this plant,

---

[1]  Daughters of the American Revolution, *The Valley of San Fernando*, San Fernando Valley Chapter (San Fernando, Calif.: DAR, 1924), 31. The land was reportedly deeded in June 1846.

[2]  Fr. Francisco González de Ibarra's Annual Report, December 31, 1832, SBMAL.

Rogério Rocha gathers the *tuna* (fruit) of the large prickly pear cacti at the mission. Photo by C. C. Pierce, July *1898*. *CCP/CHS/TICOR* (*579*).

when it attains maturity, saccharine liquor is extracted, which is manufactured into a beverage called *pulque*, and is much prized by Mexicans.[3]

The unexpected beauty of the landscape struck Lt. Robert Stockton Williamson. On their first night in the San Fernando Valley in 1853, he and his railroad survey party camped out under some fig trees north of the mission. Lt. Williamson wrote:

> On turning the point of a hill we suddenly came in sight of the mission buildings, which, with the surrounding gardens, stood isolated in the seemingly desert plain and produced a most beautiful effect. The gardens were enclosed by walls but the graceful palm trees rose above them all and groves of olives, lemon and orange trees can be seen within. Outside the walls the surface was barren and gravelly, and the fertility within is the result of irrigation.[4]

On a visit to the mission, artist Henry Miller, in Andrés Pico's absence, dined with the French gardener, who tended the orchards in exchange for the proceeds from the sale of fruits, wine, and brandy. In 1856 Miller sketched the mission landscape and wrote the following commentary, which revealed his Anglo bias:

> The day being very warm, I refreshed myself by eating all the fruit which came in my way, as pears, figs, and prickly pears (*tuna*), a fruit growing on a gigantic cactus specie[s] [*Opuntia tribuloides*, or so-called "mission" cactus of southern California],[5] which fruit is yellow and very wholesome and refreshing. . . .
>
> This mission is a fine property. With a good management, the two beautiful vineyards and orchards

---

[3] Bryant, *What I Saw in California*, 391. Bryant confused the aloe and agave, which are two different species of succulent. The aloe is from the lily family, native to Africa, and the agave is from the family *Agavaceae*, native to North and South America.

[4] Lt. Robert Stockton Williamson, *Report of Explorations in California for Railroad Routes, Explorations and Surveys for a Railroad Route to the Pacific*, vol. 5: 73–75.

[5] N. L. Britton and J. N. Rose, *The Cactaceae: Descriptions and Illustrations of Plants of the Cactus Family*, 2 vols. (New York: Dover Publications, 1963) 1: 185–86.

(*above*) Sketch of the Mission San Fernando complex by Russell Ruiz, 1978, with a raised perspective from the southwest, as the artist imagined it might have appeared ca. 1825–30. *RR/KEP.*

(*left*) An undated photo of Eulógio F. Célis, son of Spaniard Eulógio de Célis, who purchased over 56,000 acres of the valley from Pío Pico on June 17, 1846. Photographer unknown. *CHS/TICOR.*

was invited by Andrés Pico to spend the Fourth of July holiday at the mission. Pleasants wrote:

> The orchards and vineyards of the mission, including the garden, must have totaled almost one hundred acres. Pico used the buildings as a residence and maintained a large stock-ranch on what had been mission lands before secularization. . . .

> San Fernando Mission was said to have one of the largest of the stock ranges of the south as well as the tallest palm trees in cultivation in the State, these palms being a distinctive feature, besides the fame of its orchards and the groves of sweet-scented acacias and locust trees. They are located in the arroyo between the orchards and the mission grounds.[7]

alone, in which grow an abundance of grapes, pears, apples, apricots, peaches, figs, pomegranates, oranges, quinces, prickly pears, etc., being surrounded by a high adobe wall, would prove a fortune to the proprietor if he were a man of the Anglo Saxon stamp.[6]

Another description of the grounds came from Joseph E. Pleasants, a Los Angeles jurist. In 1856 he

---

[6] Miller, *Account of a Tour of the California Missions*, 42.

[7] Weber, *The Mission in the Valley*, 49–50. Weber quotes Joseph E. Pleasants' "Memoirs—1856" in *Touring Topics*, February 1930.

Twin palms north of the orchard adobe wall, on the north side of the church, ca. 1904. *UCLA.*

(*opposite*) Acrylic painting by Russell Ruiz, who built on and combined aspects of different media: a painting by H. C. Ford, a photograph by C. E. Watkins, and a plan view survey map. The prickly pear motif was suggested by the 1853 Charles Koppel sketch on page 54. Ruiz's representation of the mission, created in 1978, was as he imagined the complex might have been at the peak of construction, ca. 1825–30. *RR/KEP.*

As shown in the 1860 U.S. Survey map drawn up by Deputy Secretary Henry Hancock, the land occupied by the mission buildings, vineyards, and orchards was slightly less than 77 acres.

Benjamin Cummings Truman, former secretary to President Andrew Johnson, made many tours to the California missions between 1867 and 1872. He joined the *Los Angeles Star* in 1873, later becoming a well-known journalist and regional booster.[8] At Mission San Fernando, Truman enjoyed the hospitality of Andrés Pico, who still maintained his country home at the mission. He wrote of the orchards:

> There were two gardens attached to this mission, each containing 32 acres and respectively owned by Gen. Pico and Don Señor De Célis, Jr. The Pico garden had 300 olive trees, 12,000 grapevines, and a large number of peach, apple, pear, orange, lemon, fig, walnut, almond and pomegranate trees. The De Célis garden had 7,000 grapevines, 320 olive trees, and all other fruits mentioned above which had been planted by the missionary fathers in 1800.[9]

Henry Chapman Ford visited the California missions from 1880 to 1883. An accomplished artist, he produced sketches, an etching, a watercolor, and a magnificent oil painting of Mission San Fernando. He wrote at length of the landscape:

> There are two orchards of olives, probably containing the largest trees in the State, the trunks of some being two feet in diameter. They are of a different variety from the common mission olive, the fruit being nearly double the size and highly valued for pickling. A few years since, the large tops were cut off leaving only the trunks at the height of six feet from which new branches have sprung, being at this time literally loaded with blossoms. The large orchard contains an area of about 40 acres surrounded by an adobe wall, still standing, with only here and there a break. In the middle of this orchard are standing three large native palms (*Washingtonia filifera*) the tallest of which is about 55 feet in height, probably the highest palms in cultivation within the limits of the United States. The trunk of this is bare to the height of 45 feet, while those others are clothed with the persistent dead leaves of many years' growth forming a natural thatch. Some of the palms of Palm

8   Weber, *The Mission in the Valley,* 55.       9   Ibid., 58.

Valley east of San Jacinto Mountains, where they are indigenous, are about 80 feet in height.

In the orchard mentioned were many old grape vines, but recently they were all removed, and the whole plat is now a barley field. Another garden northeast of the mission contains about 30 acres, also enclosed with an adobe wall. There is also a large number of olive trees and three date palms of the staminate kind, which, of course, have never borne fruit. They are about 30 feet in height.[10]

In the early twentieth century, Leslie Carlton

Brand donated to the city of Los Angeles 7 acres of land located between the former vineyard and convento. The land became a park, known as Brand Park or Memory Garden. On Arbor Day in 1923, Brand dedicated a double row of olive trees, each of which bore a plaque commemorating a personage in California history. The plaques have long since been stolen, but the trees remain a visible reminder, a tribute to the magnificent orchards and vineyards that once graced the grounds.[11]

[10] Ibid., 68–69; Engelhardt, *San Fernando Rey*, 125–28.

[11] Weber, *Memories of an Old Mission*, 56–68.

(*left*) A man stands between the palms, south of the convento. A. C. Vroman (V-237), ca. 1896. *Marie Walsh Harrington Collection. ACV/ACSFM.*

(*below*) Oil painting of Mission San Fernando— view from the west in early morning, by William Keith. From the Dr. Norman Neuerburg Collection, now at the SBMAL, ca. 1881. *W. Keith/SBMAL.*

(*above*) Watercolor rendition of the church and west wing of the quadrangle
by Andrew Dagosta, 2004. The artist used the photograph on page 118 (*bottom*) as a model. *AD/KEP.*

(*below*) Lithograph—Mission and Plain of San Fernando for the Geological Report,
in *Report on Explorations in California for the U.S. Pacific Railroad Routes Expeditions and Surveys*, Plate VI
(Washington, D.C., 1857). Prepared by William Phipps Blake while traveling with
Lt. Robert Stockton Williamson in California in 1853–56. *WPB/JBG.*

(*left*) Panoramic view of the vast San Fernando Valley and the mission environs, photographed from a hill northwest of the mission, ca. 1880, by Carleton E. Watkins from his New Series Photographs No. 1216. Two large orchards north and south of the mission structures can be seen. Mt. Lee and the Cahuenga Pass are in the distance. *CEW/UCLA.*

(*below*) A modern panorama of the San Fernando Valley from approximately the same location as the one C. E. Watkins used for his photograph nearly one hundred years earlier. In 1979 Ken Pauley took two photographs from the parking lot of the Odyssey Restaurant and merged them to create this panorama. A dense cluster of deep-green trees (on the left) beyond the cemetery hides the mission buildings. *KEP.*

1070:—Resting at the Old Well, San Fernando, Mission, Cal.

(*opposite page, top*) 1066—Mission San Fernando Rey de España. Founded in California 1797—Manufactured by Longraw Card Co., 1945. *KEP.*

(*opposite page, bottom left*) Belfry and Corridor (west end)—102956—Made by Curt Teich & Co., Chicago, U.S.A. C. T. American Art Colored, n.d. *KEP.*

(*opposite page, bottom right*) Doorway to Refectory—102955—Made by Curt Teich & Co., Chicago, U.S.A. C. T. American Art Colored, n.d. *KEP.*

MISSION SAN FERNANDO—1797—CALIFORNIA.

CHURCH AND BAPTISTRY. 102951

(*this page, top*) 1070—Resting at the Old Well (actually front fountain)—San Fernando Mission—Series of Mission San Fernando, Cal. post cards. Pub. by the M. Kashower Co., ca. 1920, Los Angeles. *KEP.*

(*middle*) Church and baptistry—102951— Made by Curt Teich & Co., Chicago, U.S.A. C. T. American Art Colored, ca. 1923. *KEP.*

(*bottom*) Mission San Fernando, California— 43580—Made by Gardner—Thompson Co., Los Angeles, California, ca. 1924. *KEP.*

603:—SAN FERNANDO MISSION. BUILT 1797. CALIFORNIA.

43580

1066    SAN FERNANDO MISSION.    FOUNDED IN CALIFORNIA 1797.

FROM KODACHROME BY JUSMET

MISSION SAN FERNANDO—1797—CALIFORNIA

BELFRY AND CORRIDOR                    102956

MISSION SAN FERNANDO—1797—CALIFORNIA.

DOORWAY TO REFECTORY.                    102955

Oil painting by Henry Chapman Ford of Mission San Fernando, Rey de España, 1880.
*Courtesy of Dr. and Mrs. Lawrence B. Robinson. HCF/LBR.*

# CHAPTER 8
# LIVING QUARTERS, WORKSHOPS, AND STOREROOMS

*The planning of the mission buildings was systematized on a general plan during the administration of Lasuén. The Church, presbytery, workshops, granaries, schools, and residences of the employees were built in a square, one side being usually open. The fronts were usually arcaded, like the old cloisters of Spain and Italy, but with no attempt at architectural decoration. Adobe or stone were the materials used for the walls, and tile for the roofing. The massive walls, small openings and bright color of the tiles gave a common character to all the mission buildings, and were not unsuited to the climate of California.* —Bryan J. Clinch, *California and Its Missions*, Vol. II

ONSTRUCTION OF THE MISSIONS customarily started with the *iglesia* (church), then the *convento* (padres' living quarters), followed by the *cuartel* (living quarters for soldiers), a granary, workshops, and storerooms. These structures were usually attached to each other and arranged in a quadrangle. The church or *campanil* (bell tower—also called *campanario*) or both were usually connected to at least one wing of the quadrangle.[1] Mission San Fernando's construction generally followed this pattern, except that the convento was built as a free-standing structure.

The Plat of 8 Tracts of Land at the Mission San Fernando, drawn from the February 1860 survey of Deputy Surveyor Henry Hancock and under instructions from the U.S. surveyor general, was approved in January 1861. The plat shows the vast extent of the mission and its grounds. Tract No. 1, only a small part of all the tracts, covers $4^{3}/_{100}$ acres. Within this tract are located the main building (convento); the quadrangle buildings (the workshops, storerooms, and living quarters) and the courtyard; the church; and the cemetery and the corral area.

Fr. Engelhardt sketched a map showing the various rooms and labeled their use for storage, work, and living. He described in his book, *The Mission in the Valley*, the phases of construction from 1797 to 1822. Much of what we know about the property is taken from Engelhardt's description, which he reconstructed from previous annual reports and his own investigation in 1904. It is unfortunate that, though he described in great detail the size and use of the completed buildings, he did not record their locations. In some cases, he hypothesized locations, basing them on plat dimensions and compass directions given in the 1860 U.S. Survey.

---

[1] *California Missions: A Pictorial History*, 34–36.

Carleton E. Watkins New Series Photograph No. 1214.
Broad view of Mission San Fernando Rey from the west in 1882. *CEW/UCLA.*

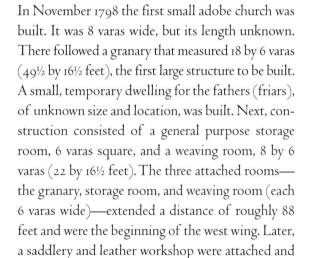

In November 1798 the first small adobe church was built. It was 8 varas wide, but its length unknown. There followed a granary that measured 18 by 6 varas (49½ by 16½ feet), the first large structure to be built. A small, temporary dwelling for the fathers (friars), of unknown size and location, was built. Next, construction consisted of a general purpose storage room, 6 varas square, and a weaving room, 8 by 6 varas (22 by 16½ feet). The three attached rooms—the granary, storage room, and weaving room (each 6 varas wide)—extended a distance of roughly 88 feet and were the beginning of the west wing. Later, a saddlery and leather workshop were attached and completed the west wing of the quadrangle.[2]

In 1799 a second, but temporary, church, 23 by 7¼ varas (63¼ by 20 feet), was constructed, apparently also of adobe. A second granary, 33 by 6.64 varas (91 by 18¼ feet); another storeroom, 6¼ by 6 varas (17.2 by 16.5 feet); and a more substantial father's dwelling, 44 by 6½ varas (121 by 17.9 feet), were built. Although Fr. Engelhardt used the annual reports, he did not give the precise locations of these buildings besides writing, "This probably formed the front wing [on the west?] next to the church and doubtless included the first *sala.*"

Friars Dumetz and Cortés wrote in 1801 that an addition measuring 106 varas (291 feet) was built. This was to become the south wing. It consisted of two granaries, which became wine and brandy factories, two small rooms for the missionaries, a weaving room, and a dormitory with its own small courtyard for girls and single women.[3] The layout of this wing is shown on a U.S. Survey map drawn

---

2   Engelhardt, *San Fernando Rey,* 15. One hundred and six varas would measure about 291 feet. The assumption here is that in 1802 the Spanish vara was still in use (1 Burgos *vara* equals 32.9096 inches), whereas after the Mexican-Spanish war, the Mexican *vara* was used (1 Mexican *vara* equals 32.9921 inches or, for all practical purposes, 33 inches).

3   Engelhardt, *San Fernando Rey,* 16.

Boys stand in front of the mayordomo's house. The weeds along the walls are gone.
It is probably summer. C. C. Pierce, ca. 1890. *CCP/CHS/TICOR* (14378).

in 1860 and was also sketched by Fr. Zephyrin Engelhardt in 1904. In addition, six houses, whose dimensions were not reported, were built. Located northwest of the church, these were assigned to the guards; they contained a storeroom, the barracks, an adobe wall for the kitchen, and a house containing a reception room and two other rooms. Called the cuartel, the six houses were actually adjoining rooms but roofed with tiles as a single structure.[4]

In 1802, construction of an addition was made "apparently so as to close up the square." According to Engelhardt, it measured 100 varas; this, however, equals 275 feet, not 292 feet as he recorded.[5] The addition included another granary, flour mill, candle factory, and carpentry shop, forming the east wing. No work was reported for the following year.

Beginning in 1804, a third church was constructed in alignment with the north wing. Shops for carpentry, carriages, and plows, a new third church, and a sacristy would account for the total length of about 133 varas (365¾ feet) for the north wing. Prior to completion of the church in 1806, a bell tower was built adjacent to the church, integrating it into the quadrangle's west wing. A staircase inside this campanil led up to the choir loft. A baptistry adjoining the northwest end of the church, opposite the bell tower, completed the north wing.

Also in 1804, about seventy rooms were constructed of adobe to house Indian neophytes. Fashioned originally in the shape of a 'U,' the complex was later surveyed as an L-shaped building, located from the southwest corner of the convento at S-58°-W at a distance of 4.32 chains or 285 feet.[6] Other structures built that year included a detached tal-

---

[4] Ibid.    [5] Ibid.

[6] Ibid. In 1804 work also began on a building at the mission's estancia, Rancho San Francisco Xavier. The construction of it and other structures built at the ranch is in Chapter 11: The Outpost.

low vat located at the northeast corner of the quadrangle and a long rectangular row of adobe and stone buildings (47 by 462 feet)—running north and south—positioned from the southeast corner of the convento at S-62°-E and a distance of 4.30 chains (284 feet). A Henry Miller sketch, dated 1856, shows this row of buildings south of the mission quadrangle. Many photographs also show ruins of this building.

Henry L. Oak, the historical writer, teacher, and librarian, visited the missions of California between February 18 and March 15, 1874, and kept a diary of his trip. He traveled by boat from San Francisco (February 18–21) to San Diego, then by stagecoach up the coast and arrived back in San Francisco on Sunday, March 15. On Thursday, March 5, 1874, Oak drew a sketch of Mission San Fernando's grounds and structures. It was a fine sketch, except for one glaring flaw. The orientation of the drawing was skewed 90 degrees counterclockwise. Using the cardinal point he drew for north (actually west) on his map, all references to the directional position of the buildings and adornments are incorrect in the journal. His diary entry for this day, edited for map corrections, can be found in the sidebar.[7]

Fr. Zephryin Engelhardt made a sketch in 1904 that shows the row of buildings mentioned earlier in Henry Miller's sketch. These buildings were the olive and grain storerooms, horse stables, a tannery, and *jabonería* (soap factory or tallow vat). In 1818 another soap factory containing two boilers and holes to accept firewood was built several yards south of the convento. It could be seen in 1927 when Engelhardt wrote about it.[8] Although all the other jabonerías at Mission San Fernando are long gone, this vat still exists and is visible today in Brand Park.

According to Fr. Ibarra's writings, all work on the convento and the adjoining quarters had been completed by 1822.[9] The result was a near-perfect quadrangle whose maximum outer perimeter measurements (according to the 1860 survey) were about 352 feet (S) by 387 feet (E) by 365 feet (N) by 352 feet (W), with *zaguanes* (passageways) placed in the middle of each wing. Also, east of the quadrangle there was a detached circular formation, 75 feet in diameter, made of adobe and thought to be a wheat threshing floor.[10]

After secularization, the original quadrangle walls, particularly on the east wing, fell into ruins. By the 1880s little remained except for some remnants of Indian dwellings and mounds of adobe, a tallow vat, and the corral a few feet east of this wing. Only a few sketches, maps, and photographs exist to give us a glimpse of the east wing's existence.

7  Henry L. Oak's diary entry for Thursday, March 5, 1874, gives one of the clearest textual descriptions of the mission complex made by a traveler in early times, except for his error in his directional orientation. All of his discussions of items with cardinal headings, therefore, are in error, and the reader must adjust his orientation in the passage in the sidebar beginning on the next page.

8  Engelhardt, *San Fernando Rey*, 24.
9  Ibid., 22–24.
10  *California Missions: A Pictorial History*, 262.

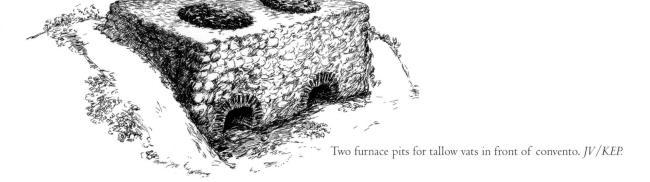

Two furnace pits for tallow vats in front of convento. *JV/KEP.*

Started by stage, on the coast line, northward at 5 A.M. passing through the hills that bound Los Angeles on the West, and over a hilly rolling country, very different from, and much less pleasant and fertile than that below the city. The weather very cold and uncomfortable. At 7½ A.M. we reached the Encino Rancho, 18 miles from Los Angeles, on the western side and about in the middle of the San Fernando Valley which extends north and south for 20 or 30 miles [*sic*, it is actually about 8–9 miles] and is about 9 miles wide [*sic*, about 20 or 30 miles. Oak reversed the distances, as evident by his sketch]. It is level and smooth [it actually slopes from 500 to 1000 feet above sea level, southeast to northwest], bounded on the east by lofty hills, but distinguished for some reason for its strong winds at this season of the year.

The Encino ranch is 3 miles square and takes its name from the numerous oak trees that dot its western hillsides. It is owned by M. [Eugene] Garnier who is engaged chiefly in the business of sheep-raising. Some 18000 [*sic*] sheep are now in his flocks, and from them $40,000 worth of wool is said to have been sold during the past year. Large numbers of horses are also raised, and we noted that most of them appeared of superior breed, size, and condition to those hitherto seen in the southern country. A general air of neatness seemed to pervade everything on this ranch which we had not yet observed elsewhere. Most of the men employed about the place are Frenchmen. The proprietor occupies a low long adobe house said to be quite elegantly furnished on the inside as it is certainly neatly plastered and painted on the exterior. A large two-story wooden house painted a light brown affords accommodations to the herders employed on the ranch. A hotel, restaurant, bar, and stable occupy three neat buildings of wood by the roadside, which cost about $10,000 and by reason of the small amount of travel, has not yet paid interest on the cost of construction. A warm spring which supplies a stream of 2 or 3 inches of water is on the place, and fills a cistern some 20 feet in diameter, running over into a heart-shaped reservoir about 700 feet in circumference and about 8 feet deep of solid cut stone. It is proposed to stock this reservoir with fish, put a boat on its surface, and perhaps build bathing houses near it.

After some delay a team was procured for a visit to the mission of San Fernando 9 miles distant across the valley eastward [northward] in plain sight from the hotel, and apparently not over 2 to 3 miles away.

Don Andrés Pico had failed to meet us at the starting of the stage as he had agreed, and at Encino Ranch; and now we found no trace of him at his home at the mission of San Fernando. From some Indians about the house we could learn nothing except the absence of Don Andrés at the pueblo, but after our visit was nearly completed Don Romulo Pico, a son of Don Andrés, made his appearance and showed us every attention, producing all the relics and MSS which in the absence of his father, he could find. The following are the mission books of San Fernando preserved in the possession of the Pico family:

*Matrimonios*—One volume 1797–1847. First entry October 8, 1797. Signed Francisco Dumet [*sic*].
*Bautismos*—One volume 1798–1852. First entry April 28, 1798. Signed Francisco Dumetz.
*Libro de Patentes y de Ynventario perteneciente a la Misión de S' Fernando Rey en la Nueva California año de 1806.*

This book, a large folio, contains doubtless some information of value and would repay an examination by Mr. Foster or some other party. In the few minutes at our disposal at the time we could not read enough of it to give even a general idea of its contents.

Another book of considerable importance was said by Sr. [Romulo] Pico to be somewhere among his father's papers but could not be found by him at the moment. Its title he thought to be something like the following: *La Fundación de la missión de San Fernando Rey, por el Padre Francisco Dumetz.* It contains a full description of the state of the country at the time when the mission was first established.

We were also shown a collection of Spanish printed works left by the missionaries, but they proved to be mostly miscellaneous theological works, printed in Spain and none of them referring at all to the Pacific States. There was one manual or catechism printed in Mexico since 1800. Among the other relics shown us was a hand-organ formerly used in church services, but it was in a sad state of decay, and all its music has long since departed. We also saw some old steelyards of the early times, and some curious little upright cannons of bronze or copper with a handle for convenience, and a touch-hole near the base. They varied in size from 4 to 6 inches in height, weighing from 5 to 20 pounds. They were used on holidays simply for the noise they could produce, much after the fashion of modern Fourth of July celebrations. One of the smaller ones was presented to us as a memento of our visit by Don Romulo.

He also promised to write down for us what he could learn from his father concerning the history of his family and of early California generally, (*continued, page 111*)

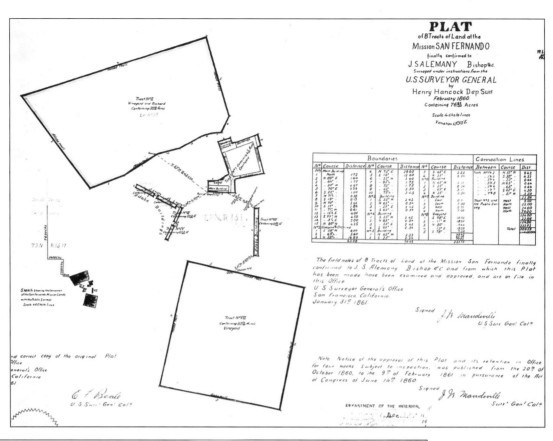

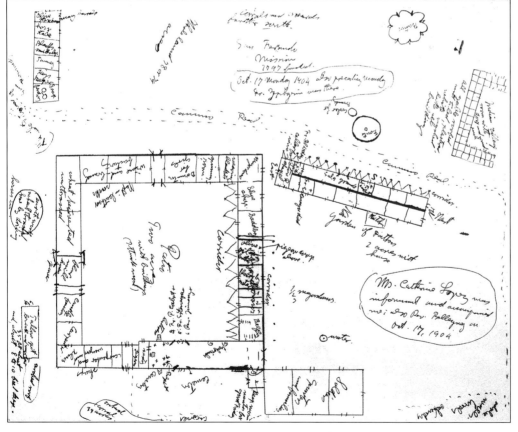

(*above*) Map of eight tracts (Alemany Plat) of Mission San Fernando confirmed to J. S. Alemany, Bishop & C[hurch], which were surveyed in February 1860 by Henry Hancock, deputy surveyor, under instructions from the United States surveyor general. Two confirmations of the maps and field notes were filed with the Department of the Interior, signed by J. W. Mandeville, surveyor general, on June 14, 1860, and January 31, 1861. Map was prepared by E. F. Beale. *Edward F. Beale/ACSFM.*

(*left*) Hand-sketched map of Mission San Fernando grounds and buildings made by Fr. Zephyrin Engelhardt, O.F.M. The sketch (with a few minor mistakes), showing a plan view of the grounds with recognizable structures, was made on Monday, October 17, 1904. *Engelhardt/ACSFM.*

and to send it to San Francisco at an early date. [Romulo Pico was another person who failed to fulfill his promise of writing something for Bancroft.]

The extent and arrangement of the mission buildings are shown by the plan [map]. [See Henry L. Oak map and attached legend.] The church walls are chiefly of adobe with brick at arches and foundations. Much of the bell wing *a*, in which hang two bells, is of brick and the walls of this part as usual are much thicker and stronger than other parts of the structure. The two buttresses *b* and *c* on the outside of the church walls are of brick and do not extend up to the eaves. The interior is ornamented by slightly projecting pillars, square with slight cornices and tinted pink. The floor is of square tiles, without plaster; and a gallery, also with a tile floor extends across the north [west] end at *d* the entrance being from the bell-wing. The church has not been used for service for many years [Actually services were moved from the deteriorating church to the large room at the east end of the convento earlier in the year this diary was written—1874], but on the inside it seems to be in tolerably good preservation, as good as many that are still occupied. Much of the church furniture remains, with one or two images of saints. On the outside the plaster is mostly fallen and the walls are said to be in a very unsafe condition. It is noticeable that no side of this church is free from other structures so as to be termed the front, nor is any side ornamented so as to indicate its right to that title. It seems probable however that the front was the north [west], and that the adobe buildings or enclosures whose ruins extend indefinitely northward [westward] at *e* have been erected in more modern times.

The court [within the quadrangle] is nearly 300 feet square and has no trace of portico pillars around its inner circumference. It has been used of late years as a corral for sheep. The court buildings are of adobe and consist of a single line of apartments for the greater part of the distance, much of them completely in ruins, especially in the southern [eastern] part. And all are in such a state that I found it impracticable to attempt to locate doors and partition walls. At *f* is a curious cistern of brick plastered on the inside with cement. Its top is arched and but little above the surface of the ground. In the top, or what remains of it is a square opening about 2 feet square, and 2 or 3 circular openings a few inches in diameter, for pipes, the holes being lined with a short burned brick pipe. The cistern is about 35 feet long, 12 feet deep and

5 feet wide. Don Romulo says it was used by the padres as a receptacle of melted tallow. At *g* detached from the other structures are the adobe foundations of a circular enclosure 75 feet in diameter, perhaps a corral. The Western [Southern] and Northern [Western] court buildings, or such apartments in them as are fit for use are occupied as stables and sheds. West [South] from the court at *h* is a detached line of adobe houses, mostly fallen; which seem never to have been joined to the court structures. In the portions about *i* [some distance off the plan map—upper left hand corner] some families of laborers live and this seems to be also a place of resort or barroom for all who live in adobe houses scattered in different directions over the ranch at short distances from the Mission. North [West] of the court building at *j.j* is a line of 8 pillars 9 feet distant from the wall and 15 feet apart. There may have been more of them originally. They are of brick, 6 of them being square and the two central ones round, the first instance of the occurrence of round pillars in the missions so far visited. They probably supported timbers for a portico along what was probably the main front of the whole edifice [west wing of the quadrangle].

The building K [the convento on Henry Oak's map] is in a perfect state of preservation and is the residence of the Pico family. The walls are of adobe, thick and well plastered, and the roof of tiles in good repair, but not entirely modern according to the statement of Sr. Pico. The building is 240 feet [actually 235 feet, 2 inches] long and 45 feet wide [actually 50 feet, 4 inches not including the 15-foot-wide arcade], being divided into 2 rows of large airy and clean rooms the exact plan of whose arrangement I did not ascertain. Along the front stretches a portico of 19 brick arches [plus one at each end] each of 10 feet 7 inches supported by 20 pillars 22 inches by about 36 inches.

The floor of the portico is paved with square tiles and is raised above the surface of the ground two or three feet. Except at the main entrances the space between the pillars is built up about three feet so as to form a balustrade 5 feet high from ground in front of the portico and before each of the 4 principal entrances is a brick pavement semicircular in shape with steps. One continuous roof covers the building and portico. The first three arches on the north [southwest] wall [west end of the convento] are walled-up. [Seen as early as 1865 in the Henry Miller sketch, page 112.] The doors in the front of the building are opposite the 3d, 5th, 7th, (*continued, page 113*)

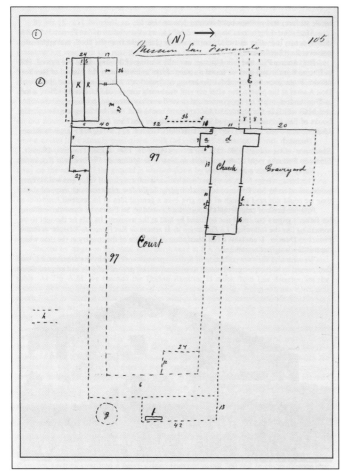

(*left*) Hand-sketched map of Mission San Fernando building complex made by Henry L. Oak on Thursday, March 5, 1874. Oak, who was visiting the missions of southern California, also made an entry in his diary for this day. Note: Arrow added to map by authors. *Henry L. Oak/SWM.*

LEGEND:

*a* bell wing (belfry)—2 bells hung

*b* church buttress (north)

*c* church buttress (south)

*d* nave and front of church

*e* *cuartel* (soldiers' living quarters)

*f* cistern (brick). According to Don Romulo a tallow vat, plastered on the inside with cement mortar (35 feet long by 5 feet wide and 12 feet deep).

*g* adobe formation of a circular enclosure—75 feet diameter; possibly a corral or grain thresher.

*h* detached line of adobe houses (incl. soap factory and graniares). Engelhardt in his 1904 sketch included keyskeeper and tannery shops.

*i* off map toward the southwest Indian barracks.

*j* array of 8 columns (6 square; 2 cylindrical). Placed 9 feet from west wall of quadrangle, 15 feet apart.

*k* *convento*

*l* 16-sided or near circular fountain

*m* 2-acre corral and gardens

(*below*) Expansive view of quadrangle shows the collapse of the east portion of the CLC church roof. Electric poles are also seen in this view looking east to west, ca. 1914–15. *SPNBPC/LAPL.*

Henry Chapman Ford made this famous etching of Mission San Fernando in 1883: A View from the West, in which the church and west wing of the quadrangle are shown in pitiful condition. By this time the convento was crowded with farm implements and supplies used by the Porter Land and Water Company. A *carreta* is seen in front of the west end of the convento. *HCF/JBG.*

12th and 19th arches. *mm* are yards [used by the padres for gardens and small stock animals] the eastern [western] walls about 8 ft. high. Under the central [i.e., eastern] portion of this building is a cellar with walls of stone about 35 feet long, 20 feet wide and 12 feet deep. It is now well filled with barrels of wine and aguardiente, the contents of which were freely offered for our tasting. In front of this building and at a distance of 75 or 100 feet is a circular fountain, *l* [near circular, in fact a hexadecagon—16-sided—fountain, see architectural drawing 12-28] about 25 feet in diameter [actually 22½ feet average outside diameter], in good preservation so far as its brick walls are concerned, but not now supplied with water. The usual adobe inclosures [*sic*] are seen on the west [south] and east [north], the latter being on the other side of a steep ravine or creek that runs along the eastern [northern] side of the ruins. Two of these inclosures [*sic*] are olive orchards whose numerous trees are very flourishing, exceeding in size those of San Diego. These are the most valuable

property on the mission grounds, and are the prize over whose possession the priests and the Pico family have been fighting in the courts for the past 20 years until as Don Andres says the whole of his fortune has been swallowed up in the quarrel. One of the orchards contains the three inevitable date palms which grow about each mission. On the lands here we noticed for the first time oxen drawing the plow by the horns, a custom universal among the Californians.

Returning across the valley late in the afternoon we passed the night at Garnier's Hotel, eating a supper and breakfast not at all in keeping with the general appearance of things at this ranch.*

---

\* Henry L. Oak, *A Visit to the Missions of Southern California in February and March 1874,* Henry R. Wagner, Ruth Frey Axe, Edwin H. Carpenter, and Norman Neuerburg, eds. (Highland Park, Los Angeles: Southwest Museum, 1981), 52–57. Henry L. Oak diary page for March 5, 1874.

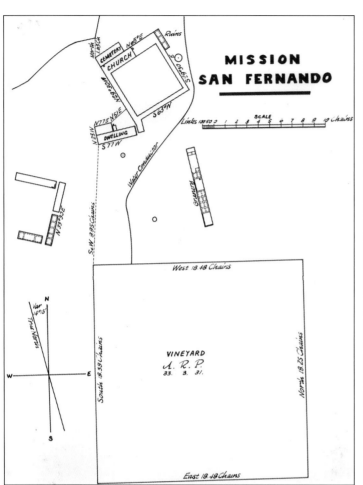

**MISSION SAN FERNANDO**

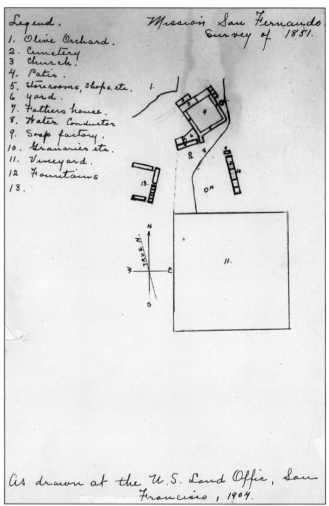

Legend.
1. Olive Orchard.
2. Cemetery
3. Church.
4. Patio.
5. Storerooms, Shops, etc.
6. Yard.
7. Fathers house.
8. Water Conductor
9. Soap factory.
10. Granaries etc.
11. Vineyard.
12. Fountains
13.

Mission San Fernando.
Survey of 1851.

As drawn at the U.S. Land Office, San Francisco, 1904.

(*above*) Map of San Fernando Mission grounds and buildings drawn at the U.S. Land Office, San Francisco in 1904. *CHS/TICOR.*

(*above, right*) Hand-sketched map of the 1851 Mission San Fernando Survey, drawn at the U.S. Land Office, San Francisco, in 1904. *KEP.*

(*left*) Panoramic view merged from three separate photographs. Broad view from within the quadrangle looking west, ca. 1915–16. *SPNBPC/LAPL.*

RUINS
MISSION SAN FERNANDO REY.

Two freehand sketches by H. C. Ford, both entitled *The Work of Henry Chapman Ford*, show the ruins of Mission San Fernando in a westerly direction, ca. 1880. The view in the sketch above was made at the same time as the one at right, but it is a little closer to the church. *HCF/ACSFM.*

(*above*) Rare photograph shows deteriorating adobe walls on the east wing of the quadrangle, ca. 1898. *CHS/TICOR* (12061).

(*below*) Mission San Fernando Ruins. A man stands in front of the west wing with all its original columns, ca. 1867.
This is one of the earliest known views of the mission. It was most likely made by Isaiah W. Taber.
Found in the Frank B. Roldolph Collection, University of California, Berkeley, Library.
*IWT/UCB* (1905.17160:4) *and SWM-P18968.*

(*above*) A rare scene of almost complete ruins of both the eastern and southern wings of the quadrangle. Hooker Collection at the Archival Center, San Fernando Mission, ca. 1893. *ACSFM.*

(*below*) Deterioration of the quadrangle and church is captured in this photograph taken from across the southern wing of the quadrangle. Charles C. Pierce, ca. 1897. *CCP/CHS/TICOR* (*5877*).

(*above*) Frederick H. Maude photo, ca. 1895. *FHM/CHS/TICOR and SWM-P18945.*

(*opposite, top*) Carleton E. Watkins New Series Photograph (No. 1215), ca. 1880, shows the church, bell tower, and quadrangle's west wing. Over a period of seventy years, many images of these structures have been produced. The following series shows the gradual deterioration and dilapidation of these buildings due to weathering and vandalism. Roof restoration of the church and convento began in late July 1897 by the California Landmarks Club. *CEW/UCLA.*

(*opposite, bottom*) This George Wharton James view, ca. 1886, shows three walls of the church's bell tower, with the southern wall showing signs of crumbling. *GWJ/CHS/TICOR (5881) and SWM-P18949.*

(*above*)This view, made about the same time as the F. H. Maude photo on the previous page, shows a close-up of the church and quadrangle's west wing, ca. 1895. *FHM/CHS/TICOR (2956).*

(*opposite, top*) Series of Adam Clark Vroman photographs, 1896–97. This view (V-232), made in 1896, shows extreme deterioration of the church due to weathering. Roof tiles have been removed and fewer brick columns remain in front of the west quadrangle. *ACV/SCWHR.*

(*opposite, bottom*) A. C. Vroman photograph (V-233) of 1897. *ACV/SCWHR and SWM P-18932.*

122

(*opposite, top*) Photo by C. F. Lummis, taken on June 1, 1897, prior to the church being roofed. Only one column remains standing in front of the west wing. *CFL/SWM-N3919.*

(*opposite, bottom*) The church shortly after reroofing in late 1897 or early 1898. The beginning of a large vertical crack can be seen on the church's west face near the choir loft window. *ACSFM.*

(*above*) The church roof is deteriorated due to weathering and the sacristy is collapsing. This photo was taken prior to Candle Day, a fundraising event for mission restoration. Ca. 1915. *SPNBPC/LAPL.*

(*left*) This is one of the earliest known photographs of the mission. This view looks east to west along the southern wing of the quadrangle. Note that the original dormer atop the convento is still intact, ca. 1860. *SBHS.*

(*opposite*) Dissolving adobe walls along the south wing of the quadrangle. One room of the mayordomo house and the dormer structure on top of the convento are gone. Only a few roof beams of the quadrangle remain, ca. 1898. *KEP.*

124

(*left*) Panorama made with two photographs taken at approximately the same time. These are the remnants of the west wing, the church, north wall and a storage hut, which contained a large tallow vat, on the quadrangle's east wing. The collapsed belltower, weathered church sacristy, and temporary support beams on the south wall can also be seen, ca. 1923. *UCLA*.

Ruins, San Fernando Mission. East end of the convento and the mayordomo's house, ca. 1897.
*WGP (M3-5)/HL - photCL 188 (87).*

(*above*) Ruins of San Fernando Mission. Francis Parker photo, ca. 1898. *FP/KEP.*

(*below*) The south wall of the quadrangle is reduced to ruins and rubble, ca. 1900. *ACSFM.*

(*left*) The church altar and reredos were damaged from the earthquake in 1971. *By Keystone Photo Services, Inc. KP/ACSFM (LA129-121).*

(*below*) The bell tower's exterior wall cracked and its limestone covering came loose in large pieces after the 1971 temblor. *By Keystone Photo Services, Inc. KP/ACSFM (LA129-109).*

(*opposite, top*) Damage to the church's interior and its southern wall at the west entrance, 1971. *By Keystone Photo Services, Inc. KP/ACSFM (LA129-120).*

(*opposite, bottom*) After the Sylmar earthquake, artist Fred Rolla is seen in 1972 using his many talents to restore an ancient icon. The statue of Saint Ferdinand and paintings are in the background. *ACSFM (10289-2).*

(*above*) Very early view, looking south, of the large granary in the west wing of the quadrangle. This photo is probably by Henry T. Payne, although Edward Vischer has often been given credit for it. Ca. 1875. *HTP/CHS/TICOR (7230) and SWM-P18926.*

(*below*) The second story wall on the east side of the west quadrangle after its collapse, ca. 1875. *HTP/UCLA.*

(*above*) View of the convento from the west. By Carleton E. Watkins, 1880. Photograph was made in the cabinet format (4 by 6 inches) New Series and was sold from the photographer's Yosemite art gallery, Portraits and Landscapes, in San Francisco. *CEW/HL—photPF 1035.*

(*right*) The west wing of the quadrangle and the convento are pictured with Porter Land and Water Company farm equipment, ca. 1895. This is a rare view of the buildings, since most photographs taken at this time faced north. *IWT/UCB (1905.17160:27).*

131

A DISTANT VIEW OF THE CONVENTO BEFORE RESTORATION.
Only a stump remains of the pepper tree that grew in front of it, ca. 1897.
*CHS/TICOR (173) and SWM-P19008.*

(*top*) The storeroom in the west wing of the quadrangle has a unique beam-and-truss construction and limewash on the interior wall. Photograph by Charles F. Lummis on October 17, 1897. *CFL/SWM-N3921.*

(*bottom*) A room in the west wing with its roof gone and beams and trusses exposed. The **T** structure shown here is an example of center bolster-girder construction, a popular building method in the Japanese culture for many centuries. Whitewash limestone can be seen covering the interior walls. Ca. 1899. *KEP.*

(*opposite*) View from the quadrangle shows rubble in the workshop rooms on the west wing, ca. 1904. By C. C. Pierce. *CCP/CHS/TICOR (5878).*

(*below*) Two early twentieth-century large-format views, taken by William M. Graham (Photos), are joined to form this wide-angle panorama. The photographer swiveled his camera on his tripod, taking both pictures from a position on the north wall of the quadrangle east of the church, facing west. The panorama scans from the mayordomo house and convento, left, sweeping past the west wing of the quadrangle, past the church sacristy toward the cemetery, right, across the orchard and beyond, ca. 1905. *WGP/HL—photCL 188 (89 and 90).*

*Port Holes in 'Dobe Wall through which Many a shot was fired at attacking Indians. Mission San Fernando.*

*The Burial Ground San Fernando*

Two Photographs by G. W. Hazard.

(*above*) From the vantage point of the belfry, the workshop ruins and the convento are viewed.
An inaccurate and misleading caption, typical of Hazard, is on his negative, 1908.

136

(*below*) San Fernando Mission's cemetery, ca. 1908.

The convento with a gaping hole where the dormer once stood (*above, top*) and after reconstruction (*above, bottom*). A portion of the mayordomo's house was restored with a slanting flat roof. These two photos were taken by the same unknown photographer, ca. 1922.

The altar is colorfully decorated with flowers for dedication services after the 1974 church reconstruction.
Photograph by Rolf H. Hoog. *Hoog/ACSFM.*

## CHAPTER 9
# THE CHURCH

*In December 1806, an adobe church, with a tile roof, was consecrated, which on the 21st, 1812, was severely injured by the earthquake that did damage to almost all the missions of the chain. Thirty new beams were needed to support the injured walls. A new chapel was built, which was completed in 1818.*
—George Wharton James, *In and Out of the Old Missions*

OVEMBER 28, 1797, was a significant day, for Fray Francisco Dumetz recorded the forty-third baptism of a child born and baptized in the church on the same day.[1]

Fr. Dumetz's description of the church is sketchy. It was 8 varas (22 feet) long—its width unknown as he did not record it—and constructed of adobe. There is no record of a dedication, but it is believed that the first church was probably blessed on the same day as the baptism.[2]

Within two years the first church was too small for services. Thus, a second church was begun, apparently also made of adobe. Measuring approximately 23 by 7¼ varas (63 by 20 feet), it served the mission for five more years.[3]

In 1804 construction began on the third church. Manuel Gutiérrez, a peninsula-born Spaniard and carpenter who was at the mission from 1805 to 1806, is considered the architect of this church.[4] Perhaps because of strong winds from the Mojave Desert, thirteen of the eighteen windows may have been intended as false decorative windows. A contrary view, however, is that most of the windows on the north wall and several on the south wall were later blocked in. Eight large arched niches, alternating with pilasters, were constructed on the interior walls. The inside walls appeared to lean outward because they were constructed of adobe bricks five to seven feet thick at the base and tapered to three feet at the top, while the exterior wall surfaces remained relatively vertical. Various decorative designs—rounded, scalloped, flat, and sloping—were painted on doorways and were different on the entrances and exits.[5]

1   The first forty-two baptisms at Mission San Fernando were mostly of children and were performed in the *enramadita* (little arbor), since there was no chapel or church for two months after the founding. Engelhardt, *San Fernando Rey*, 14. In Fr. Francisco Dumetz, *Libro Primero de Bautismos* (First Book of Baptisms) *de la Misión el Sor S. Fernando, Rey de España*, November 28, 1797, the forty-third recorded baptism takes place *"en la iglesia de esta Misión de San Fernando Rey"*; Berger, *Franciscan Missions*, 170.   2 Engelhardt, *San Fernando Rey*, 14.
3   Ibid., 15.

4   Mardith K. Schuetz-Miller, *Building and Builders in Hispanic California 1769–1850* (Tucson, Ariz.: SMRC/Santa Barbara, Calif.: SBTHP, 1994), 198.
5   Francis J. Weber, "Appears to Lean—Adobe Sides Taper at San Fernando," *San Fernando Valley Times*, April 18, 1964; Weber, *The Mission in the Valley*, 11–12; Berger, *Franciscan Missions*, 171–72.

(*above*) Latter-day roof tile mold.
(*right*) Worn out bench in convento corridor.
*JV/KEP.*

The roof was built with timbers from the nearby Tujunga canyon. According to legend, the width of the church building depended on the dimensions of the beams. The length and diameter of the beams used depended on the distance between the timber source and the building site. As was the custom, large logs were cut in the mountains and dragged overland. By turning the logs from time to time, their surfaces became partially planed due to dragging. At the building site, the final shaping and trimming of the roof beams, corbels, and purlins were accomplished with an adz. Long rawhide strips, soaked in water, bound the beams, and, upon drying, produced rigid, almost indestructible joints. This type of joint, not requiring ferrous connectors, was commonly used throughout most of the mission period.[6]

Skilled artisans were contracted by the Franciscans to come to Alta California to build furnishings and to create adornments for the new church. One such person was the master carpenter and mason José Antonio Ramírez, who was at the mission in 1809; it is believed that he tutored neophytes while the church was under construction.[7] Woodworkers produced chairs, benches, and tables whose joints were interlocked with a mortise and tenon or fastened together with a dowel. Blacksmiths wrought works out of iron that was shipped from Mexico.

A master blacksmith, Rafael Arriola, was living at the mission during 1812–13. He taught smithery to the natives and is credited with creating the window grilles, door hinges, latches, and decorative ironworks for the church and convento that have lasted to this day.[8]

Construction of the third church was completed in 1806. Built of adobe and roofed with tile, it measured 60 varas (165 feet) in length and approximately 14 varas (38 feet) in width. It was blessed on December 6, 1806, by Fr. Múñoz, who came down from Mission San Miguel.[9]

Decorations for this church were completed by neophytes. Lesser-skilled neophytes used stencils

---

6 Daughters of the American Revolution, *The Valley of San Fernando*, 19.

---

7 Schuetz-Miller, *Building and Builders*, 198.
8 Ibid.
9 In addition to the appearance of Fr. Pedro Múñoz, who officiated at the third church's blessing and dedication, other visiting padres were in attendance. According to Msgr. Weber, *The Mission in the Valley*, 11, Fr. Múñoz wrote that "the new church of the Mission of San Fernando, Rey de España was blessed; and on the following day [December 7, 1806], its solemn dedication, for the greater honor and glory of God, was celebrated with the invocation of the glorious King San Fernando and under his tutelage and protection." Berger remarked in *Franciscan Missions*, 171, that "a large musical band was formed, comprised of native musicians from Missions Santa Barbara and La Purísima Concepción. These musicians and singers entertained the assemblage with the melodious chants they had learned from the padres."

brought from Mexico by the friars to make the decorative designs. Those who were more skilled painted the imitation columns and floral bouquets on the reredos and geometric designs on the dados in the church's interior.[10] After the church was completed, an artisan substituted a more elaborate decoration of two painted marble columns for the earlier, colorful Indian decorations in the nave and on the reredos.[11]

A baptistry was situated on the north side of the church and a bell tower on the south, both close to the church's west entrance. The bell tower was also incorporated into the quadrangle's west wing. The third church building remained very nearly intact until an earthquake struck the Southland on December 21, 1812. Thirty beams were required to support the damaged walls and it took six more years of restoration work to bring the chapel back to its full serviceability.[12]

The names of some of the neophytes who were skilled in their craft have come down to us. Pre-1812

(*above*) Detail of iron grillework. (*right*) Outside and inside door handle and lock. *JV/KEP.*

earthquake, Juan Francisco and Fortunato were carpenters, and post-earthquake, Joaquín, Gerónimo, Francisco Xavier, and José Miguel were artisans. Others were Rogerio, a blacksmith; Basilio, a mason; and Juan Antonio, a painter. Tradition has it that Juan Antonio painted a set of the Stations of the Cross on ship's canvas while at Mission San Fernando; these paintings are now housed in the museum at Mission San Gabriel.[13]

---

[10] Unskilled but trained natives made the initial decorations to the church's interior since only a few skilled artisans were willing to travel to distant Alta California in the early period. When the padres came north, they brought with them books with patterns from which they taught the neophytes how to craft decorations.

[11] *California Missions: A Pictorial History*, 161; Engelhardt, *San Fernando Rey*, 16. This *trompe l'oeil* painting of the marble columns deteriorated and was replaced in the restoration of 1938–41.

[12] George Wharton James, *In and Out of the Old Missions* (Boston and Cambridge, Mass.: The University Press, 1905), 246.

---

[13] Schuetz-Miller, *Building and Builders*, 198; Norman Neuerburg, "Paintings in the California Missions," *American Art Review* 4, 1 (1977): 72–88.

Original key for door to room in the convento. *KEP.*

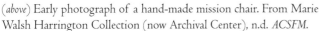

(*above*) Early photograph of a hand-made mission chair. From Marie Walsh Harrington Collection (now Archival Center), n.d. *ACSFM.*

(*right*) Original Mission San Fernando sanctuary chair. Now at the Mission Inn—Riverside, 3649 Mission Inn Avenue, Riverside, California 92501. *N.d., SWM-N14833A.*

In the 1850s, the church was reported to be in good condition. Artist Henry Miller wrote in his journal:

> In the morning I returned to the Mission, of which there are a number of buildings remaining and some in good order. The Church and the building in which the proprietor (Don Andrés Pico) lives, are in good condition, built of adobe and white washed.[14]

Surviving the ravages of time, pilfering, and acts of vandalism, the church served the mission until the late 1860s. Early in the next decade, however, the roof of the nave began to sag and disintegrate. In 1874 religious services had to be moved to a temporary chapel situated in the large first-story room at the east end of the convento. After many decades for restoration efforts, on September 7, 1941, Mass was once again celebrated in the mission's third church.[15]

Two more earthquakes struck in the twentieth century. The 1971 Sylmar earthquake devastated the church, which demanded considerable reconstruction, and the 1994 Northridge earthquake also damaged the church and required extensive restoration efforts to retain the church's historical characteristics, while bringing it up to modern building codes.

---

[14] Francis J. Weber, "Wells Fargo at San Fernando—1858," in *Memories of an Old Mission*, 22–23; Bancroft, *History of California*, 7: 145, 264.

[15] Weber, *Memories of an Old Mission*, 26.

Earliest known photograph of the church interior, ca. 1875. Seen in this view are the altar, wooden rails, and painted pseudocolumns forming the reredos. The last Mass was performed in the nave in 1874 when the roof and walls began to show signs of their slow decay and later collapsed. Absent are items noted in the final mission inventory of 1849, viz., paintings, mirrors, and statues of Saint Joseph and La Purísima Concepción, and the crucifixes that were all moved to the convento. *UCLA.*

(*above*) A group dressed in their Sunday best take a tour through the church about 1888. *CCP/CHS/TICOR* (*125*).

(*left*) In the ruined church, a woman sits near the entrance to the baptistry. George W. James, ca. 1895. See Charles Francis Saunders and J. Smeaton Chase in the Bibliography.

(*above*) Rubble covers the floor of the church. Note that the CLC roof has been newly installed, October 17, 1897. *CFL/SWM-N743.*

(*above, right*)W. C. Dickerson photograph of the interior of the church, which had not been used since 1874. Patchwork from the 1897 CLC roof restoration can be seen, ca. 1905. *WCD/SWM-N1492.*

(*right*) Mission San Fernando Rey de España, view of interior— north wall at chancel. Photo by Henry F. Whithey, March 1936. Reproduction from the collection of the Library of Congress now at the Archival Center. *HFW/ACSFM.*

(*right*) (3206)—San Fernando Mission. Visitors tour
the roofless church, Charles F. Lummis, October 4, 1896.
*CFL/SWM-N3433.*

(*below*) The desolate altar at the east end of the church,
1924. *CHS/TICOR (4494).*

-3206- SAN FERNANDO MISSION

146

SERVICES WERE HELD IN THE NEWLY RESTORED CHURCH, CA. 1947.
Note that the decorations are different from the 1875 version on page 143.
The St. Ferdinand statue above the altar on a cantilevered shelf was a
potentially dangerous missile later in the Sylmar 1971 earthquake. *NN/ACSFM.*
For color images of restored church after the earthquake, see page 192.

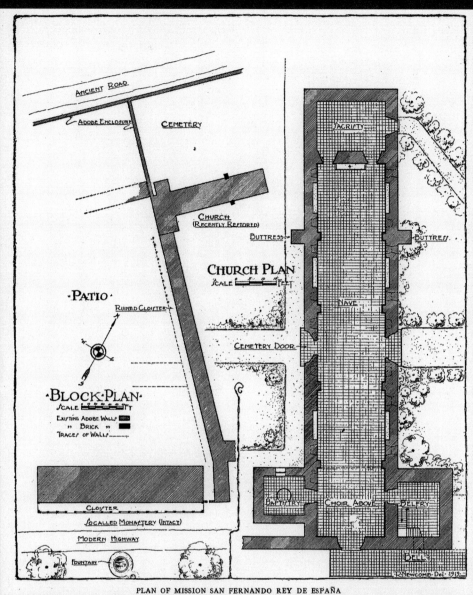

PLAN OF MISSION SAN FERNANDO REY DE ESPAÑA

(*this page*) Plan of Mission San Fernando, Rey de España, found in *The Old Mission Churches and Historic Houses of California* by Rexford Newcomb, ca. 1919. *RN/ACSFM.*

Church—San Fernando, Rey de España—Historic American Building Survey—(*opposite, top*) [West and South Elevation Views], (*opposite, bottom*) [North Elevation and Floor Plan Views]. Redrawn from U.S. Department of the Interior Office of National Park Service, Branch of Plans and Designs, 1936. Published by Learning Windows Publications, P.O. Box 455, Santa Margarita, CA 93453-0455. Prepared by Robert McCumsey, 1993. Printed with permission of publisher. *McCumsey/JBG.*

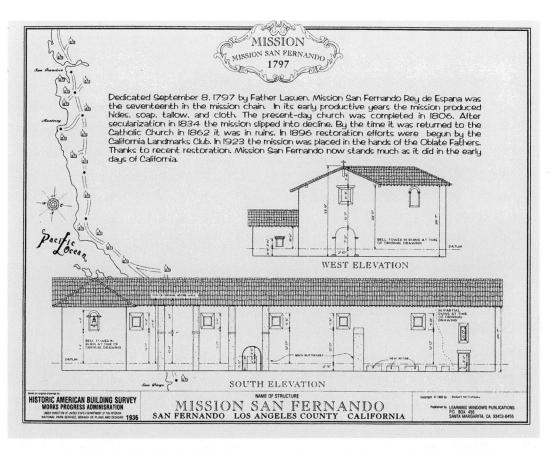

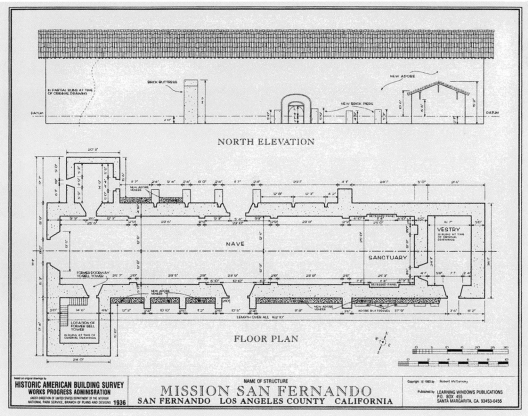

One of the earliest known photographs of Mission San Fernando.
Attributed to Henry T. Payne (or possibly to William Godfrey or Edward Vischer), ca. 1875.
Original view was placed on a stereocard and shows a portion of the cuartel,
baptistry, church, and bell tower. *HTP/CHS/TICOR* (7227).

The sacristy just prior to its collapse and a portion of the east wing of the quadrangle as they appear ca. 1893.
Hooker Collection at the Archival Center, San Fernando Mission, ca. 1893. *ACSFM*.

Two ladies stand at the south side of the church. Fraisher Collection
(now at the Lopez Adobe Archives), by unknown photographer, ca. 1903. *LAA*.

V iew taken by C. C. Pierce from the stone ruins of buildings
south of the quadrangle. The church is seen with its newly-
installed CLC roof and the still-ruinous west wing of the quadrangle,
ca. 1904. *CCP/CHS/TICOR (9862) and SWM-P18938.*

(*opposite, top*) The California Landmarks Club reroofed the church,
ca. 1905. This view looks from the southeast to the northwest. *KEP.*

(*opposite, bottom*) View shows the CLC roof beginning to wear. Holes in
the roof allow light to shine through at the east end of the church
and the crack on the west wall has widened. Photo ca. 1914. *ACSFM.*

Two Views of the Church from the South by W. C. Dickerson.
The church before (*above*) and after (*below*) the sacristy collapsed.
*Ca. 1905 WCD/SWM-N1495, and ca. 1915 WCD/SWM-N1497.*

Mission San Fernando
Showing Port Holes for defence

THE REROOFING OF THE CHURCH, CA. 1908. A view by Los Angeles photographer George W. Hazard: The sacristy at the east end of the church, looking southeast to northwest. Hazard's handwritten caption on this photograph is erroneous. He labels the windows in the sacristy "port holes for defence," which is a misleading and inaccurate description. *GHZ/KEP.*

In 1916 the sacristy fell into a state of ruin. *ACSFM.*

View shows the CLC roof beginning to wear. Holes in the roof allow light to shine through at the east end of the church and the crack on the west wall has widened, 1917. The roof was removed soon after this photo. *ACSFM.*

North orchard was leveled by farm equipment. This view shows north palms, church, and baptistry.
At this time, the belfry collapsed. Newly-built high-wire electric towers are seen in the distance, 1923. *ACSFM.*

The same unknown photographer who took photos on pages 124 and 137 also made
this photograph, ca. 1930, in which the east sacristy wall has completely collapsed. *UCLA.*

The Old Church—Mission San Fernando—433.
Made by Los Angeles Post Card Co., Brookwell Photo, ca. 1937. *KEP.*

Repairs on the church wall begin, in Dr. Mark R. Harrington's restoration project, ca. 1940.
Tree growth assists in determining time sequence. *ACSFM.*

160

Two Views Looking Through the Door from Mid-Center of the Church's South Wall
(*left*) Adam C. Vroman (V-235), 1897. *ACV/CHS/TICOR* (2578) and *SWM P-19044*.

(*below*) View during the 1920s by an unknown photographer. *KEP.*

(*opposite, top*) North exterior wall of the church, baptistry, and fenced cemetery plots. By the same unknown photographer who made the panorama on pages 114–15, ca. 1915–16. *LAA.*

(*opposite, bottom*) A similar view by the same photographer. Further to the right looking west, this view is across the sloping hill to the orchard wall, the adobe wall, twin palm trees, olive trees and beyond, ca. 1915–16. *LAA.*

Edwin Deakin oil painting of Mission San Fernando, Rey de España, ca. 1880.
*Courtesy of the History Collections, Los Angeles County Museum of Natural History. ED/LACMNH G. P. F. 730.*

## CHAPTER 10
# THE CONVENTO

*The building K [the convento on Henry Oak's map] is in a perfect state of preserva-
tion and is the residence of the Pico family. The walls are of adobe, thick and well plastered, and the roof of tiles in good repair, but not entirely modern according to the statement of Sr. Pico. The building is 240 feet [actually 235 feet, 2 inches] long and 45
feet wide [actually 50 feet, 4 inches not including the 15-foot-wide arcade], being divided into 2 rows of large airy and clean rooms the exact plan of whose arrangement I
did not ascertain. Along the front stretches a portico of 19 brick arches [plus one at each
end] each of 10 feet 7 inches supported by 20 pillars 22 inches by about 36 inches.*
— Henry L. Oak, *A Visit to the Missions of Southern California—1874*

A NEW HOUSE WAS BUILT for the friars. Father
Pedro Múñoz and Father José Antonio
Urrestí first wrote about its construction
in their annual report dated December 31, 1810.[1] Little is known about the house, as these priests did
not provide details of its dimensions and location,
or about its builders, except that two names have
come down to us. The master carpenter Salvador
Carabantes, according to Mardith K. Schuetz-
Miller, was employed to work on the convento as
early as February 1811, though he may have been there
a year earlier, and continued to work there until his
death in February 1813. Probably assisting him as an
apprentice was Vicente Lorenzana, who was an
orphan brought from Mexico City in 1800.[2]

Successive annual reports from the resident friars revealed building and remodeling efforts for the
next dozen years. In the years 1812 and 1813, Fr.
Múñoz and Fr. Joaquín Pascual Nuez, who was the
late Fr. Urrestí's replacement, informed Fray Fermín Francisco de Lasuén that a corridor was added
to the house.[3]

Many years passed without any construction
activity. In December 1819, Fr. Marcos Antonio
Vitoria wrote that the living area for the friars had
been repaired and renovated.[4] The next year Fray
Román Francisco Fernández de Ulibarri, who was
in charge at the mission, and Fr. Vitoria's replacement, Fray Francisco González de Ibarra, reported
that a staircase leading from the interior kitchen to

---

1  Fr. Pedro Múñoz and Fr. Urrestí's Annual Report, December 31, 1810, SBMAL. The padres wrote: *"Se ha echo una casa
nueva para los P.P. (padres) y se a renovado la vieja."*

2  Schuetz-Miller, *Building and Builders*, 198.

3  Fr. Pedro Múñoz and Fr. Nuez's Annual Report, December 31, 1812–13, SBMAL. The padres reported: *"Se ha puesto un
corredor a la casa y se ha renovado lo viejo, 1812"*; *"Se ha puesto un
corredor a la casa de los Padres, 1813."*

4  Fr. Marcos Antonio Vitoria's Annual Report, December
31, 1819, SBMAL. Vitoria wrote: *"Se ha compuesto y renovado la
mayor parte de la casa donde habitan los Padres."*

(*above*) (3219)—San Fernando—"Long Building" or convento at its worst. The chimney and a portion of the wall collapsed and there are holes in the roof. Photo by C. F. Lummis on June 1, 1897. *CFL/SWM-N3145.*

(*left*) (3203)—Large door to kitchen on north wall of convento after it and the dormer completely collapsed. By Charles F. Lummis, October 4, 1896. *CFL/SWM-N3146.*

the second floor had been added and a section of the house was enlarged.[5]

In 1819 and 1820, some construction took place, but details are lacking. The work may have been the construction of the external kitchen located next to the smokehouse or possibly modifications to walls, doors, or windows. Evidence of a kitchen extension on the convento's north side is clearly indicated in old photographs, which show the cavity for the ridgepole and two recesses of the sloping roof.

---

[5] Fr. Román de Ulibarri and Fr. González de Ibarra's Annual Report, December 31, 1820, SBMAL. The padres reported: "*Se ha aumentado un tramo de la casa de los PP.*"

(3211)—San Fernando—View taken from inside the
convento. Through a large splintered opening, we see
a dilapidated church and Porter Land and Water
Company equipment. By Charles F. Lummis, June 1,
1897. *CFL/SWM-N742.*

The following year Fr. Ulibarri died. But Fr. Ibarra continued to work on the convento and reported that the inner walls were heightened on the second floor and the building was roofed.[6] An adobe
wall was built on the north side of the convento to
enclose an adjacent service yard for a corral and gardens. Fr. Ibarra later reported that all construction
on the convento was completed by 1822.[7]

❁          ❁          ❁

After the arcade and a flat section at the west end
were roofed, the convento was completed. The
building measured slightly more than 235 feet long
and about 65 feet wide (including the portico). It
was two rooms deep on the first floor, except at the
east end, where a single large room about 20 by 50
feet and two stories high was built. Consisting of
twenty-one rooms, it contained quarters for the friars, guest accommodations, a sala or reception
room (the largest in Alta California's mission chain),
an interior and exterior kitchen, a storehouse, a winery, a refectory, and numerous storage rooms in the
attic.[8]

6   Fr. González de Ibarra's Annual Report, December 31, 1821,
    SBMAL. Fr. Ibarra reported: "*Se ha levantado y techado la casa de
    los PP.*"
7   Fr. González de Ibarra's Annual Report, December 31, 1822,
    SBMAL. Fr. Ibarra reported: "*Se ha concluida toda la fabrica de la
    casa de los PP^S y demas quartos inmediatos. Se a hecho otra cerca de la
    casa con mucha comodidad para todos los oficios.*"

8   Room designations were established in restoration plans
    for 1936–1938, drawn up from instructions by the Reverend
    Charles Burns and Dr. Mark R. Harrington. Plan views of
    the first and second floors were made by the Historic Amer-
    ican Building Survey, prepared by the U.S. Department of
    the Interior Office of National Parks, Buildings and
    Preservation Branch of Plans and Design, Survey No. 37-
    5, ca. 1936. See Plan Views of First and Second Floors and
    accompanying legend on pages 188 and 189. Beautiful
    reproductions of these architectural drawings were made
    from copies of the original and were provided by Troy
    Greenwood.

Large door to kitchen on north wall of convento and the dormer were repaired by the CLC. By Charles F. Lummis, October 11, 1897. *CFL/SWM-N3434.*

This building is best known as the convento, but it is often called the Fathers' Dwelling or the Long Building. Architecturally speaking, it is perhaps the most distinctive non-ecclesiastical structure of all the Alta California missions, with its attractive arcade of twenty-one arches and huge tile roof. The only other structure comparable in length and type is the Fathers' Dwelling at La Purísima Concepción, located near Lompoc. The difference between the two, however, is that La Purísima Concepción's arcade has piers instead of arches.

It was not clear to art historian Dr. Norman Neuerburg why the decision was made to build such an ambitious residence separate from the quadrangle when the one existing prior to 1810 would have been considered adequate. However, he believed the building was envisioned to be the start of a new and larger quadrangle and a grander church, as there was optimism for expansion at the time it was being built.[9]

The convento was constructed whenever materials and resources were available. Construction details are not explicit from the friars' writings but the phases of building can be pieced together by inspecting the contemporary structure and comparing photographs, both new (those taken after the 1971 and 1994 earthquakes) and old.

Dr. Neuerburg reconstructed how the building might have appeared at various times from 1810 to 1822.[10] Room numbers shown below correspond to those on the 1936 Historic American Buildings Survey prepared by the Department of the Interior, and redrawn by Troy Greenwood (see pages 186–188).

1810–1811    First-story rooms, 11–20, on the north (rear) side and the east end room (No. 1) formed an L-shaped structure with flat roof. The larger room (No. 1) was above the subterranean wine cellar (No. 21), which contained a wine vat and a ramp for receiving grapes from the outside.

9   Dr. Norman Neuerburg's unpublished research paper, entitled *Biography of a Building: The Fathers' Dwelling, "Long Building," or Convento of Mission San Fernando, Rey de España,* was given to the authors in 1986. A revised, shortened version of this manuscript was published as "Biography of a Building: New Insights into the Construction of the Fathers' Dwelling, An Archaeological and Historical Resume," *Southern California Quarterly* 79, 3 (Los Angeles: HSSC, 1997): 291–310.
10   Ibid.

Room 20 was not yet built. The window opening allowed the dumping of grapes directly into the vat. A mirador was constructed on the flat roof above room 16. A gate was built in the fashion of a *zaguán* (portico or doorway) going into room 16 and out a large opening on the north wall.

1811–1812    A corridor was built, most likely between the church and convento. The front row of rooms for the convento was built so that rooms 2 through 8 lined up with the southern face of the large east room (No. 1). The window opening to the wine cellar was blocked. Doors between rooms 4 and 16 were blocked.

1812–1813    Rooms 9 and 10 were added to the west end of the first floor. Walls were built up to partition attic rooms on the second floor. On top of the southern edge, a brick parapet over rooms 1 through 5 was built approximately one vara high. Two small square windows were placed on the south side of room 25 above the parapet wall. This allowed one to look out onto a southern view of the entire valley. The far east adobe wall in room 26 had two similar small square windows built, but no window was made in the west-facing walls of rooms 24 and 33. A door opening was made in room 33, allowing access to the flat roof over rooms 7–12. The first

Double-exposure of the soldiers quarters: One exposure is a view from the large door in the hall stairway on the convento's north wall, October 1899. The other, a mysterious one, is of a young boy. *CHS/TICOR (9863).*

gabled, tiled roof was placed over all rooms made above the second floor (No. 24 through No. 33).

The famous portico was built about 15 feet wide. It consisted of nineteen arches facing south and one arch at each end. Areas above rooms 7–12 and the roof above the portico (No. 23) were flat. The flat roof necessitated construction of a sophisticated water drainage system (see Chapter 12: The Mission Water System).

Centennial celebration held Thursday, September 9, 1897 (one day and one century after the official founding date).
These two "then" photographs show crowd gathered in front of the convento for the celebration.
By this time, work was completed on roof restorations of both the convento and church by the
California Landmarks Club. *CFL/SWM-P18913* (top) *and CFL/SWM-P18984* (bottom).

1819–1820  The convento was repaired and remodeled. A stairway to the second floor was built. It led from the zaguán, which was converted into a kitchen (No. 16), and then to the mirador (a lookout, used here as a solarium, room 31) on the second floor. An adobe wall was constructed north of the convento for a possible service area. Details of construction are lacking.

1821  The roof was raised several feet to the present height. The partial roof over rooms 24 to 33 was removed and existing walls on the second story were raised by laying adobe bricks on a slope matching the original roof slope. Buttresses were required for strength to form rooms 22 and 34 and the extreme west wall was built up with adobe bricks laid horizontally. At the end of construction, the new roof extended over the entire convento, including the arcade. The drainage system built in the 1812–13 phase therefore became non-functional.

1822  Doors between rooms 3 and 4 and 6 and 7 were blocked and moved to the side. Work on the convento was now complete.

A towerlike structure built on top of the convento prior to any roofing is a curiosity and its function is a mystery. The east and west sides of this structure, seen as Room 31, were made of solid bricks, and the north wall, which may have had a small window, was made of adobe. The south-facing wall, also made of brick, had a large arched opening and all

(*above, left*) Window grille under the southern arcade of the cloister. Ca. 1904. *CCP/CHS/TICOR* (*11397*).

(*above, right*) This photo was taken shortly after whitewash had been applied to the south wall of the convento, n.d. *FAP/SWM-P19040.*

(*opposite*) Father McGuire peers out from behind grille on the southern window of the convento. From the Feynes Collection, Southwest Museum. Photograph taken by C. C. Pierce, ca. 1932. From Marie Walsh Harrington Collection (now Archival Center). *CCP/SWM-P19093.*

of the walls were covered with lime plaster, inside and out. The structure was built with an open-air top. The west wall was adjacent to the smokehouse, allowing the room to retain the warmth of the sun and the smokehouse. Dr. Neuerburg surmised that it was used as a mirador by the sickly Fr. Urrestí. The facts leading to this conclusion are circumstantial but were convincing to Neuerburg: Fr. Urrestí died at the young age of thirty-six on January 4, 1812; the room had a southerly or sun-exposed opening; and the open-air roof of the convento was covered over soon after his death.[11]

After secularization, the church and other mission buildings slowly and steadily deteriorated, but some-

[11] Ibid., 297–99.

how the convento was spared. About this time, a two-room residence for the *mayordomo* (mission foreman or steward) was constructed at the southwest corner of the quadrangle. The rooms were an appendage to the west wing of the quadrangle. On the southeast corner of the convento, an adobe wall connected the convento and the mayordomo's house, and a door in the wall allowed access between the two.

As detailed earlier, an adobe wall closed off the convento's north side. The buildings and the wall created an enclosure of about two acres, an area for gardens and a corral for raising chickens, pigs, and goats. The convento's two kitchens were conveniently located within this enclosure.

In 1845 Andrés Pico and Juan Manso jointly leased the mission and took care of its maintenance. Pico made the convento his summer residence and the site of numerous parties. He used its ample storage rooms and facilities for his ranching needs, while Manso used the surrounding lands for cattle operations and farming.[12] Pico made only minor changes to the convento, such as replacing some doors and windows, and he is said to have built the small fireplace in the sala, which remained as he had left it until the convento was restored a century later.

Turmoil embroiled the mission in 1847. Lt. Col. John C. Frémont and his four hundred troops, on their way south to engage the Mexican army in battle, occupied the convento, where they committed acts of thievery and left behind visible scars of their presence. Fr. Blas Ordaz, the priest in residence, attested in a certificate to the following facts: Lieutenant Colonel Frémont and his troops were at the mission in January 1847; implements and other things, missing from the workshops and storerooms, were reclaimed by Ordaz; and Frémont's troops had, during the days they were there, "maintained themselves on the sheep and cattle of said establishment, taking more than two of the tame horses it had."[13]

The troops vandalized the property, burning roof beams and leaving drawings and inscriptions on doors and on a pier of an arch. The graffiti were uncovered after the 1971 Sylmar earthquake but are no longer visible, as the walls were covered over with plaster during restoration.[14]

___

[12] Engelhardt, *San Fernando Rey*, 67–68.

[13] Ibid. In a letter from Fr. Blas Ordaz to Andrés Pico (now a military general spearheading Californio forces in the Mexican War), Ordaz wrote about Lt. Frémont and his battalion: "Fr. Blas Ordaz, Missionary Apostolic of the holy Mission San Fernando. I certify in the form permissible that in the month of January of the year 1847, [Lt.] Colonel J.C. Frémont and his troops were at this Mission. He entered the workshops and rooms of this Mission, and the lessee reclaimed from Señor Frémont the implements and other things which he told him were missing. I certify likewise that during the days when the troops remained at this Mission they maintained themselves on the sheep and cattle of said establishment, taking more than two of the tame horses it had. At the request of the persons concerned I sign this at San Fernando on January 14, 1847—Fr. Blas Ordaz." The effect of this certification was nil, since Gen. Andrés Pico had capitulated to Frémont at Cahuenga the day before. See Daughters of the American Revolution, *The Valley of San Fernando*, 33, for a description of a more cordial association between Lt. Col. J. C. Frémont and the mission's mayordomo, Pedro López.

[14] Neuerburg, "Biography of a Building," 308.

Old pepper trees in front of the convento —1885. Bell is seen in the small corporal or "guard's" tower. *SWM P-18997.*

By 1856 the last three bays of the convento's west arcade were walled in and fitted with windows and a lean-to was added.[15] From 1857 to 1861 the Butterfield Overland Mail Stage company used three rooms at the far west end as a depot for mail and passengers on the Los Angeles–San Francisco route. By 1865 the lean-to was removed but the walled-in arches remained. In the far west wall of the convento, two doors were made, each allowing entrance into its own room.[16] (In 1861 the Butterfield line moved its station operations from the convento to the López Station, a few miles to the northwest. At this location, the valley's first post office was established in 1869. The area was covered over by the Van Norman Reservoir in 1913.)

In 1873 George K. Porter acquired the land surrounding the mission and later converted the convento into the headquarters for his Porter Land and Water Company. The next year, the convento was used as a storage facility for the company's farm equipment and supplies and the large room at the east end doubled as a chapel when the church became so dilapidated that it could no longer be used for services. (Room 1, page 188.)[17]

During the next few decades, the rooms in the convento were used for different purposes. Doors and windows were either blocked or opened up and sometimes their functions were reversed. There were no attempts to maintain or repair the building but it remained in relatively good condition throughout the 1880s. The three western arches were reopened sometime before 1883, and the convento's west doors were sealed sometime after 1912.[18]

[15] Henry Miller, *Account of a Tour of the California Missions,* 49, in which his famous 1856 sketch, *M. San Fernando,* appears.

[16] Jeanne Van Nostrand, biography of the artist Edward Vischer, *Drawings of the California Missions, 1861–1878* (San Francisco: The Book Club of California, 1982). The Edward Vischer sketch (Plate 32) on page 272 clearly shows the convento's condition at the west end in 1865.

[17] Neuerburg, "Biography of a Building," 308.

[18] Ibid. See William Adam oil painting on page 191.

(*top*) One of the earliest views of the convento's east end that shows the extended adobe wall and the mayordomo's house. Gaps at each end of the roof reveal the original, flat roofline over the second-story convento rooms. *Hervé Friend photograph, ca. 1886.*

(*bottom*) Old pepper trees in front of the convento—1887. Corporal bell is still seen in the tower at the west end of the convento. The Porter Land and Water Company raised pigs on the property. Photographer unknown, ca. 1900. *HL.*

Old pepper trees in front of the convento, ca. 1897.
The original adobe wall between the convento and mayordomo house is now missing.
The Porter Land and Water Company's barns and farm equipment are seen at far end of convento.
*Harry Franz Rile photograph.*

The west end of the convento with new maturing pepper trees in front.
A Father looks at the entrance to the convento, ca. 1925. *LAA.*

(*above*) Fresh whitewash beautifies the
convento. Photograph by C. C. Pierce,
1904. *CCP/CHS/TICOR* (2269).

(*right*) East to west view through the arcade
of the convento. W. M. Graham Photos,
ca. 1905. *GP/HL—photCL 188* (91).

3201—Mission San Fernando, Rear of Monastery

(*opposite, top*) (3201) Mission San Fernando—Rear of Monastery. Photographed by Charles F. Lummis on October 4, 1896. *CFL/SWM-N3931.*

(*opposite, bottom*) A Californio cook stands in front of the door leading into the sala. Photo by A. C. Vroman, 1896. *ACV/SCWHR (V-226).*

(*right*) Porter Land and Water Company farm implements rest inside the arcade of the convento, ca. 1884. *KEP.*

(*below*) Palms north of adobe wall. A view of the convento through a break in the wall. By W. C. Dickerson, ca. 1905. *WCD/SWM-N1482.*

View from the east interior doorway into the sala.
The "River of Life" door is open on the left. This is the sala before restoration work
began under the direction of the Oblates of Mary Immaculate, ca. 1926. *KEP.*

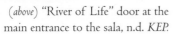

(*above*) "River of Life" door at the main entrance to the sala, n.d. *KEP.*

(*above, right*) Sketch of the exterior "River of Life" door, which leads to the sala in the convento, n.d. *JBG.*

(*right*) Interior side of door leading to sala in the convento. Photo by Warren C. Dickerson, ca. 1922. *WCD/SWM-P19055.*

Sala (reception or parlor room) of the convento, ca. 1950. *KEP.*

(*right*) The small fireplace, reportedly built by Andrés Pico during his residency, in the sala of the convento. By C. C. Pierce, ca. 1904. *CHS/TICOR* (*11399*).

(*below*) Mission San Fernando—Interior Chapel by Adam Clark Vroman, 1896. Dr. Mark R. Harrington, in his restoration elevation plan of 1938–1940, labeled this the "House Chapel" (eastern-most room on the first floor plan, page 188). *ACV/SCWHR V231*.

(*above, left*) Stairway leading from the kitchen to the second floor of the convento, ca. 1904. *CHS/TICOR (11393).*

(*above*) (3221)—San Fernando, C. F. Lummis. Large second-floor room over the chapel at the east end of the convento is at its worst. The chimney and wall collapsed and there are holes in the roof. This photo is prior to roof restoration, June 1, 1897. *CFL/SWM-N3918.*

(*left*) The wine vat and steps leading to the cellar, ca. 1923. *CHS/TICOR (4491).*

(*above*) (3212) San Fernando, by C. F. Lummis. View of the convento rooftop. Tiles and rafters were beginning to sag, June 1, 1897. Four thousand tiles were eventually recovered from surrounding ranchos to reconstruct the convento roof. *CFL/SWM-N739.*

(*right*) The tile roof and beams of the convento collapsed shortly before the 1897 restoration. *LAA.*

(*below*) The sala, ca. 1940, after Dr. Mark R. Harrington's restoration. *KEP.*

Two ladies stand in front of the convento. Fraisher Collection, ca. 1903. *LAA.*

(*left*) Looking through the interior door into the sala. Photo by James B. Gulbranson, 1950. *JBG/JBG.*

(*below*) Door, arch, and niche surrounding the "River of Life" door leading into the sala. *ACSFM.*

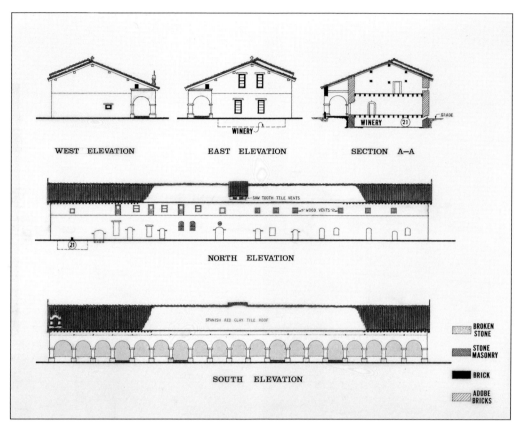

WEST ELEVATION      EAST ELEVATION      SECTION A–A

NORTH ELEVATION

SOUTH ELEVATION

BROKEN STONE

STONE MASONRY

BRICK

ADOBE BRICKS

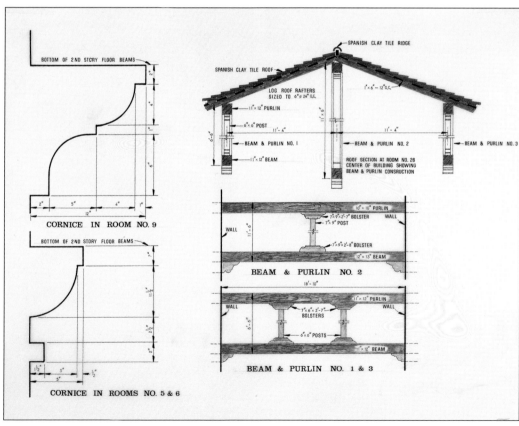

CORNICE IN ROOM NO. 9

CORNICE IN ROOMS NO. 5 & 6

BEAM & PURLIN NO. 2

BEAM & PURLIN NO. 1 & 3

186

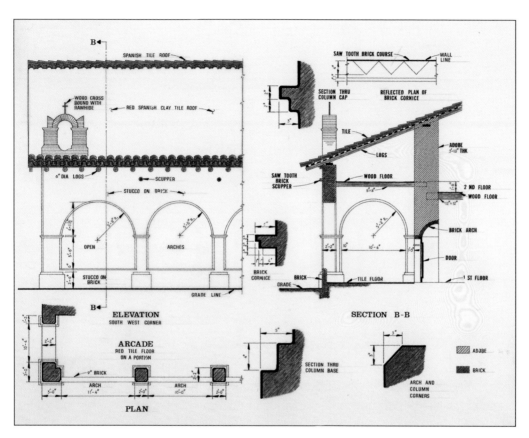

Monastery—San Fernando, Rey de España—
Historic American Building Survey
(*above*) Details of southwest corner—elevation
views; (*opposite, top*) elevation views; (*opposite, bottom*)
details of cornices in rooms (5), (6), and (9), beam
and purlin construction at room (26). *Redrawn by
Troy Greenwood from U.S. Department of the Interior Office
of National Parks Buildings and Preservations Branch of
Plans and Design, Survey No. 37-5, ca. 1936. TG/KEP.*

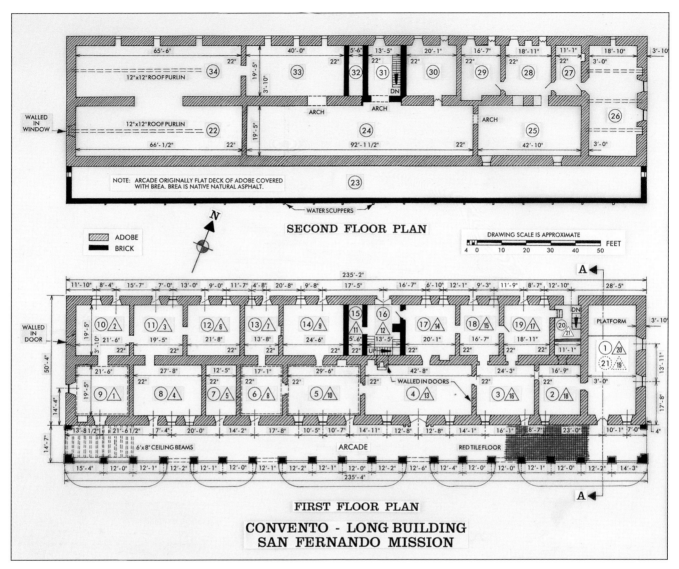

**SECOND FLOOR PLAN**

NOTE: ARCADE ORIGINALLY FLAT DECK OF ADOBE COVERED WITH BREA. BREA IS NATIVE NATURAL ASPHALT.

WATER SCUPPERS

ADOBE
BRICK

DRAWING SCALE IS APPROXIMATE
FEET
4 0    10    20    30    40    50

WALLED IN WINDOW

12"x12" ROOF PURLIN

12"x12" ROOF PURLIN

ARCH    ARCH    ARCH

N

**FIRST FLOOR PLAN**

**CONVENTO - LONG BUILDING
SAN FERNANDO MISSION**

WALLED IN DOOR

WALLED IN DOORS

6"x8" CEILING BEAMS

ARCADE

RED TILE FLOOR

PLATFORM

A

A

Monastery—San Fernando, Rey de España—Historic American Building Survey
Plan Views of First and Second Floors; (*opposite*) legend.
*Redrawn by Troy Greenwood from U.S. Department of the Interior Office of National Parks Buildings and Preservations Branch of Plans and Design, Survey No. 37-5, ca. 1936. TG/KEP.*

(*opposite, top*) Impressionist acrylic painting of the front fountain and southwestern corner of the convento, n.d. Artist unknown. *JBG.*

(*opposite, bottom*) Early morning at the cloister looking toward the east. Oil on canvas, owned by the San Fernando Valley Historical Society and displayed at the Andrés Pico Adobe, Mission Hills, California, n.d. *SFVHS.*

| INTERIOR DEPARTMENT REPORT | | M. HARRINGTON RESTORATION (1938-1940) | |
|---|---|---|---|
| 1 | STORE ROOM | 20 | HOUSE CHAPEL |
| 2 | STORE ROOM | 18 | STORAGE ROOM |
| 3 | CHAMBER | 16 | PRIVATE PARLOR |
| 4 | SALA | 13 | RECEPTION ROOM |
| 5 | LIBRARY | 10 | PADRE'S STUDY |
| 6 | CHAMBER | 8 | PASTOR'S BEDROOM |
| 7 | STORE ROOM | 5 | STORAGE (BAGGAGE ROOM) |
| 8 | CHAMBER | 4 | HOSPICE |
| 9 | CHAPEL | 1 | GOVERNOR'S ROOM |
| 10 | CHAMBER | 2 | HOSPICE |
| 11 | CHAMBER | 3 | HOSPICE |
| 12 | CHAMBER | 6 | HOSPICE |
| 13 | CHAMBER | 7 | FOOD STORAGE |
| 14 | CHAMBER | 9 | BAKERY |
| 15 | SMOKE ROOM | 11 | GRILL (LARGE FIREPLACE) |
| 16 | STAIR ROOM | 12 | KITCHEN |
| 17 | DINING ROOM | 14 | REFECTORY |
| 18 | CHAMBER | 15 | ASSISTANT PRIESTS' ROOM |
| 19 | CHAMBER | 17 | MISSION OFFICE |
| 20 | WINE VAT ROOM | 21 | WINE VAT ROOM |
| 21 | WINERY - BELOW ① | 19 | WINERY - BELOW 20 |
| 22 | ATTIC | | |
| 23 | ATTIC | | |
| 24 | ATTIC | | |
| 25 | ASSEMBLY ROOM | | |
| 26 | ASSEMBLY ROOM | | |
| 27 | ANTE - ROOM | | |
| 28 | CHAMBER | | |
| 29 | CHAMBER | | |
| 30 | CHAMBER | | |
| 31 | STAIR - HALL | | |
| 32 | SMOKE ROOM | | |
| 33 | ATTIC | | |
| 34 | ATTIC | | |

Only a remnant of The Old San Fernando Mission, founded 1797.
A colloidal on cardboard (*carte-de-visite*) by William H. Fletcher, ca. 1885–90. *WHF/KEP.*

A view of the convento from the southeast, across San Fernando Mission Boulevard, 1979. *KEP.*

Henry Chapman Ford watercolor of the convento's west end, 1883.
From the Dr. Norman Neuerberg Collection, now Santa Barbara Mission Archive-Library. *HCF/SBMAL.*

Oil painting of the mission by William Adam, ca. 1912.
This picture is displayed at the Andrés Pico Adobe. *Adam/JBG (SFVHS).*

(*right*) Details of the convento's west wall, corporal (guard's) bell tower, sandstone parapet and arcade. By A. C. Vroman, 1890. *ACV/SCWHR (V-230).*

(*below*) The convento arcade, the near-circular fountain, and, in the distance, the adobe workshops and storerooms in ruins. By George Wharton James, 1884. *CCP/ CHS/TICOR (5879) and SWM-P19033.*

(*opposite, top*) Reredos in the nave of the church. Photograph and postcard by Ken Pauley, 1978. *KEP.*

(*opposite, bottom*) Church altar and reredos in Mission San Fernando Rey nave. Photograph by Larry Underhill on July 29, 2004, completes a sequence chronicling the church's interior conditions over nearly 130 years. *LU/KEP.*

193

Adam Clark Vroman's portrait of himself while seated
(left) on a bench with his friends, in the arcade of
the convento, 1896. *ACV/SCWHR* (*V-227*).

West end of the convento corridor after
repairs had been made to columns and
whitewashing of walls, ca. 1917. *UCLA.*

Front of the old ranch house at Camulos Ranch, legendary home of Helen Hunt Jackson's Ramona.
It was actually the home of Antonio del Valle, his son Ignacio, and their heirs from the
Estancia San Francisco de Xavier, ca. 1916. The Mentor Association,
courtesy of the Lopez Adobe Archives, San Fernando. *LAA.*

CHAPTER 11

# THE OUTPOST

*With the necessity for removing flocks and herds from the immediate vicinity of the mission in order that fruit and vegetables might be raised there, and with the pressing need to find land most suitable for the cultivation of various crops to feed the ever increasing number of neophytes, the mission estancias came into being. . . . Occasionally, when the distance from the mission was too great for the proper attendance at religious services, a capilla was built in connection with the ranch buildings for the benefit of the Indians living there.*

—Edith Buckland Webb, *Indian Life at the Old Missions*

MISSION CATTLE RANCHES, or *estancias*, came into existence near many Alta California missions as a result of ranching and agricultural expansion driven by population growth. Ranches were usually at a distance of ten to forty miles from their associated mission and consisted of Indian barracks, a few workrooms, a storage area, corrals for the flocks and herds, and lands for cultivating crops and raising livestock.[1]

At some estancias, a room was set aside or added later and reserved for use as a *capilla* (chapel). An estancia with a chapel was an *asistencia* (sub-mission) if specific Church requirements were also met. In a discussion of whether a building site at San Bernardino was an estancia or a sub-mission of Mission San Gabriel, Fr. Engelhardt defined an asistencia as a "[m]ission on a small scale with all the requisites for a [m]ission, and with Divine Services [Holy Mass] held regularly on days of [Holy] obligation, except that it lacked a resident priest."[2] To perform these religious duties, friars would travel periodically from the parent mission to the sub-mission when there was a great distance between the two.

An asistencia was a branch or extension of a fully established and flourishing missionary foundation.[3]

---

1  Francis J. Weber, *El Caminito Real—A Documentary History of California's Estancias* (Hong Kong: Yee Tin Tong Printing Press Ltd., 1988), xiv; Francis J. Weber, "The Mission Ranchos," *Rancho Days in Southern California: An Anthology with New Perspectives*, Brand Book 20, Kenneth Pauley, ed. (Studio City, Calif.: Westerners, Los Angeles, 1997), 45–61 (hereafter referred to as "Mission Ranchos"); Webb, *Indian Life at the Old Missions*, 92–93.

2  Engelhardt, *San Gabriel Mission*, 347, argues that the San Bernardino Rancho, though commonly thought to be an asistencia for San Gabriel Mission, was not an asistencia since it "lacked all the prerequisites." The estancia at San Bernardino did have a small chapel for services for the local Indians, but since there were usually only two priests at San Gabriel and the asistencia at Los Angeles Plaza had priority, only occasionally could the friars provide Sunday services to the estancia at San Bernardino.

3  Francis J. Weber, *El Caminito Real—A Documentary History of California's Asistencias*, in which there are sixty-three short articles on Alta California's asistencias, Santa Margarita de Cortona, San Antonio de Pala, and Santa Isabel.

(*left*) Adobe ruins of Rancho San Fernando de Xavier located near Castaic Junction. By Arthur B. Perkins, ca. 1910. *Courtesy of the Santa Clarita Valley Historical Society. ABP/SCVHS.*

(*below*) (472) Adobe ruins of Estancia San Francisco de Xavier, ca. 1915. *Puck and Colton/HL.*

There were only five asistencias in Alta California meeting the above conditions: Santa Ysabel (founded 1818) near Mission San Diego de Alcalá; San Antonio de Pala (founded 1810) near Mission San Luis Rey; Nuestra Señora la Reina de los Angeles (founded 1784) near Mission San Gabriel;[4] Santa Margarita de Cortona (founded 1787) near Mission San Luis Obispo; and San Rafael Arcángel (founded 1817 and granted mission status in 1823), across the bay from Mission Dolores.[5]

The area at the confluence of the Santa Clara River and Castaic Creek, near today's Castaic Junction, was under consideration as the site for a mission. On the so-called "Sacred Expedition" of 1769, both Fr. Crespí and Captain Portolá had made favorable remarks in their diaries about the site. Their early opinions, however, did not influence the decision-makers, and the site was ultimately rejected, based on several weighty reasons that Fr. Santa Maria noted in his August 1795 report to Fr. Lasuén.

The area was close to the Chaguayabit ranchería, which the Spanish soldiers called Ranchería del Corral because, Fr. Crespí said, "the people lived without cover, for they had no more than a light shelter fenced in like a corral . . . , and I called it Santa Rosa

---

4　The asistencia in the Pueblo Nuestra Señora de la Reina de Los Angeles began in 1784 and grew into "Plaza Church" in the 1820s and 1830s. It is located across the street from Los Angeles Plaza and Olvera Street in downtown Los Angeles.

5　Weber, *History of California's Asistencias,* xv.

de Viterbo."[6] One of the reasons the area was reject-ed was that it was not close enough to El Camino Real. (It was thirteen miles northwest of the future Mission San Fernando. By 1795, El Camino Real was repositioned along the Conejo Corridor, six leagues south of Castaic Junction. It is virtually the same path that today's Highway 101 takes westward out of the San Fernando Valley.)

It is very likely that Friars Dumetz, Uría, and Múñoz were convinced by Fr. Crespí's and Captain Portolá's earlier, favorable descriptions of the area to establish a ranching and agricultural outpost there. The outpost became San Francisquito, one of Mission San Fernando's four ranch sites, the other three being Las Virgines, La Amarga, and La Huenga.[7]

In 1804 the mission friars vigorously protested the rancho grant to Francisco Avila for the Camulos Ranch, located at the western limit of the Santa Clarita Valley. They were successful in their protest and hastened to start building during that year at Estancia San Francisco de Xavier, as the outpost was then called.[8]

After Mexico's expulsion of the Spanish from Alta California, Carlos Antonio Carrillo, a sergeant stationed at the Santa Barbara Presidio, attempted to make a *denuncio* (claim registration) for the Camulos rancho, at the westernmost portion of Rancho San Francisco, but was unsuccessful. The Fernandino Franciscans thwarted his attempt at wresting mission properties from their control. Fr. González Ibarra admonished Carrillo in a letter of April 1825:

> That one should serve and respect him who is of benefit is very proper and just; but that one should feed him who not only does not protect, but positively destroys, requires a stout heart. In effect, what benefit do I receive, or have I and the Mission received

from your presidio? None. What damages, on the other hand? Incalculable. Yes, yes, if the presidio did not exist, I could figure on my labor and toil. In that case, I should mind neither the Tulares nor the sierras, the refuge of wicked men. The second sierra, or bawdry (alcabuetaria), your presidio, it is that annoys me. If a low man should behave in a low manner one should not be surprised; but that men who regard themselves as honorable act thus, this is what stuns.[9]

Colonists, *politicos*, and soldiers seized upon opportunities to acquire mission land, and one of these acquisitive individuals was Lt. Antonio del Valle, the scion of a wealthy family from Jalisco, Mexico. He served under the Spanish army in Alta California and later was commissioned to secularize Mission San Fernando in October 1834. Appointed by the Mexican government, he became administrator of the mission. On May 29, 1835, del Valle was appointed the mayordomo of the mission. On July 26, 1835, he inventoried the mission's wealth. The property, except for sacred vessels and vestments, and the lands came to $41,714. The Indian population was 541.[10]

Lt. Antonio del Valle filed a petition for owner-

---

6   Arthur B. Perkins, "Rancho San Francisco: A Study of a California Land Grant," *Southern California Quarterly* 39, 2 (Los Angeles: HSSC, 1957): 100.

7   Engelhardt, *San Fernando Rey*, 63.

8   Ibid., 20; Bancroft, *History of California*, 2: 115–16; Perkins, "Rancho San Francisco," 102.

9   Engelhardt, *San Fernando Rey*, 41, in which Engelhardt erroneously refers to Carlos Carrillo as "apparently the storekeeper for the [Santa Barbara] presidio." Carlos Antonio Carrillo and many of his family members, in fact, played very important roles in 1818–1838 California history. See, for example, Bancroft, *History of California*, 2: 236, where Sergeant Carrillo leads a charge of soldiers and civilians from the Santa Barbara presidio up to Santa Inés to confront the pirate Hipólito Bouchard and his hoodlums in 1818; see Rose Marie Beebe and Robert Senkewicz, eds., *Lands of Promise and Despair*, 325–26 and 386–89, for Carlos' involvement with the February 1824 Chumash revolt at missions Santa Inés and La Purísima Concepción. Also, on October 3, 1830, he was appointed Alta California's first *diputado* (delegate) to the congress in Mexico City, where he delivered a message to the congress, urging modernization of the judicial system (from a colonial system to a republican government). These are some of Carrillo's contributions to California. He was more than a "storekeeper" at the presidio. See Perkins, "Rancho San Francisco," 104.

10   Engelhardt, *San Fernando Rey*, 50–51.

ship of Rancho San Francisco de Xavier in 1833 but it was rejected. The Franciscans opposed his land ownership, and, on behalf of the missionaries and local Indians, they filed a protest that was successful in keeping the property out of del Valle's hands. In 1839, however, the lieutenant filed a second petition, which was approved.[11]

❈        ❈        ❈

The first building at the outpost was built of adobe and measured 38 by 6 varas (105 by 16½ feet). There is some disagreement about the use of the building. A few historians and archaeologists have suggested that in its early days, the building was used for religious services and therefore the rancho had the status of an asistencia. Their suggestion is disputed as the original building did not fulfill the requisite of having a chapel.[12]

The estancia eventually did gain the status of an asistencia, after Lieutenant del Valle, who was successful in acquiring a land grant with his petition of January 22, 1839, built a second adobe structure near the first one and integrated a chapel into it. The building was slightly larger than the first, measuring 39 by 8¼ varas (107 feet 4 inches by 22 feet 8 inches).[13] During this time, Fr. Blas Ordaz, the last resident Franciscan, would have traveled to

the ranch and performed Holy Mass for members of the del Valle family and their Indian workers. Since the estancia became an asistencia after secularization, it was never counted among asistencias in the Alta California mission chain.

The very fault that Fr. Vicente de Santa María found with the Castaic Junction area—the steepness of San Fernando Pass—was considered an advantage for herding livestock. The pass provided a natural fence to keep animals within its steep confines. It was reported that three places required only minimal fencing: at the narrow outlet of Grapevine Canyon, a single bar from one side to the other; at Piru Creek, a fence across the riverbed; and at the boundary line between the San Francisco and Triunfo ranches. There is some dispute, however, that a fence between the San Francisco and Triunfo ranches was actually needed, since there was a steep ridge between the two.[14]

From the beginning of Mexican rule, Commandant José de la Guerra of the Santa Barbara presidio, which had military jurisdiction over Mission San Fernando, constantly feuded with Fr. Gonzáles Ibarra. Disputes between the two continued from the time of Mexican independence in 1821 to secularization in 1835. The commandant and his soldiers were always demanding more and more from the mission in the form of food stuffs (meat, beans, barley, and wheat), handcrafted leather goods, soap, tallow, and blankets. Fr. Ibarra protested to De la Guerra that the demands were unreasonable. He bemoaned the fact that Indian labor was being used to indulge the personal needs of the presidio soldiers. In addition, he complained constantly to the commandant that drought and insect infestations at both the mission and estancia had significantly reduced plant production for the year 1821. The fol-

[11] Manuel P. Servín, "The Secularization of the California Missions: A Reappraisal," *Southern California Quarterly* 47, 2 (Los Angeles: HSSC, 1965): 133–49. For more on this subject, see the discussion in *Secularization and Political Intrigue* regarding the Franciscans' opposition to land acquisitions by *gente de razón*.

[12] Perkins, "Rancho San Francisco," 97–126; David Whitley, "Intensive Phase I: Archaeological Survey of the West Ranch Area, Newhall Ranch, Los Angeles County, etc.," in *Ethnographic Background, CSUF Archeological Information Center* (Fullerton: California State University at Fullerton, 1994), Chapters 2.2–5.2; Weber, "Mission Ranchos," 50.

[13] Whitley, "Archaeological Survey," Chapter 2.4; Gerald (Jerry) Reynolds, *Santa Clarita: Valley of the Golden Dream* (Granada Hills, Calif.: World Communications, Inc., 1992), 17.

[14] Perkins, "Rancho San Francisco," 103. In a personal interview in June 2002, archaeologist David Whitley told the authors there is a steep ridge between the two ranches which serves nicely as a natural boundary and that probably the fence mentioned was not needed.

"The Old Milk House" at the bottom of the hill on which the estancia stood, ca. 1915. *Puck and Colton/HL.*

lowing are excerpts, translated by Fr. Engelhardt, of the original *De la Guerra Papers*: [15]

On September 17:

It seems to me impossible to supply seventy or eighty fanégas [*sic*] of corn, because the harvest of this year may yield only a hundred.

On September 21:

I just came from the Rancho de San Francisco. Things are as I said. There are only sixty or seventy fanégas [*sic*]. Rabbits and hares and worms have done damage to the crop. In effect, on Monday I shall order twenty-nine fanégas [*sic*] to be husked, which will be taken as far as San Buenaventura.

On September 25:

Fifteen pack mules would leave the Rancho de San Francisco with thirty fanégas [*sic*] of corn for San Buenaventura to be forwarded to the Santa Barbara presidio.

In a letter to De la Guerra dated May 2, 1825, Fr. Ibarra expresses indignation and sums up years of frustration:

Who can read the extravagance of that letter without indignation? Hence you can imagine what must be the indignation which I suffer from such foolishness. . . . The government, you say, demands aid for the presidio from the pueblo [Los Angeles] and the Mission. This is a sacred duty, as you call it. Well, from this obligation of the Mission to support the presidio follows the duty of the presidio to aid the Mission, so that it can advance spiritually and temporally; but the very opposite obtains, so much so that the Mission is now in a worse condition than at the beginning, because at that time the troops would follow runaway Indians and bring them back.[16]

Though Fr. Ibarra was unhappy with the presidio soldiers and their commandant, he persevered and continued to provide supplies to the military up until his departure in 1835. He was able to meet the military's demands principally due to the assistance

---

[15] Engelhardt, *San Fernando Rey*, 38–40. Fr. Engelhardt consistently and incorrectly adds an accent mark to the word fanegas when one is not needed in his translation of Fr. Ibarra's correspondence.

[16] Ibid., 41–42.

of Estancia San Francisco de Xavier, which became a productive outpost.

Scant physical information about this remote outpost is available and comes mainly from descriptions by early explorer William Lewis Manly, historian Arthur B. Perkins, and contemporary archaeologists.[17] After his arrival with John Rogers at Rancho San Francisco in 1849, Manly wrote:

> A house on higher ground soon appeared in sight. It was low, of one story with a flat roof, gray in color, and of a different style of architecture from any we had ever seen before. There was no fence around it, and there were no animals or wagons in sight, nor person to be seen . . . but a mule tied to a post told us there was some one about. . . . Rogers now began looking around the house, which was built of sun-dried bricks about one by two feet in size, and one end was used as a storehouse . . . [located] down the hill . . . [where there was a] small, poorly, fenced field which was sometimes cultivated.[18]

What little we know about the appearance of the site comes from a few early 1900s photographs from the John B. Colton and Charles Puck collections at the Huntington Library. The estancia with its adobe walls in ruins is shown at the top of the terrace near Castaic Junction. Photographs by Perkins and Colton show the house referred to as the "Old Milk House," which is the same one located "down the hill."[19]

A later archaeological excavation of the site revealed the following about the estancia-turned-asistencia:

> A Dig at the site in 1935, indicated five rooms, those for storage and dormitory use having whitewash interior. The living quarters had tiled floor, and whitewash[ed] walls. Roof was of Mission tile, burned at [a] kiln [at the] easterly end of [the] rear building. This rear adobe structure, parallelling [sic] the larger front building, apparently divided into small rooms for trades, cobbler, smith, sempstress, etc. There was little recovery from the dig, which was abandoned after vandals ruined the tile floors and remaining adobe walls [while] searching for Mission treasure about 1937. The buildings stood on the high mesa overlooking Castaic Junction.[20]

The area was hit by a natural disaster common in California. On January 9, 1857, an earthquake struck at 8:20 A.M. and lasted anywhere from one to three minutes. Its epicenter was not known, but the area of strongest reported shaking was at Fort Tejon. It was felt from Marysville south to San Diego and east to Las Vegas. It was later learned that the quake, with an estimated magnitude of 8.0 on the Richter scale, cracked open the earth's surface for 350 kilometers (220 miles) along the San Andreas fault. The asistencia, located thirty-four miles south of El Tejon, suffered so much damage to its adobe structures that it was totally abandoned.

The Estancia (Asistencia) San Francisco de Xavier is recorded as site CA-LAN-962H in the files of the UCLA Archaeological Information Center and is registered as California Historical Landmark No. 556. It is also listed as a historical landmark in Los Angeles County in *Historic Landmarks in Los Angeles County* (County Superintendent of Schools, Los Angeles, 1956).[21]

[17] William L. Manly, *Death Valley in '49: An Important Chapter of California Pioneer History* (Bishop, Calif.: Chalfant Press, Inc., 1977), 176–77. Originally published as *Death Valley in '49* (San Jose, Calif.: The Pacific Tree and Vine Co., 1894); Perkins, "Rancho San Francisco," 97–126; Whitley, *Archaeological Survey*, Chapter 2.4.

[18] Manly, *Death Valley in '49*, 176–77. Manly reached Rancho San Francisco after he and John Rogers had traveled for twenty-six days on a treacherous journey out of Death Valley to seek relief for the stranded Bennett-Arcane overland party that was left behind.

[19] The John B. Colton and Charles Puck collections reside in the Rare Books Department of the Huntington Library; Perkins, "Rancho San Francisco," 112–13.

[20] Perkins, "Rancho San Francisco," 123 n10.

[21] Whitley, *Archaeological Survey*, Chapter 5.2.

CHAPTER 12

# THE MISSION WATER SYSTEM

*Water for irrigation of the gardens and fields is supplied by a large reservoir [dam] about a half-mile east of the buildings. Here is collected water from innumerable springs that rise from two to three miles distant from the mission. The ditches from the different localities radiate directly at the gate of this basin so that water can be furnished to every place at the same time.* —Daily Alta California, *June 26, 1865*

THE FRIARS DISCOVERED a source of water, the vital resource needed to establish a mission. For about a league they followed a trickle of water from the foothills and found a large *ciénega* (swamp or marsh) with several natural springs rising from a deep fountainhead.

The friars began their aqueduct by building a settling basin, "the intake," to catch water issuing from the natural springs. The basin was made of mission masonry, which consisted of burnt-brick and rock, was mortared with concrete and then covered with limestone.[1] The square-like basin, whose inner dimensions are 11 feet square and 5 feet deep, is in excellent condition today, considering its age. There was an inlet at the top on the north face, in the direction facing the ciénega, and a 4-inch outlet mission-pipe at the bottom of the south side, from which flowed the drinking water. A catchment inside the basin filtered mud and other sediments before water entered the aqueduct. The water flowed by gravity for a little less than a mile (0.34 league) to a masonry dam. Pipelines then carried the drinking water

over the dam and down the slope a little less than ½-mile (0.16 league) to the mission.

According to Engelhardt, there was nothing on record regarding building activities after 1806, except for the following:

> December 31, 1808, Fathers Landaeta and Múñoz reported a dam built of masonry—*se ha hecho una presa de cal y canto*; but they gave no details whatever. On December 31, 1811, Fr. Múñoz reported the construction of an aqueduct, half a league in length [1⅓ miles from the filtering basin to the mission]. This explains the item regarding the dam.[2]

A rock and cement dam was constructed across the Cienega Wash, which was located northeast of the mission, creating Cienega Lake. Unfiltered water from the dam flowed out of a large pipe at the base of the dam where it was metered and gravity-fed the short distance to the mission. A mill was said to have been built next to the dam; some structure was still there in 1952 (when Edith Webb wrote about the mission water system), but without excavation it was not possible to determine its actual

---

[1] Webb, *Indian Life at the Old Missions,* 77.

[2] Engelhardt, *San Fernando Rey,* 21.

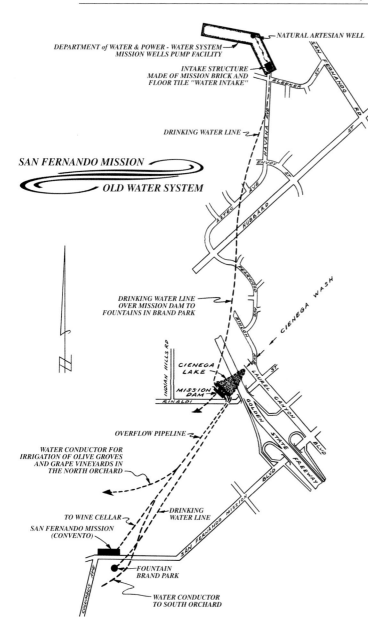

DEPARTMENT of WATER & POWER - WATER SYSTEM
MISSION WELLS PUMP FACILITY

NATURAL ARTESIAN WELL

INTAKE STRUCTURE
MADE OF MISSION BRICK AND
FLOOR TILE "WATER INTAKE"

DRINKING WATER LINE

SAN FERNANDO MISSION
OLD WATER SYSTEM

DRINKING WATER LINE
OVER MISSION DAM TO
FOUNTAINS IN BRAND PARK

CIENEGA
LAKE

MISSION
DAM

OVERFLOW PIPELINE

WATER CONDUCTOR FOR
IRRIGATION OF OLIVE GROVES
AND GRAPE VINEYARDS IN
THE NORTH ORCHARD

TO WINE CELLAR

SAN FERNANDO MISSION
(CONVENTO)

DRINKING
WATER LINE

FOUNTAIN
BRAND PARK

WATER CONDUCTOR
TO SOUTH ORCHARD

The San Fernando Mission's old water system, drawn ca. 1970. *KEP.*

must have been involved with the building of the aqueduct and the two fountains.[4]

Subsidiary pipelines drained down from the water basin and supplied the two fountains in front of the convento, a few small, circular water reservoirs, and another mill situated to the southeast. Traces of the mill and its piping have long disappeared.

Before a roof was built over the entire convento, a simple system was used to drain rainwater. A gabled roof covered only rooms 24 through 33 (see page 188) on the second story. A flat roof was over a large area at the west end and on the arcade. Rain from the gabled roof drained onto the flat roof, then ran southward toward the arcade perimeter. On the perimeter was a two-brick-high sandstone wall carved on the outside to look like a sawtooth cornice. On the inner side, a long trough was chiseled at the base of the wall to form a gutter along the entire length of the convento. Rainwater from the arcade roof flowed into the gutter, where it was channeled into terra-cotta drainpipes (water scuppers) that pointed diagonally downward to the outside, above each pillar of the arcade. Water then exited to a ditch in front of the convento along its entire length.

Large wooden beams used in the attic restoration after the 1994 Northridge earthquake have completely obscured the sandstone gutters and drainpipe system. Today, only the exits for the terracotta drain pipes can still be seen from the outside.

In 1919 the Los Angeles Department of Water and Power (DWP) purchased from the San Fernando Land Company, for $40,000, six acres on which the

purpose.[3] Smaller pipelines and *zanjas* (ditches or trenches) led the water to the orchards, the olive groves, the two vineyards, and the cellar.

In the years 1811 to 1813, a neophyte mason who was known only as Tomás was working there and

---

[3] Webb, *Indian Life at the Old Missions*, 77.

[4] Schuetz-Miller, *Building and Builders*, 198.

(*right*) View of the collapsed old dam shows the concrete drainage basin, ca. 1900. *CHS/TICOR* (6622).

(*below*) The Mission San Fernando dam, ca. 1965. *ACSFM.*

(*below, right*) Boulders, rocks and concrete are all that remain of the mission dam, ca. 1945. *LAA.*

(*left*) Mission cement and clay water pipes from the mission water system. *CHS/TICOR (11285) and SWM-P19037.*

(*below*) Sections of pipes that carried water from the wells to the mission, 1949. *Intake* (DWP) *Magazine.*

mission well was located. Seven new deep-well pumps, sunk by the DWP, have now replaced the five early artesian wells. Today, only three of the DWP well pumps provide water to residents in the general Pacoima area. The DWP calls the mission well their #1134 Regulated System. From October 1, 1999, to September 30, 2000 (the DWP's "water period"), the system supplied 2,493 acre-feet of water, which translates to 2.23 million gallons per day.[5]

The actual date of construction for the catch basin is not known, but the DWP believes it to be around 1800. The Native Daughters of the Golden West placed a historic marker on the site, near the corner of Bleeker and Havana Streets in Sylmar. For the inscription, see the plaque on page 210.

On December 3, 1904, Leslie Carlton Brand, an insurance, real estate, and banking tycoon, and a group of Los Angeles businessmen organized the San Fernando Mission Land Company.[6] They bought out the remaining interests of the Porter Land and Water Company, an estimated 16,000 acres, for a reputed $524,000. Brand subdivided most of his holdings for later development and sale but retained a small section of land adjacent to the convento.[7]

A civic-minded group of women in San Fernando, fearing the fruit packing industry's encroachment on the land directly in front of the mission, successfully persuaded the San Fernando Mission Land Company to set aside seven acres for a public park. In early 1920 Brand donated the land and two fountains—the Cordova or "Rosette" fountain and another one, which was near-circular—to the city of Los Angeles. On November 4, 1920, the Los Angeles City Council dedicated the land, naming it Brand Park.[8]

The Cordova fountain, previously a pool since it did not have a centerpiece, was originally located at a different site from where we see it today. It was situated 600 to 700 feet south of the convento until June 6, 1922, when Leslie Brand had it moved approximately 500 feet across Brand Boulevard to the west end of Brand Park. It was placed 160 feet in front of the convento and became a fountain when an *españolado* (Spanish-style) stone centerpiece graced it shortly after its relocation.

---

[5] Recent water data for the Mission Well supplying the Pacoima area near San Fernando was provided by Department of Water and Power representatives Le Val Lund, former chief water engineer, and Tom La Bonge, director of community relations.

[6] Leslie Carleton Brand was born in St. Louis, Missouri, in 1859. Departing for California at the age of twenty-seven, he left behind a title insurance business. Arriving in California in 1886, he teamed up with Edward Sargent and founded the Los Angeles Abstract Company, but both men sold the company when the real estate industry suffered a severe decline in 1882, with Brand returning to Missouri. He married in 1894 and returned with his wife to California where he resumed a real estate career and founded the successful Guarantee Title and Trust Company. In 1912, together with Edward Doheny, Brand also founded the Mortgage Guarantee Company, which became even more successful than Guarantee Title and Trust. Brand and other entrepreneurs made one successful acquisition after another. With the help of the Huntington Land Improvement Company, he purchased most of the land in Glendale on what is now Brand Boulevard from Broadway to Mountain Street, east to Louise. He organized the water companies in both Glendale and San Fernando and built a rail line from Los Angeles near the roadway land described. He put in the electric light company,

the telephone company, and the First National Bank of Glendale. He helped build both the Elks Lodge and the Tuesday Afternoon Club clubhouses. Brand bought 1,000 acres along the foothills in Glendale and built "Brand's Castle," or "El Miradero," the name he gave to his family home (now a public library). (Data provided courtesy of the Brand Library & Art Center, Glendale, Calif.)

[7] W. W. Robinson, *The Story of San Fernando Valley*, 40, describes Brand becoming interested in developing the San Fernando Valley. Associates affiliated with the formation and purchase of the valley were Henry E. Huntington (who was building an electric railway from Los Angeles to San Fernando), W. G. Kerckhoff, J. F. Sartori, E. T. Earl, F. H. Taft, and other influential businessmen. They formed the San Fernando Mission Land Company, which made the purchase.

[8] Weber, *Memories of an Old Mission*, 55–58.

*(right)* Fred Martine (at left) and Gordon Lease (at right) measure the old catch basin near the corner of Bleeker and Havana Streets in Sylmar, 1949. *Intake* (DWP) *Magazine.*

*(below)* The filtering basin "water intake" of Mission San Fernando's water supply system, 1979. *KEP.*

It is due to Charles Fletcher Lummis's staunch efforts that the fountain remained intact during its relocation. His appreciation for this fountain, which he described as "extraordinary," prompted him to insist that this large fountain, with a basin measuring 30 feet in diameter, not be "pulled apart while I live" but moved "as a solid entity" to a new location within the park.[9]

On the Fourth of July, 1922, the Cordova fountain was dedicated amidst considerable fanfare and speeches from dignitaries, including Leslie C. Brand, who flew out from Glendale in his own airplane and officially donated the fountain to the city of Los Angeles.[10]

The second fountain, situated 57 feet from the steps leading into the sala of the convento, is located at the same spot on which it was originally built. The fountain appears to be circular but is actually a hexadecagon, with a mean outer diameter of 22½ feet. This fountain has always had its decorative *españolado* centerpiece, and at one time had a thick coating of limestone. A sequence of photographs shows this fountain in various states from ca. 1865 to the present.

A basin, located a few feet east of the near-circular fountain, was a brandy cooler. It was a reservoir, 6 feet, 10 inches, in diameter, which had long fallen into disuse and had to have its brickwork restored to make it a decorative pedestal. In 1924 Sallie James Farnham's statue of Junípero Serra and the Indian boy Juan Evangelista was placed on top of it.

---

[9] See the sidebar on the next page for a partial diary of Charles Fletcher Lummis for Wednesday, September 7, 1921.

[10] Weber, *Memories of an Old Mission*, 55–58.

## Wednesday, September 7, 1921—
## Partial Diary in Charles Fletcher Lummis's Hand

Much marketing and Chores, and readying the camera. At 1 [P.M.] Mrs. Park, Commissioner McCan and Sumner Hunt and Park Supt. Shearer arrove [*sic*]. And I hopped into the old cords while they were waiting for Charlie Britton in another auto. Took the camera head in my lap, away from the tripod which is much safer and handier; and we had a fine trip up [to] San Fernando, good talk with Sumner whom I don't often get a chance with and Mrs. McCan who is always interesting. I promptly started in to photograph that extraordinary [Cordova] fountain while Hunt began prospecting to find out how deep the foundations were, and got Charlie Britton and others with pick and spade to go down to it. And in his occasionally brash way he told them that it was all right to take the fountain to pieces and rebuild it in the new place. I heard this from under the focusing cloth, and promptly advised him "where to head in"— that no 2 bricks of the fountain will be pulled apart while I live; if the fountain is moved at all it will be as a solid entity. And Sumner knows me for 25 years in an official capacity, and promptly headed in and staid right. In fact an hour later he was assuring Charlie Britton—who was one of my helpers on my house [El Alisal], and is now with the Park Dept., and will have charge of the transference—that he felt sure it could be moved bodily just as cheap as torn to pieces and rebuilt!

They found the foundation as expected only about 2 feet below the surface; and it will be a very simple matter to "get under" this; and with 4 12×12 timbers parallel and under the critical lines, and 4 3×12s crossing them at right angles—the whole thing can be jacked up and slid across the 500 ft. like nothing at all.

Meantime I was having bad times with my attempts to photograph. The ground falls away on every side. I made one from the coping itself, which takes in exactly half the foundation. But I wanted a bird's eye view—and there were no beautiful tufa slabs such as I dragged about one-armed [Lummis had broken his left arm while trekking across the country from Cincinnati to Los Angeles in 1885] in 1890 and built me a platform 4 ft. high from which to make the only photo ever made showing the Stone Mountain Lions of Cochiti complete in their curious Stonehenge. And you bet, that tired as I was, I made Bandelier [the archaeologist who accompanied Lummis to Peru] wait while I dragged everyone of those big tufa slabs away to scattered places, so that no one else should get that picture without working for it. But I poked up Shearer for a hayrick or something; and the one-lung gardener brought his push-cart and 2 carpenter's trestles, and we sat the cart up on those, after steadying them in the plowed ground 6 ft. from the fountain, south; and a man at each end steadied the cart while I mounted into the narrow bed and balanced the tripod and got my picture, taking in the whole business in its 30 ft. diameter, and the outside wall down to the ground 6 ft. away. Then we went around on the other side and I photoed in the same way looking south, first with Charlie Britton behind the further wall as a standard of measure, and then a little Mexican boy on the coping in the second—and both show in the distance the ancient twin palms of 1797.

———

\* Lummis diary provided courtesy of the Southwest Museum, Los Angeles.

In 1949 the California Historical Landmarks Advisory Committee designated Brand Park as California Historical Site No. 150. Today the park, also known as Memory Garden, contains the two fountains, the basin with its statue, a gazebo that was formerly a train depot, a central pergola with columns and latticework, the two-hole jabonería,

and a well-manicured garden. On the perimeter there is a partial wall facing San Fernando Mission Road. Because of the garden's scenic beauty and the quaintness of its fountains, Brand Park is frequently used as a backdrop for weddings and visitors' photographs. Unfortunately, however, over the years graffiti on the archways and other types of vandalism

(*left*) Inlet hole for water into the intake.

(*below*) Plaque placed by the Daughters of the American Revolution at the filtering basin (water intake).

have plagued the park and have spoiled some of that beauty.[11]

A third fountain, a replica of the Cordova Fountain, also with an españolado centerpiece, is located inside the mission quadrangle near its center. In 1962 it replaced an octagonal fountain that had been built there in the late 1940s.

Today, there is little evidence of the mission water system that brought its vital resource to those who

lived and worked at the mission in its heyday. An empty, dusty, rock-and-limestone catch basin, some rock and mortar fragments of the dam, broken sections of clay pipes which were saved and placed in the mission museum, and two fountains in front of the convento are all that remain. Remnants of the dam can still be seen in Mission Hills at Rinaldi Street, west of Laurel Canyon and just west of the Golden State Freeway (Highway 5). Among these reminders, only the fountains—the decorative component of the water system—have survived intact and are still in use.

---

[11] Lawrence C. Jorgensen, ed., *The San Fernando Valley—Past and Present* (Los Angeles: Pacific Rim Research, 1982), 160–61.

Cordova (Rosette) fountain in its original location about 700 feet south of the convento, ca. 1910.
By C. C. Pierce. *CCP/CHS/TICOR (12006).*

Charlie Britton poses behind the Cordova (Rosette) fountain.
By C. F. Lummis, September 7, 1921. *CFL/SWM-N6404/P19017.*

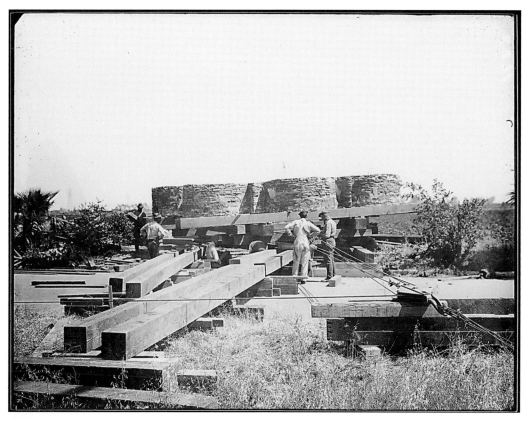

Just as Charles Fletcher Lummis had insisted on in his diary regarding the photo session of September 7, 1921, the Rosette fountain is dug up and carried on 12-by-12-foot timbers to its new location in toto. Leslie C. Brand had the fountain moved about 500 feet, across Brand Boulevard, to within 160 feet of the west end of the convento, on June 6, 1922. A series of photographs (*opposite and above*), possibly by C. F. Lummis, shows the progress of the fountain's move to its new location. *CFL/LAA.*

(*right*) View of the Cordova fountain. It was moved from its original position to a few hundred yards closer to the west end of Brand Park, 1922. Marie Walsh Harrington Collection (now Archival Center). *ACSFM.*

(*above*) The Cordova fountain replica built in 1964,
with the church in the background, before the
1971 earthquake. *ACSFM.*

(*opposite, top*) Octagonal fountain built sometime around
the mid-1950s inside the mission quadrangle.
*By Bill Murphy of the* Los Angeles Times. *ACSFM.*

(*opposite, bottom*) The replica fountain is in a serene setting
within the quadrangle. October 1979. *ACSFM.*

*181 Stone Fountain, San Fernando*

PLATE 64

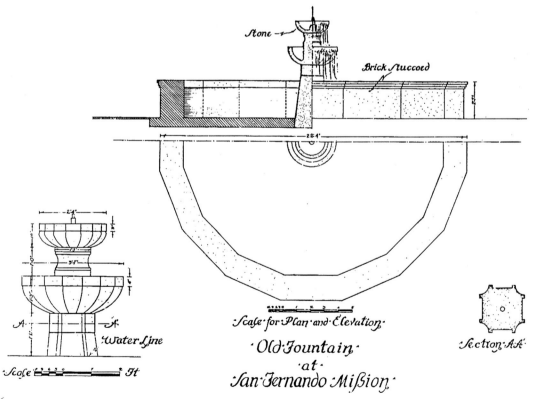

Stone

Brick Stuccoed

Water Line

Scale _____ ft

Scale for Plan and Elevation.

·Old·Fountain·
·at·
·San·Fernando·Mission·

Section·AA·

216

(*opposite, top*) One of the earliest known photographs of the mission on a stereocard, with the inscription "181 Stone Fountain San Fernando." The photograph is labeled "H.T. Payne, Los Angeles" but is possibly by William Godfrey, whose photos were purchased by Payne and oftentimes relabeled. Ca. 1860. *HTP/SCWHR (A.6457.53-28).*

(*opposite, bottom*) Architectural drawing of the circular "Old Fountain" in front of Mission San Fernando. This fountain is hexadecagonal (sixteen-sided). By Rexford Newcomb, ca. 1919. *KEP.*

(*above*) Two boys sit on the circular fountain in front of the convento. By W. M. Graham Photos, ca. 1898. *WGP/HL—photCL 188 (93).*

(*right*) Farnham statue of Fray Junípero Serra and the Indian boy, Juan Evangelista. By K. Kaminsky, May 23, 1964. *KK/ACSFM.*

Seven-acre expanse of Brand Park in front of the mission, just after it was donated to the City of Los Angeles by Leslie C. Brand. View shows ground preparation, prior to planting an assortment of flower and plant species taken from other Alta California missions. Circular fountain is seen at the end of the path, early 1920s. *LAA.*

From Brand Park with its newly-planted roses, the convento and the collapsing mayordomo's house can be seen. By W. C. Dickerson, ca. 1921. *WCD/SWM-N1474.*

(*above*) The train depot at Brand Park before park development. W. M. Graham photos, ca. 1922. *WGP/HL—photCL 188 (94).*

(*right*) The train stop in Brand Park. By W. C. Dickerson, ca. 1930. *WCD/SWM-N1472.*

(*below*) The train depot at Brand Park was redesigned to have more arches, raised flooring, and a roof by 1940. *UCLA.*

B RAND PARK AS IT APPEARED IN 1923. (*opposite, top*)
A small pond was in the middle of Memory Garden. *LAA.*
(*opposite, bottom*) This view was at the corner of two new roads,
Columbus Avenue and Brand Boulevard. Unknown photographer. *LAA.*

(*above*) The pergola at the extreme west end of Brand Park
leads toward the convento. The Cordova fountain can be seen
toward the right, ca. 1932. *CHS/TICOR* (*11873*).

(*left*) This is the first in a series of Frederick H. Maude photographs, ca. 1882. *FHM/SPNBPC/LAPL and SWM P-18914.*

(*below*) The old pepper trees have been cut down and their stumps remain for use as hitching posts, ca. 1890. *SWM P-19023.*

(*bottom*) Weeds and grass have grown up around the front fountain, ca. 1893. The Hooker Collection. *Courtesy of the Archive Center, San Fernando Mission. ACSFM.*

(*top*) The mission is in a desperate state. The front fountain is dry and the convento is dilapidated, with its roof in need of repair. This is prior to CLC reconstruction, ca. 1896. Possibly by C. C. Pierce. *CCP/CHS/TICOR* (7868).

(*above*) One of the tree stumps has been dug up and was most likely used for firewood. Roof restoration on the convento has begun, ca. 1897. *KEP.*

(*right*) A barn belonging to Porter Land and Water Company is west of the convento. The front fountain is dry, ca. 1898. *UCLA.*

(*above*) The convento with its roof repaired, the El Camino Real bell, the deteriorated mayordomo's house, and young pepper trees are seen in this view, ca. 1923. *KEP.*

(*left*) The near-circular fountain is framed by the open River of Life door. This is a view from inside the convento sala, looking south toward Brand Park, ca. 1930. *KEP.*

(*opposite, top*) A vintage photo of two women sitting on the coping of the Cordova (Rosette) fountain, 700 feet south of the convento. Fraisher Collection (now at the Lopez Adobe Archives), ca. 1903. *LAA.*

(*opposite, bottom*) THE SANDSTONE GUTTER— A panorama from two merged photographs. The gutter, carved from sandstone, is atop the arcade at the southern perimeter. It is no longer visible to the public, as restoration work on the convento after the 1994 Northridge earthquake obscured it from view. Prior to a slanted roof being built over the arcade in 1822, rain fell on its flat roof, collected into the gutter and traveled down a number of terra-cotta pipes—one at each arch of the portico, 1986. *KEP.*

E. Fraisher                    Mission San Fernando Rey de España
                                            1797

Reconstructed fourth church after the Sylmar earthquake,
with the Cordova fountain in the foreground, 1979. *KEP.*

(*opposite, top*) Dr. Norman Neuerburg rests on the coping of the
circular fountain during a break at the 1988 California Mission
Studies Association Conference, held at Mission San Fernando.
*Photo courtesy of Edna Kimbro.*

(*opposite, bottom*) Modern view of the Cordova fountain at the
west end of Brand Park. Ken Pauley photo, 2003. *KEP.*

Oil painting of Fray Junípero Serra and the Indian boy, Juan Evangelista,
with the fountain and convento in the background. Painting by Ben Abril, 1987.
The original painting was presented to John Paul II on his visit to Mission
San Fernando and now resides in the Vatican. *BA / Vatican.*

View from Brand Park looking along the main path in the park toward the circular fountain and the convento.
Fraisher Collection (now at the Lopez Adobe Archives), ca. 1945. *LAA.*

Carillon bells hanging in the belfry. Ken Pauley photograph, 1979. *KEP.*

# CHAPTER 13

# MISSION BELLS

*Very little is known about the bells of San Fernando Rey de España. . . . But of the large bells which once hung in the mission tower, the only definite word, via inventories, is that contained in an inventory of March 12, 1849, in which it is mentioned that the "belfry contained three bells; one large and two small ones. Three others were elsewhere."* —Marie T. Walsh, *The Mission Bells of California*

IT WAS THE CUSTOM for the king of Spain to present each newly-founded mission with two bells. It is reasonable to believe that since the missions served the dual purpose of administering to spiritual as well as temporal needs, one bell was used to signal prayers and devotions and the other to signal work, meals, and other activities. This belief is supported by an *informe* (report) of 1773, sent to the padres of Mission San Antonio by the padre *presidente*, Fr. Junípero Serra, which referred to a large bell and a smaller one that was used for calling the workers in the field to assign them to their tasks.[1]

Over the years, Mission San Fernando possessed several bells, some of which were received in trade and others given as gifts. An inventory of bells was taken on March 12, 1849. The Reverend Dr. Sebastian Bongioanni, who arrived in Los Angeles that year, was appointed *cura* (substitute parish priest) not only of Our Lady of the Angels at Los Angeles Church but also of Mission San Fernando. He and Fr. Blas Ordaz were requested by the new administrator of the church at San Fernando, Fr. José

Maria González Rúbio, O.F.M., to take an inventory of all possessions at the mission. Their inventory list included vestments and articles for ecclesiastical purposes, linens, books, and a total of six bells. They wrote: ". . . the belfry contained three bells, one large and two small ones. Three others were elsewhere."[2]

During the 1920s, bell aficionado Mrs. Alice Harriman conducted an extensive search for the bells of all twenty-one California missions. She recorded their names, approximate weights, dates of arrival, and foundries, and noted the stories that accompanied them. Unfortunately, she died in 1925 before she could publish her work.[3]

In the next decade, Marie T. Walsh (who later became Mrs. Mark R. Harrington) picked up the search where Mrs. Harriman left off. Just as her predecessor did, she traveled along El Camino Real to find the bells. She described their distinguishing characteristics and compiled a record of their history and location. She admitted that very little was

---

1 Webb, *Indian Life at the Old Missions*, 31–32.

2 Marie T. Walsh, *The Mission Bells of California* (San Francisco: Harr Wagner Publishers, 1934), 66; Engelhardt, *San Fernando Rey*, 144.

3 Engelhardt, *San Fernando Rey*, 151.

(*left*) One of the earliest known photographs of Mission San Fernando's bell hanging under the eaves of the mayordomo's house. Photo probably by H. T. Payne, although oftentimes attributed to Edward Vischer, ca. 1870. *CHS/TICOR* (7229).

(*below, left*) The bell near the entrance to the convento. It hangs from a wooden beam placed between two columns in the portico. The Hooker Collection, Archival Center at San Fernando Mission, ca. 1893. *ACSFM.*

known about Mission San Fernando's bells, but she did discuss four of the six bells listed in the 1849 inventory in her book, *The Mission Bells of California.*

A story retold by Walsh connects the bells to one of the seven daughters of Gerónimo and Catalina López. The tale from the late 1890s goes that a member of the López family saw a *carreta* (cart) laden with three Mission San Fernando bells heading for Los Angeles. Gerónimo López and some friends quickly followed and went to Los Angeles, where they bought back the bells that had been sold previously to some unknown scavenger.[4]

One bell recovered in that episode was the original large one in the belfry. This bell had the inscription "AVE MARIA PURÍSIMA S. JUAN NEPOMUCENO 1809." A heavy yoke fixture replaced the original handle, which might have been either an elaborate crown handle denoting royalty or an eyelet. This bell was brought back to the mission and has been there ever since.

After the bell tower totally collapsed during the early 1920s, the 1809 bell was hung from a makeshift frame-and-truss wooden structure. In the 1930s it was placed near the north wall of the convento and later, next to a buttress shoring up the church wall where the belfry once stood. After World War II, the bell tower was reconstructed and the 1809 bell, which had a heavy yoke with four circular canons,

---

4   Walsh, *Mission Bells,* 66–71, esp. 67.

Two views of the bell with its inscription AVE MARIA PURISIMA S. JUAN NEPOMUCENO. (*above, left*) Photo from 1926. *CHS/TICOR* (*11870*). (*above, right*) The 1809 (not 1808 as stated on the photo) bell is affixed to a braced wooden stand. By G. W. Hazard, ca. 1908. *GHZ/LAA.*

(*left*) The "Camulos Bell," or mystery bell, which was formerly at Mission San Fernando, was purloined by Antonio del Valle and remained at his Camulos Ranch. It was turned over to Marie T. Walsh by Reverend August A. Rubel, who was assigned to Camulos Ranch, and subsequently returned to Mission San Fernando in 1948. Photo by Carl Wallace, ca. 1932. *ACSFM.*

and two large bells from the Ezcaray Collection were hung in the belfry.

The Ezcaray Collection, which arrived at the mission around 1940, was a lavish one. Shipped to the United States from Ezcaray, Spain, after 1925, it included not only the two large bronze bells but also an elaborate reredos, backdrops, wooden confes-sionals, carved structures, an organ, pulpit, and several paintings.[5]

The Right Reverend Martin Cody Keating dedicated the bells and rebuilt tower on April 28, 1946.

---

5   Weber, *Memories of an Old Mission*, 134–39, and *The Ezcaray Altar Pieces at San Fernando Mission* (Mission Hills, Calif.: Mission San Fernando, 1997), a pamphlet.

(*above*) Carillon bells forged at the foundry of Felix Von Aerschodt in Belgium, ca. 1925. The bells were used in the belfry at Mission San Fernando after the 1971 Sylmar earthquake. Tuned on the chromatic scale, the bells played in all keys. In February 2001 the bells were removed and sent to Philadelphia for cleaning and tuning. They now reside at the Archdiocese's new cathedral in downtown Los Angeles. *ACSFM.*

(*above, right*) Marie T. Walsh (Harrington) in 1932 with an old Russian bell (not the Kodiak) that formerly belonged to Mission San Fernando. The bell was removed and sent to the Los Angeles Orphanage sometime prior to 1934 and was later returned to the mission. *ACSFM.*

The 1809 bell and the two Ezcaray bells hung in the tower until 1971 when the Sylmar earthquake struck and caused extreme damage to the church and belfry. All three bells were put into storage in a room in the west wing of the quadrangle.

In 1974 Msgr. Eugene Frilot had the two Ezcaray bells hung from a wooden standard that was made from original rafters taken from the convento. The rectangular frame was placed on the grounds close to the north wall of the convento, but it had to be removed in 1999 because its old beams were about to collapse from extensive termite damage. At this time the Ezcaray bells went back into storage.

Also in the year 1974, after reconstruction of the fourth church and bell tower, the mission acquired a thirty-five-bell carillon taken from St. Monica's Church in Santa Monica. The carillon, using a modern electrical system that activated push rods to the clappers, has a range of three octaves. The bells weigh from twenty to one thousand pounds. Under the direction of Felix Von Aerschodt, each bell was cast of three-quarters copper and one-fourth tin in Louvain, Belgium, in 1931. The mission's carillon was the first of the complicated Belgian design installed west of the Rockies.[6]

---

[6]   Weber, *Memories of an Old Mission,* 100–104.

(*left*) Russian bell hangs below eaves in the quadrangle's west wing, ca. 1965. *ACSFM.*

(*right*) Russian bell in the west corridor. *KEP.*

On the morning of November 4, 1974, a dedication ceremony for the fourth church took place. The strains of the *Cantico de Alba*, sung much earlier by the mission Indians, were heard once again. The peals of the new carillon greeted the large assembly that gathered at the mission church that morning.

The Belgian carillon was removed from Mission San Fernando's bell tower on February 8, 2001. Sent to Philadelphia to be cleaned and tuned, it was returned to southern California and installed at the new Cathedral of Our Lady of Angels, located in downtown Los Angeles. The bells were dedicated on the same day as the cathedral, on Labor Day, September 2, 2002.

The 1809 bell and the two Ezcaray bells were removed from storage and returned to the belfry. The 1809 bell now hangs between the two Ezcaray bells in the south-facing belfry niche.

✹        ✹        ✹

Two of the three bells hauled off to Los Angeles and recovered in the late 1890s were small; the third of the trio was the large San Juan Nepomuceno 1809 bell. The two small bells, it was said, were taken to Monterey, but no trace of them could be found there. Later on, when Walsh was looking through a C. C. Pierce collection, she happened to find two old pictures, one taken in 1890 and the other of the old Plaza Church. She was thus able to trace one bell, described as small and crudely shaped, with a heavy clapper, a single, three-eyeleted handle, and the inscription AVE MARIA PURÍSIMA 1802. The bell was taken to the old Plaza Church, but when the

(*left*) Two Ezcaray bells, originally in the third bell tower, hang on a frame made from original rafters removed from the convento. These bells were placed in the mission's west garden near the convento's north wall in 1974. They were removed from this location in 1999 and now hang in the belfry. Ca. 1975 *ACSFM*.

(*below*) One of two Ezcaray bells hanging from an A-frame made of convento rafters, 1977. Photo and postcard by Ken Pauley. *KEP.*

church museum was dismantled, it was taken from there to a small Pechanga Indian church near San Diego, where it was removed to nearby San Antonio de Pala, Mission San Luis Rey's asistencia. In 1918 the bell was stolen and to this day has not been found.[7]

The other small bell eventually ended up in Boyle Heights. This Russian bell, weighing about seventy-five pounds, had no inscription but did have two fine lines of scrollwork circumscribing its upper perimeter. This is the bell shown with Marie T. Walsh in the 1934 photograph.[8] On her insistence, after the bell was returned to the mission, a weld-

---

[7]   Walsh, *Mission Bells*, 68–70.

[8]   Ibid., 160–61 (see photo on p. 234).

Ezcaray bell being reinstalled in the western niche of the belfry on the same day, February 8, 2001, that the Belgian carillon bells were being removed. Note the loudspeaker for the new autobell electronic Novabell™ system. Ken Pauley photograph, 2001. *KEP.*

ment was made to repair a large vertical crack. She was convinced that the bell was the companion to a second Russian one, the famous Kodiak bell.[9]

The Kodiak bell, also known as the Mystery or Camulos bell, was used at the mission but was not listed in the 1849 inventory. It is possible that this 100-pound bell was one of the two brought to California by Count Nicolai von Rezanof and used to trade for food while he was in the San Francisco area. In 1806 Capt. José Argüello, commander of the port at San Francisco, was transferred to the presidio at Santa Barbara. The popular notion is that Argüello took the two Russian bells, along with his personal effects, to the new post. Since Mission San Fernando was under the

jurisdiction of Santa Barbara's presidio, it is believed that both Russian bells were deposited at Mission San Fernando between 1808 and 1815, after petitions for them were made by the missionaries.[10]

The Kodiak bell remained at Mission San Fernando until mission mayordomo Antonio del Valle appropriated it for his Camulos Ranch sometime after 1839 when he received his land grant. The bell had the crudely punched inscription "Sn DE FERN"

---

[9] Ibid., 70–71; Francis J. Weber, "Historic Mission Bell: Mystery Shrouds Its Past," *San Fernando Valley Times*, May 9, 1964, and repeated in Weber, *The Mission in the Valley*, 94–95. The bell truly resided at one time at Mission San Fernando, and later at Los Angeles Plaza Church, then the Los Angeles Orphanage. Msgr. Weber believes this bell to be the one-hundred-pound Kodiak or Mystery Bell. But, in fact, the smaller of the two Russian bells now hangs in the corridor between the church and convento. Like the Kodiak, it, too, had a serious crack and might have been confused with it after the repair mentioned. It is not clear just when Marie Walsh returned the smaller Russian bell to the mission. As to the Kodiak, Msgr. Weber acknowledges that Marie Harrington "returned it to the restored Mission San Fernando in 1948." What has happened to it since is not clear.

[10] Engelhardt, *San Fernando Rey*, 148–50.

and a cross on its surface. Mrs. Harriman found this bell in 1923 on a wood frame standard next to the chapel at Camulos Ranch. It had a large crack, around which holes were bored in an attempt to repair it with a plate and rivets, both of which were missing at that time.[11]

The term "mystery" has been associated with the bell because there have been numerous explanations over the years regarding its inscription and origin. A representative for Camulos Ranch, the Reverend August A. Rubel, gave the bell to Marie Walsh. It is said that she, in turn, gave it to Mission San Fernando in 1948. Today, however, there is no evidence of the Kodiak bell at the mission. A bell of similar shape but twenty-five pounds lighter than the Kodiak bell hangs from a girder in the west wing of the quadrangle. Its heavy weldment along one vertical edge leads one to think it might be the cracked Kodiak bell, but the bell's weight, surface and scroll design, and lack of an inscription clearly disqualify it from being the Kodiak bell, whose location to this day remains a mystery.

One of the last set of three bells that were described as "elsewhere" in the 1849 inventory might have been the corporal or "guard's" bell. It hung in the bell-archway atop the roof at the west end of the convento. Its whereabouts have not been known since 1888.[12]

The corporal bell-archway was without a bell for about eighty years. Two devastating earthquakes caused the archway to be removed. It was reconstructed in 1996. This distinctive, historic feature of the convento was restored to public view after a long absence. Unfortunately, though, in place of the corporal bell there hangs a small brass bell that is decorative but has no historical significance.

Other bells can be seen in early photographs. One bell hung next to the mayordomo's house and another from a makeshift girder on the left of the

[11] Ibid.

[12] Walsh, *Mission Bells*, 67.

Small (75-pound) Russian bell (not the Kodiak) with large weldment hangs from the girder along the west wing of the quadrangle, between the church and the convento. Ken Pauley photo, 2002. *KEP.*

Msgr. Weber and more PLAS-TAL Manufacturing Co. personnel before Ezcaray bell is returned to the belfry. Ken Pauley photo, February 8, 2001. *KEP.*

Sketch made by artist known only as Viole, of the west face of the church as it might have appeared ca. 1850, n.d. *Viole/JBG.*

sala entrance into the convento. There are no details available of these bells' provenance or even of their existence at the present time.

A commemorative bell, distinctly American and early twentieth century, was placed in front of Mission San Fernando and all the other Alta California missions by the El Camino Real Association. Mr. and Mrs. Armitage S. C. Forbes, the association's founders, secured the design patent and copyright for the Bells of El Camino Real in 1906.[13]

The bells were intended to be a symbolic reminder of the history of the chain of Alta California missions and placed approximately one mile apart along the King's Highway, which today is roughly U.S. Highway 101. The first bell was placed at the Plaza Church in Los Angeles on August 15, 1906. One was placed at the front of the convento at Mis-

sion San Fernando in 1909, but was later relocated to the east end of the building, where it can be seen today.[14]

More than four hundred of these decorative, non-ringing, cast-iron bells were hung from iron tubing standards, each set in a concrete base. Each bell has a simple brass plate identifying the route of El Camino Real, along which the twenty-one missions are located.

Today the mission has entered the digital age. It currently uses a Novabell™ III Carillon digital auto-bell electronic system, which replaces the clanging of the original bells. The digital system, made by Schulmerich Carillon, Inc., accurately simulates the sound of bells using amplified, pre-programmed melodies. The modern marvel of electronic sound reproduction obviates the need to ring the bells physically and protects the three irreplaceable old bells in the belfry from further wear and cracking.

[13] Mrs. A. S. C. Forbes, *California Missions and Landmarks—El Camino Real* (Los Angeles: [copyrighted by A.S.C. Forbes], 1915), 275–80.

[14] Weber, *Memories of an Old Mission,* 43–45.

(*left*) (3220)—San Fernando. The bell tower, the chimney and wall of the convento collapsed and there are holes in the roof. By C. F. Lummis, June 1, 1897. *CFL/SWM-N3930.*

(*below*) Dissolved adobe of the east and south walls of the bell tower, ca. 1899. *CHS/TICOR (9860).*

(*opposite, top*) Concrete choir loft stairs are covered with wood planks to protect them from the elements, ca. 1900. *CHS/TICOR (4490).*

(*opposite, bottom*) Warren C. Dickerson photograph of the church with its new CLC roof, ca. 1905. *WCD/SWM-N1494.*

(*left*) Details of the choir loft stairway. "The Choir climbs the stairs no more." By G. W. Hazard, who frequently wrote incorrect or misleading captions on his negatives. Ca. 1908. *GHZ/KEP.*

(*below*) After the bell tower's partial collapse, the stairway is exposed to view. In the summer of 1912, two tourists pause at the top of the stairway which leads into the choir loft. *ACSFM.*

(*opposite, top*) The church was in a perilous state when this photo was taken on August 11, 1924. *ACSFM.*

(*opposite, middle*) West face of the reconstructed church and baptistry. This photo was taken ca. 1940, at the start of Dr. Mark R. Harrington's restoration. From Marie Walsh Harrington Collection (now Archival Center). *MWH/ACSFM.*

(*opposite, bottom*) A triangular section of adobe, built in place of the original bell tower, helps to buttress the church wall. The 1809 bell is suspended from a make-shift wooden stand, ca. 1943. *ACSFM.*

(*left*) Reconstruction of Mission San Fernando bell tower, under Dr. Mark R. Harrington's direction. The tower incorporates the temporary triangular adobe section built earlier. Photo by Thomas J. Taylor, ca. 1944. *TJT/SWM-P19106.*

(*below*) Newly reconstructed third church once again serves parishioners, ca. 1947. From Marie Walsh Harrington Collection (now Archival Center). *ACSFM.*

The southwest corner of the convento—
An inkwash by Henry (Harry) Fenn, ca. 1890.
*HAF/UCB.*

The bell in the corporal bell tower was missing after
1888. Photo ca. 1940. *CHS/TICOR (4489).*

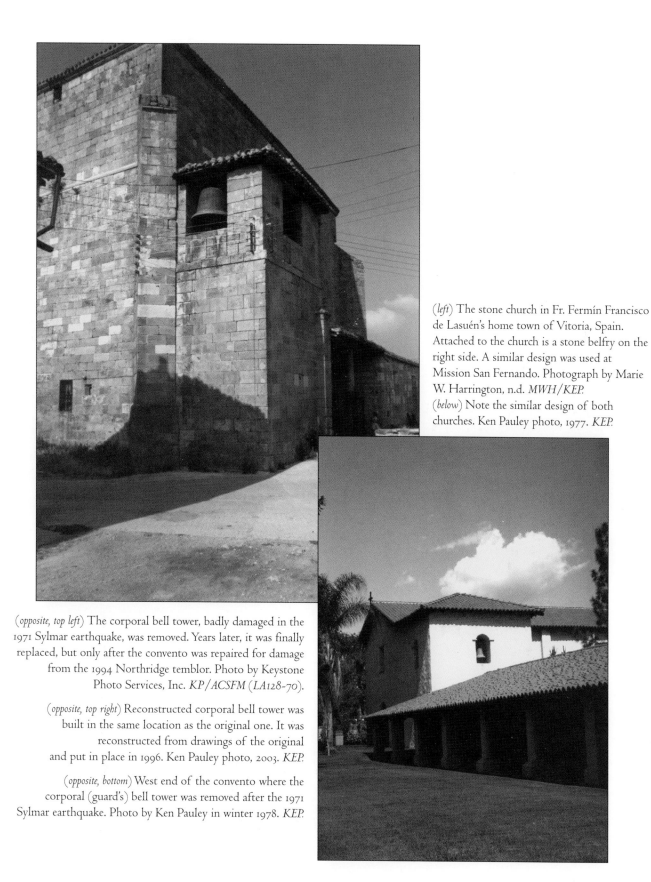

(*left*) The stone church in Fr. Fermín Francisco de Lasuén's home town of Vitoria, Spain. Attached to the church is a stone belfry on the right side. A similar design was used at Mission San Fernando. Photograph by Marie W. Harrington, n.d. *MWH/KEP.*
(*below*) Note the similar design of both churches. Ken Pauley photo, 1977. *KEP.*

(*opposite, top left*) The corporal bell tower, badly damaged in the 1971 Sylmar earthquake, was removed. Years later, it was finally replaced, but only after the convento was repaired for damage from the 1994 Northridge temblor. Photo by Keystone Photo Services, Inc. *KP/ACSFM (LA128-70).*

(*opposite, top right*) Reconstructed corporal bell tower was built in the same location as the original one. It was reconstructed from drawings of the original and put in place in 1996. Ken Pauley photo, 2003. *KEP.*

(*opposite, bottom*) West end of the convento where the corporal (guard's) bell tower was removed after the 1971 Sylmar earthquake. Photo by Ken Pauley in winter 1978. *KEP.*

# PART IV

# TRANSFORMATION—
# 1834 TO THE PRESENT

Pío Pico, by unknown photographer, ca. 1900.
*Courtesy of the Daughters of the American Revolution—San Fernando Valley Chapter*
*and the San Fernando Valley Historical Society. DAR/SFVHS.*

CHAPTER 14

# SECULARIZATION AND POLITICAL INTRIGUE

> *. . . there is a tragic as well as a glorious side to the mission history of New Spain, namely secularization. The term, secularization, originally meant the substitution of secular priests for the religious order priests and the conversion of the mission into a parish. Later it also meant the raising of the Indian community to the status of a self-governing pueblo and, finally, in practice it often resulted in the confiscation of the mission property and lands by white settlers or government officials.*
> —Gerald J. Geary, *The Secularization of the California Missions*
> *(1810–1846)*

DURING SPAIN'S COLONIZATION period it was understood early on that the missions were never intended to be permanent. They always were presumed to have a deadline of ten years, or sometimes even longer. At the end of this time, the missionaries would turn the church over to parish priests, the land over to the Indians, and then move on to the next frontier.[1] The understanding of non-permanence implied that secularization always meant two things: (a) the handing over of the church itself from the religious order priests (in the case of California, the Franciscans), who, since they lived according to a rule or regula-

tion (written by their founder, Saint Francis of Assisi) were often called "regular" clergy—after the Latin term for rule—to the diocesan clergy under the control of the bishop, who were usually called the "secular" clergy (hence the term secularization); and (b) the land would be handed over to the Indians, who would, as a result of the mission process, have developed a knowledge of agriculture and the practice of Catholicism. This was the intent.[2]

The modern struggle over secularization began in 1749 with a law that was directed, as James Ivey states, not at missions, but at *doctrinas* and *curatos*. Doctrinas were semi-parishes, where the church was administered by an order priest. The land did not belong to the Church but allegedly to the local Indians. Curatos were full-fledged parishes. This law had

---

[1] Gerald J. Geary, "The Secularization of the California Missions (1810–1846)," Ph.D. diss. (Washington, D.C.: Catholic University of America, 1934), 16–19, 29–30; C. Alan Hutchinson, *Frontier Settlement in Mexican California: The Híjar-Padrés Colony and Its Origins* (New Haven, Conn.: Yale University Press, 1969), 129–30.

[2] James E. Ivey, "Secularization in California and Texas," in *Boletín: The Journal of the California Mission Studies Association*, 20, no. 1 (2003): 23–36.

an effect in Baja California and Sonora, but not in the Alta California mission areas.[3] The Alta California missions were included when an 1813 law was passed by Spain's parliament (*cortes*), which ordered the secularization of all missions in New Spain. The law never really went into effect, but it remained on the books when Mexican independence arrived in 1821, and the Mexican congress (*congreso constituyente*), in its various laws, followed up on it. Some in New Spain and Mexico were frustrated by the slowness of the process, and thought that the missionaries were stalling.[4]

### Spanish Laws, Decrees, Etc.

In the mid-1700s, the Spanish Crown had begun issuing decrees (*cédulas*), laws or edicts (*bandos*), and written orders (*instrucciones*) to the provincial authorities, viceroys, counts, and magistrates, ordering them to secularize provinces in the New World. For the next eighty-five years, secularization laws were passed by both Spain's Cortes and Mexico's Congress. The many laws, though idealistic about freedom and self-governance for the natives, did not achieve their intended results, and, through the twists and turns of circumstance, led to the confiscation of mission lands and property. Ultimately, they became the death knell for the missions of Alta California.[5]

On October 4, 1749, King Ferdinand VI issued a bando secularizing all churches and missions under his jurisdiction. This law was broadly interpreted to mean that regular clergy and the missions were exempted from Episcopal jurisdiction under a bishop, thus secular priests were substituted for the religious order priests. But it appears that under Viceroy Francisco de Güemes y Horcasitas, subsequently the first count of Revillagigedo (1746–55), his instruc-

ción from Mexico City gave the following meaning to secularization—a wider one than was originally laid down under the law:

> . . . the turning of the missions over to the bishops, the replacing of the regulars by diocesan priests, the distribution of the mission lands and properties to the Indians, the transfer of the Indians from the control of the missions to a form of pueblo government and laws, and finally, a two-fold boon to the treasury in the form of tributes to be paid by the Indians and of *sínodos* [*sic*] no longer to be paid by the government to missionaries, the new diocesan priests now being obliged to look to their Indian parishioners for support.[6]

Viceroy Revillagigedo's broad interpretation of the law of 1749 gave rise to the modern belief that secularization, early on, meant the substitution of the missionaries by diocesan priests after ten years and, in addition, that the mission would become a parish, mission lands and properties would be distributed to the Indians, and the natives would be organized in pueblos and made citizens.[7]

The key element of secularization in Alta California was the eventual emancipation of the natives after their conversion and education. Governor Diego Borica, in a 1796 letter to Lt. Col. Pedro Alberni, commandant at the San Francisco Presidio, said that the natives were to be freed from tutelage at the end of ten years and the missions were then to become doctrinas (Indian communities converted to Christianity, but lacking a parish). He expressed doubt about the outcome of emancipation: ". . . those [natives] of New California at the rate they are advancing will not reach the goal in

---

[3] Ibid., 25–27.

[4] Hutchinson, *Frontier Settlement*, 70–71.

[5] Webb, *Indian Life at the Old Missions*, 282–309.

[6] Geary, "Secularization," 28–29. In summarizing Count Revillagigedo's *instrucción* on secularization, Geary used the word *sínodos*, which should have been *sinodáticos*, which were the annual donations made by the government to the bishop or missionaries. The *sínodos* (synods) were ecclesiastical governing or advisory councils.

[7] Ibid., 29.

ten centuries; the reason, God knows, and men know something about it."[8]

According to James Ivey's interpretation, the doctrina was somewhere between a mission and a parish. Ivey, who researched and wrote about secularization over the entire borderlands, also argues that the Texas missions often became doctrinas in the late eighteenth century and that the establishment of doctrinas helped smooth the transition to secularization.[9]

On September 13, 1813, the Cortes passed legislation to secularize all missions under its jurisdiction. The law included missions in the old colonies and in the Americas that had been in existence for ten years or longer, and directed that they "should at once, be given up to the bishop 'without excuse or pretext whatever, in accordance with the laws.'"[10] The Cortes is here expressing its frustration that the handovers, which were supposed to have been going on regularly, had not occurred.

On January 20, 1821, Viceroy Juan Ruiz de Apodaca (who was also known as Conde del Venadito) published the royal confirmation of secularization in his *Bando de la Reforma* (Law of Reform), which included as one of its provisions the secularization law of 1813. News of the law was forwarded by Fr. Baldomero López, guardian of San Fernando College, to the president of the California missions, *Comisário-Prefecto* Fr. Mariano Payeras, with instructions for immediate compliance by the nineteen existing missions in Alta California.[11]

Soon after, in September 1821, Mexico won its independence from Spain. Gen. Agustín de Iturbide, the new president, entered Mexico City in triumph and celebrated his coming to power with huge fanfare. The political turmoil and change in leadership would have a huge impact on secularization of the Alta California missions.[12]

The 1813 secularization law had been in effect for many years but compliance was nowhere in sight. In his letter of December 20, 1821, the bishop of Sonora, Bernardo del Espíritu Santo, informed California Prefect Payeras that "secularization had not been enforced anywhere in America; that they [the California padres] might remain in charge of their missions; and that it would be time enough to think of new conversions when the imperial independence should be firmly established."[13] This is another indication that though the secularization process was legally in force, it did not exist in fact before Mexican independence.

## Post-Mexican Independence

The newly-appointed California governor, José María Echeandía, was chosen by Mexico's new administration in mid-February 1825 to carry out the 1813 secularization decree. Echeandía selected Lt. José María Padrés, Second Lt. Agustín Zamorano, and four others from the Corps of Engineers to accompany him to California. On the trip from Acapulco to Baja California, their ship was damaged and taken in at San Blas for repairs. Echeandía and his entourage continued on to Loreto, Baja California, on another vessel, finally reaching Lower California on June 22, 1825. After an arduous journey by land, they arrived at San Diego at the end of October.[14]

Even before Echeandía got to Alta California, he was hailed as a hero by the natives in northern Baja California because he removed one of the Dominicans they disliked.[15] Echeandía was appointed by a

8   Bancroft, *History of California*, 1: 535, 540–41, 580.

9   Ivey, "Secularization in California and Texas," 25–27.

10  Webb, *Indian Life at the Old Missions*, 288–89; Zephyrin Engelhardt, O.F.M., *Missions and Missionaries*, 4 vols. (San Francisco: The James H. Barry Company, 1915), 3: 95–97, for wording of the decree.

11  Geary, "Secularization," 72; Bancroft, *History of California*, 2: 431.

12  Michael C. Meyer, William L. Sherman, and Susan M. Deeds, *The Course of Mexican History*, 6th edition (New York: Oxford University Press, 1999), 285; Geary, "Secularization," 78.

13  Bancroft, *History of California*, 2: 433; Geary, "Secularization," 73.   14  Hutchinson, *Frontier Settlement*, 127–28.

15  Beebe and Senkewicz, eds., *Lands of Promise and Despair*, 341–42.

liberal Mexican government, and he came with liberal ideas, including secularization. He started with a gradual approach, since he knew that there were not many secular priests ready to come to the north and take over for the Franciscans.

Echeandía's first order of business when he arrived in San Diego was to put into motion the 1813 law, which called for the disposition of mission lands and the liberation of the Indians. Upon his arrival, however, he found that many of the conditions needed to comply with the 1813 secularization law were missing because of poor territorial finances, troop dissatisfaction due to pay insecurity, and the aforementioned lack of secular priests to replace the padres. In addition, he learned that the missions that he was sent to California to scale down were supporting most of the territory's needs. This was not the time to be disposing of lands and allowing the labor force to leave at will.

What followed was, in effect, the governor creating and installing his own program of "partial emancipation," which he announced on July 25, 1826. He was following the precedents of Gov. Pablo Vicente Solá and Canon Agustín Fernández de San Vicente, who, before Echeandía arrived, had taken it upon themselves to make unauthorized changes to the formal bando and to the generally accepted 1813 secularization law.[16] The actions of Solá and Fernández indicated that everyone knew that secularization was imminent in the near future. It was not a question of whether it would happen, but when.

Echeandía's program permitted married, adult Indians south of Monterey to leave their missions, provided that they had been Christians for at least fifteen years or from childhood and could support themselves. The Indians had to petition the commanding officer of the presidio that they wanted to leave.

Not many Indians availed themselves of the offer

to leave the missions, as they were caught between their own culture and the Spanish culture imposed on them. Some of those who did leave were unbridled in their new-found freedom, gambling away all of their property and committing acts of thievery and beggary. The military brought these Indians back to the missions, where they were punished by being placed in shackles and put to hard labor.[17]

The traditional view of mission neophytes' emancipation—that they were unable to adjust to their new circumstances—has been challenged by historian Lisbeth Haas.[18] She argues that the indigenous peoples had an awareness of their new-found freedom. She expounds on their acceptance or rejection of freedom and recounts their acts of rebellion against those who oppressed or exploited them. Haas details the natives' strong desire to return to their *patrias*, or place of ancestral origin and birth, and their resistance to being coerced to live in reservations, places that were not their own.

During the transition from empire to republic, anti-clerical sentiment in Mexico grew. Mexico City's Congress issued the law of 1827 calling for the expulsion of all Spanish friars from the republic. Governor Echeandía felt pressure from Mexicans and aggrieved *Californios* who were envious of the wealth of the missions to remove the friars. He was faced with carrying out a law which would bring about serious and ruinous consequences for the region if not handled correctly. Expulsion of the friars, along with secularization, would further erode the mission institution, which by this time

[16] Hutchinson, *Frontier Settlement*, 110.

[17] Ibid., 130–31; Bancroft, *History of California*, 3: 104.

[18] Lisbeth Haas, *Conquests and Historical Identities in California, 1769–1936* (Berkeley: University of California Press, 1995), and "Emancipation and the Meaning of Freedom in Mexican California," in *Boletín: The Journal of the California Mission Studies Association*, vol. 20, no. 1 (2003): 11–22.

generated most of the region's wealth, primarily in the form of farm produce.[19]

In 1827 Governor Echeandía recognized that his 1826 experiment of partial emancipation was a failure and began writing his new 1828 plan, which he submitted to the territorial assembly (*diputación*). In early August 1830, the diputación approved his *Plan para convertir en Pueblos las Misiones, 1829–30*. Next, he immediately sent it to Mexico for approval. The revised plan had additional regulations beyond the 1828 version. It called for the appointment of commissioners and specified their duties and salaries, together with those of the administrators of the pueblos; limited the number of missions that were to be converted into towns to San Gabriel and San Carlos; and provided for the establishment of two schools, one at Santa Clara and the other at San Gabriel. The Indians were to learn the basic skills of reading, writing, and arithmetic. Echeandía issued these regulations in his secularization decree of January 6, 1831.[20]

Unchecked, Governor Echeandía continued to carry out his partial version of secularization. Since the friars had not been expelled under the earlier 1827 law, they were to be given the choice of staying on as curates or to follow other clerical paths.[21] Those who remained in California were required to take an oath of allegiance to the new republic. Fray Vicente Francisco Sarría, *comisario-prefecto* of the missions, did not comply and was arrested and detained for some time. *Misión presidente* Fray Narciso Durán, however, went through the motions of taking the oath. Fray Francisco González de Ibarra, the feisty and intransigent resident priest at Mission San Fernando since October 1820, took the oath of allegiance but emphasized that, in doing so, it "did not militate against Christian conscience."[22] Fr. Ibarra later became a dissident, incurring the scorn and hostility of the new authorities. (Fr. Ibarra and Fr. Francisco Suñer, curate at Mission San Buenaventura, both wrote about the exploitation and plight of the Indians and causes of the missions' demise, but from divergent perspectives.)[23]

Echeandía's decree for the secularization of all the California missions was made under the false pretense that he was still governor in January 1831. It was issued before he turned over command to Manuel Victoria, his successor and the legitimate governor, who had been appointed on March 30, 1830. Victoria, appointed by a conservative Mexican government, came to Alta California with conservative ideas. The emerging *Californio* elite, who expected to stake their claim to mission lands that remained after the Indians had received their due as a result of secularization, did not like the fact that he attempted to halt the secularization process. For this reason, the elites opposed him and aligned with Echeandía.

Echeandía, in a plot to seize power and carry out his plans, lured Governor Victoria to Santa Barbara and delayed him there. In the meantime, Echeandía and the Monterey Council (*ayuntamiento*), headed by former lieutenant José María Padrés, selected commissioners to begin secularizing seven northern missions. Governor Victoria, realizing that he was being duped, hurried to Monterey and demanded that his office be surrendered to him. Angered by the situation, Governor Victoria nullified Echeandía's 1831 secularization plan. He believed that Padrés, now a politician, was the cause of his increasing difficulties with the Californios. He thus had him exiled, sending him back to San Blas aboard the vessel *Margarita* on November 8, 1831.[24]

---

[19] James, *In and Out of the Old Missions*, 89–90; Charles E. Chapman, *A History of California—The Spanish Period* (New York: The Macmillan Company, 1926), 467–68.

[20] Hutchinson, *Frontier Settlement*, 131–33; Bancroft, *History of California*, 3: 106.

[21] Bancroft, *History of California*, 3: 301–06; James, *In and Out of the Old Missions*, 90.

[22] Engelhardt, *San Fernando Rey*, 45.

[23] Hutchinson, *Frontier Settlement*, 129–30.

[24] James, *In and Out of the Old Missions*, 91; Hutchinson, *Frontier Settlement*, 145; Geary, "Secularization," 108–13. *(continued)*

Governor Victoria's tenure came to an abrupt end after only two years in California. More an infantry officer than a politician, he was dictatorial and unpopular. He refused to call together the diputación, which he knew would oppose him, and ordered the imprisonment and execution of individuals with whom he disagreed. Dissident Californios Juan Bandini, Pío Pico, and José Antonio Carrillo rallied around Echeandía. They revolted and were about ready to engage Victoria in a skirmish.

Victoria rounded up fourteen soldiers and left Monterey, arriving at Mission San Fernando on December 4, 1831. The next day he and his band, now numbering about thirty, continued south where they met the rebels near the Cahuenga Pass. About 150 rebels who had trekked north from the Pueblo de Los Angeles met the governor's small army. On the battleground of Lomitas de la Cañada de Breita, two men were killed—on the governor's side, Capt. Romualdo Pacheco, and on the rebels' side, José María Ávila. Before he expired, Ávila managed to inflict serious injury by his sword on Governor Victoria, who was wounded five times and taken to the nearest mission, San Gabriel. While he was recovering, Victoria requested and received permission from Echeandía to return to Mexico. He left early the following year.[25]

After Victoria's ouster, Echeandía re-assumed power. His supporters, the rebel Californios, had issued on November 29, 1831, in San Diego a plan that was apparently drawn up by Juan Bandini, Pío Pico, and Jose Antonio Carrillo. Under the plan, Echeandía was to assume both the civil governorship and military command of the territory. But the territorial assembly thought otherwise and intended that the power should be divided between two people they appointed.

Echeandía and the diputación became embroiled in a feud after he excused himself from attending the assembly's meetings. At Los Angeles on January 10, 1832, in accordance with an old law passed in 1822, the diputación appointed its senior officer, Pío Pico, *jefe político* (civil governor). Echeandía vehemently objected to this appointment.

While the political squabbles between Echeandía and the territorial assembly ensued, Capt. Agustín Zamorano, who was as politically ambitious as Echeandía, entered the fray. He issued a statement at Monterey that northern California, from San Francisco to Santa Barbara, did not accept the plan of San Diego. He and his supporters decided that acts of the diputación were null and void. Zamorano refused to recognize Echeandía's command. He rallied the support of a group of foreign residents of Monterey, whose interests were aligned with his; this group and another company of citizens were organized for the defense of Monterey. Lieutenant Ibarra, who served under Zamorano, started with his military band to Santa Barbara about February 9. Zamorano, too, went south to Santa Barbara with all the forces he was able to muster to uphold his authority there. On his arrival, he was less bellicose than when he left from Monterey.

Though Zamorano and Echeandía actively prepared for war, it appears they were not eager for bloodshed. Echeandía was willing to make arrangements for peace. Zamorano, after arriving at Santa Barbara, was inclined to consider proposals for a truce, which he had previously ignored. On May 8 or 9, 1832, an arrangement was made between the two men and the diputación. Power would be shared between Zamorano and Echeandía in the interregnum, until Mexico could send north a new civil governor.

Captain Zamorano agreed to remain in military command of the district from Mission San Fer-

---

(*continued*) A more expanded account of Manuel Victoria's short-term governorship is best described in Bancroft, *History of California*, 3: 184–212; see especially 197 n32 and 383 for a description of the vessel *Margarita*.

[25] Hutchinson, *Frontier Settlement*, 150–51; Bancroft, *History of California*, 3: 206–08.

nando north to Sonoma and Echeandía was to have military control of the district south of the mission to San Diego.[26] In a separate action from their power arrangement, Echeandía was acclaimed the territory's civil governor by his cohort of Californios, although the diputacíon did not recognize him as such.

The political squabbles over power and succession meant that little happened in the way of secularization until a new governor whom everyone would recognize as legitimate came to Alta California. This would soon materialize with the arrival of José Figueroa in early 1833.

In November 1832, Echeandía implemented a modified form of his January 6, 1831, secularization law, one in which there was a resurrection of the 1830 plan to emancipate the population. Set free at the four southern missions of San Diego, San Luis Rey, San Gabriel, and San Juan Capistrano, Indians who were rebellious to the missionaries united and planned a major uprising. They acclaimed Echeandía their liberator and hero. Historian Lisbeth Haas puts this into modern perspective, calling Governor Echeandía "a liberal in favor of Indigenous citizenship rights."[27] The natives' response to the governor's provisional emancipation was the almost immediate preparation of petitions. Some natives wrote their own petitions, while others had them prepared by the missionaries. The documents written by the natives used the word *freedom* and those written by the fathers used the phrases "released from *neofia*," "scratched off the mission roll," or "allowed to disaffiliate" from the mission. The clerics' choice of words revealed the consternation they felt.[28]

The missionaries were opposed to Echeandía's plan. Fr. Francisco González de Ibarra, at Mission San Fernando, did not approve and stated that he thought the Indians were being deceived by Echeandía's experiment in bestowing freedom. Fr. Narciso Durán, president of the missions, expressed dismay and pointed out that the Indians were most useful to the mission, and if they were all released, the mission (San Buenaventura) might not be able to support itself. Exacerbating the situation, Echeandía began arming the Indians in the south to augment his small but growing rebel army, and even provoked minor skirmishes to the north at Santa Barbara. Fr. Durán expressed outrage at Echeandía for fomenting these actions and remonstrated that there were earlier attacks by freed Indians in the north, and, if the Indians were not controlled, "before many years had passed the whites would have serious trouble on their hands."[29]

President Anastasio Bustamante and his government in Mexico City had earlier confirmed José Figueroa as inspector and *comandante general* of California and on May 9, 1832, appointed him governor. Governor Figueroa arrived in San Diego in January 1833, at which time he devised, with Fr. Durán, a new plan for secularization. The new governor observed that the Indians were unhappy with Echeandía's promises of liberty. Figueroa's own plan was called "Provisional Steps for the Emancipation of Mission Indians" and was issued on July 15, 1833. Very much like Echeandía's first secularization attempt in 1826, Governor Figueroa's plan required that Indians who were to be freed be selected by an appointed commissioner working with the missionary at his mission. Emancipated neophytes were to be given food and lots in a nearby town, but were expected to work at mission harvests and other times. These and many other stipulations were attached to the new plan and sent off to the minister of relations in Mexico City on July 20.[30]

[26] Hutchinson, *Frontier Settlement*, 151; Chapman, *Spanish Period*, 462–63.

[27] Haas, "Emancipation and the Meaning of Freedom," 13.

[28] Ibid.

[29] Hutchinson, *Frontier Settlement*, 153.

[30] Ibid., 224–25.

Governor Figueroa interviewed both legitimists, Echeandía and Zamorano. He immediately retained the affable Zamorano as his own secretary, in gratitude for his and his adherents' undeniable loyalty to Mexico, but sent Echeandía packing back to Mexico, never to return. It became clear to Governor Figueroa that Echeandía had gone too far with "his form of secularization," as the governor called it, and that "his mischief was beyond repair."[31] Figueroa was in favor of secularization; he was also very close to the emerging landed elite, and his secularization was more closely aligned to their interests.[32]

Shortly after his arrival in California, Governor Figueroa became ill and asked to be retired from his governorship. In May 1834, he learned that his petition to retire was accepted and that his successor, a federalist, Don José María de Hijar, was coming north to California with a large band of colonists. Governor Figueroa had members of the Vallejo family survey plots for the colonists in the north (San Francisco) bay region. Earlier, the exiled Lt. José María Padrés and his associate, Hijar, hidden in Mexico City, seized the opportunity to advance Echeandía's version of secularization. Padrés influenced the Mexican Congress to pass a law of secularization on August 17, 1833.

In July 1834, Hijar and Padrés headed by sea for Monterey with 120 colonists. Hijar, having been appointed governor of Alta California by the federal government in Mexico City, had every expectation of becoming the new leader to carry out the new secularization law and of Padrés' filling the subordinate post of vice-director of colonization after they arrived.[33] Terrible seasickness forced Hijar to disembark at San Diego, whence he and some colonists continued on to Monterey on an overland journey.

Governor Figueroa's attitude toward the arriving colonists underwent a considerable change after he learned of the upheaval taking place in the Mexican government and the cancellation of Hijar's appointment. President Anastasio Bustamante, presiding at the end of his first term, was being replaced by Antonio López de Santa Anna. Santa Anna sent a speedy courier, Rafael Amador, to Governor Figueroa in Monterey, with an urgent note informing him of the cancellation of Hijar's governorship. Amador arrived in California well before Hijar, and Figueroa anticipated the ire and frustration that Hijar and Padrés were going to experience when they finally arrived in Monterey, but he was also suspicious of their intentions. When they did arrive, on the 24th of September, 1834, Governor Figueroa, Hijar, and Padrés began a tumultuous power struggle with the territorial assembly lasting 230 days! The detailed and complex set of circumstances surrounding just who was in control in California is discussed quite thoroughly by historian C. Alan Hutchinson in his work.[34] In the end, Governor Figueroa exiled both Hijar and Padrés—for the second time—on the grounds that they were plotting his overthrow, a questionable allegation. The two were also accused of instigating a minor outbreak at Los Angeles, together with their ally, a doctor named Francisco Torres, whom Hijar had commissioned to take important documents with him back to Mexico in March 1835.[35]

A frustrated Governor Figueroa penned his lengthy, self-serving polemic *Manifiesto a la República Mejicana* (*Manifesto to the Mexican Republic*), completing it on September 4, 1835, about three weeks before he died. He put forth the reason for the dispute he had with Hijar, Padrés, and several colonists. It was the mission lands. The existing Californio elites, who had supported secularization à la Figueroa because

[31] Ibid., 153–54; Chapman, *Spanish Period*, 464–69; Bancroft, *History of California*, 3: 243–44.

[32] Haas, "Emancipation and the Meaning of Freedom," 17.

[33] Chapman, *Spanish Period*, 464–65.

[34] Hutchinson, *Frontier Settlement*, 216–392.

[35] Ibid., 356–59; Chapman, *Spanish Period*, 466.

he had been generous to their interests on the land issue, were not about to welcome a group of new immigrants and share with them the land they had been confident of receiving.

Figueroa's manifesto contains many letters written between him and Hijar. These letters were damning to Hijar and Padrés, exposing their plan to confiscate mission properties and their physical wealth for themselves, at the expense of the Indians.[36]

## OF SECULAR REPLACEMENTS, PUEBLOS, AND INDIAN EMANCIPATION

By the beginning of 1834, secularization, in essence the Figueroa plan of 1833, had begun in ten of the Alta California missions. Among them was Mission San Fernando. In October 1834, Lt. Antonio del Valle was appointed commissioner to secularize Mission San Fernando. In May 1835, del Valle became mayordomo of the mission, a position he held until March 1837. Fr. Francisco González de Ibarra, who had been at Mission San Fernando for fourteen years, adamantly opposed the appointment of Lieutenant del Valle as mayordomo. His frustration of losing the mission's estancia at Rancho San Francisco to del Valle was now being compounded with having to serve under his stewardship. Fr. Ibarra was bitter with the Californios and the chiefs he called *paisanos*, the officials sent from Mexico to execute secularization and hasten the expulsion of Spaniards from Alta California.

He and Fr. Tomás Eleuterio Esténaga, who had been at Mission San Gabriel for about a year, opposed all secularization plans—Echeandía's and Figueroa's. They believed that the Indians were being deceived by the prospect of freedom and that those who left the missions would be exploited because of their naïveté. In 1835, conflicted by con-

science and their personal situations, and aggrieved by the actions of the paisano chiefs and the demanding military, the two abandoned their posts as resident priests and fled to Sonora, Mexico.[37]

Fr. Pedro Cabot, Fr. Ibarra's successor, served at Mission San Fernando until a grave illness beset him in August 1836. Fr. Ibarra returned to the mission to serve in his stead. After Fr. Cabot died and was buried in October, Fr. Ibarra left Mission San Fernando for Mission San Luís Rey. Meanwhile, Fr. Esténaga returned to Mission San Gabriel in August 1836, a year after leaving his post, and from there went to Mission San Fernando to fill the vacancy left by Fr. Ibarra.[38]

In May 1837, Fr. Blas Ordaz arrived and remained as the mission's curate until June 30, 1847. He was the mission's last resident Franciscan. During Ordaz's tenure at the mission, he was a controversial priest and a colorful personage.[39] Fr. Ordaz left to take charge of Mission San Gabriel, but since there was no priest at San Fernando, he occasionally returned to perform religious services there until February 1849. The Reverend José M. Rosales, who officially took charge on May 28, 1848, became the diocesan replacement for the religious order priest. This fulfilled the requirement for secular priest replacement under secularization and Mission San Fernando took its place among other curatos in Alta California.

Another major requirement in satisfying secularization was that the mission settlement be replaced with a pueblo. Most mission buildings in the Alta California string were to be placed in the hands of civil administrators for public services to the pueblo. A few buildings were allowed to be retained by the Catholic Church for its own use. The mission set-

---

[36] Hutchinson, *Frontier Settlement*, 268–69. The *Manifiesto a la República Mejicana* was the first printing in California, made on a new press sent to Agustín Zamorano in Monterey in 1835.

[37] Engelhardt, *San Fernando Rey*, 36–44, 52–54.

[38] Ibid; Geiger, *Franciscan Missionaries*, 111–12.

[39] Doyce B. Nunis, Jr., "The Franciscan Friars of Mission San Fernando, 1797–1847," *Southern California Quarterly*, 79, no. 3 (1997): 242, where Fr. Blas Ordaz's philandering is discussed and substantiated.

tlement at San Fernando, however, was not replaced with a pueblo, or any form of township, but became part of a hacienda under private ownership. The convento was turned into storage rooms and became living quarters for lessees, squatters, and finally purchasers, and through neglect, the premises became dilapidated over the next three decades.

In 1861, Bishop Jose S. Alemany, O.P., filed a lawsuit on behalf of the missions in Alta California to have certain Church properties reinstated. At Mission San Fernando, the Catholic Church won its suit and retained the church, the convento, and other minor dwellings. The land associated with these buildings amounted to about 77 acres. Another 100 acres of land, including the cemetery, was regained. President Abraham Lincoln signed the confirmation of Mission San Fernando's patent on May 31, 1862.[40]

Secularization was conceived as a plan with the humane goal of emancipating the Indians. It provided that each male Indian connected to a mission would assume his role as a full citizen of the Mexican Republic. Indians were entitled to receive seed and a plot of land for residence and cultivation in order to enable them to become self-sufficient. Unaware of the value of their land acquisition rights, however, most Indians lost them through trickery, gambling, or speculation. The majority of Indians, in the end, worked for the very landowners who had appropriated their lands.

The Spaniards' original plan for civilizing indigenous peoples in ten years was, from the start, doomed to failure. The padres opposed the secularization plan(s), which they harshly criticized for not allowing a sufficient amount of time to achieve its ends. They argued that the Indians were far too primitive and childlike, and were not ready to earn their own living outside the mission.[41]

Some contend that the fault rested with the friars and the paternalistic institution in which they operated. It was a system which discouraged individualism and encouraged a dependency that made it virtually impossible for the natives to start anew on the outside or return to their former way of life. The friars and the mission system did not allow for preparing the "flock" (the Church's figurative reference to its congregation) for a citizen's life in a pueblo. Others contend that the Indians, if given a chance, would have survived on the outside.[42] Despite the odds, a number of them did manage to survive and preserve their identity and culture.[43]

The debate regarding the purpose and activities of the missions, clerics' secularization, and emancipation of indigenous peoples rages on. It is not the intent of the authors to explore all of the complexities and controversies about the success or failure of secularization, but merely to recognize some of these arguments.

Secularization was arguably the major cause of failure of the missions but was, by no means, the only reason for their demise. The diminishing population at the missions was another reason and was, for the most part, due to disease. Popular discord caused by Mexico's wars with Spain and the United States, the growing anti-clerical sentiment of the Mexican populace under the republic, the corruption and greed of the Californios and politicos, and the growing hostility against the Franciscans were other causes.

The last of these possible causes has been attributed to the Franciscans' own desire to exclude non-Franciscans and their wards from acquiring partial lots of mission lands for farms and ranches as missionization went forward. The friars did, in fact,

---

[40] Engelhardt, *San Fernando Rey*, 69–81.

[41] *California Missions: A Pictorial History*, 42–44.

[42] See Webb, *Indian Life at the Old Missions*, 282–309, for one of the best descriptions of the tragic fate of the mission Indians.

[43] Jackson and Castillo, *Indians, Franciscans and Spanish Colonization*, 111.

allow groups of outsiders to inhabit pueblos (with some exceptions during Fr. Serra's time) and presidios, but did not allow individuals to settle on mission property.[44] Fr. Ibarra upheld the prevalent view, evident from the beginning of Franciscan control in Alta California, that lands held for the missions should be used solely by missionaries and their subjects. (See Chapter 11: The Outpost, where Francisco Avila and Carlos Carrillo are examples of individuals who were not allowed to settle mission lands. Lt. Antonio del Valle met with great opposition from the Indians and the friars for his land grant of Camulos Ranch, as reported by Visitador General William Hartnell.) This stance, which can be interpreted partly as self-interest, partly as altruism, engendered hostility in the newly arriving colonists, *politicos,* and soldiers toward the Franciscans. Outside forces eventually prevailed to bring about the completion of secularization and the closing down of the missions, except for Santa Barbara, which remained a functioning mission.

Manuel P. Servín, in his article "The Secularization of the California Missions: A Reappraisal," concludes: "the Fernandinos [friars] hastened their loss of control over the land, the system, and the *gente de razón.* Despite fervor, inflexibility, and protest, the missionaries would not continue to hold back the tide of secularization and settlement."[45]

On his official visit between June 17 and June 24, 1839, to appraise mission status, Visitador General William Hartnell inspected the lands and inventories of Mission San Fernando. He wrote: "June 17— I began examining the documents presented to me relative to this Mission's accounts: everything is in the greatest confusion." In his remaining time at Mission San Fernando, Hartnell required the mission's ex-administrator, Sr. Don Francisco del Castil-

lo, to round up "a paralyzing lack of documents" and make a tally for livestock, plantings—which he finds "very healthy," except that the wheat has rust—and the Indian population, now limited to 161 men, 146 women, 27 boys, 39 girls, and 43 infants. He reported in his journal that the Indians' primary complaint was that their lands were taken away from them and that they would go hungry from that time onward, as Rancho San Francisco was recently acquired by ex-mayordomo Antonio del Valle.[46]

Both Gov. Juan Alvarado (1836–1842) and Gov. Pío Pico (1845–1846), the last Mexican governor of California, greatly hastened secularization and guided its course during their tenures. Their plunder brought ruin to the mission. Their acts of despoliation and self-aggrandizement through the illegal leasing and sale of mission lands and properties, especially by Pío Pico, were rampant, and ultimately contributed to the breakdown of the Alta California missions.[47]

Secularization could not achieve its intended objective of local self-sufficiency as long as politicians, the military, and Californios stripped the missions and the Indians of everything of value; by the late 1840s, Gold Rush plunderers had added to the physical decline of the missions. The new Californians' inertia and apathy allowed most mission structures, including those at Mission San Fernando, to fall into ruin for the next forty years.

---

[44] Manuel P. Servín, "Secularization: A Reappraisal," 133–49.

[45] Ibid., 142. Fernandinos, as the term is used here, were the friars (not the Indians) who studied at the College of San Fernando in Mexico City and were serving in Alta California.

[46] Hartnell, *The Diary and Copybook of William E. P. Hartnell,* 41.

[47] Bancroft, *History of California,* 4: 49–50, especially n49, where the historian writes of the methods of spoliation and ruin that were substantial during Alvarado's governorship: "The governor and subordinate officials by his authority used the cattle and grain of the missions as freely as they used the revenues from other sources. If the government contracted a debt to a trader, the governor gave in payment on any mission for wheat, tallow, or hides, just as he would draw a check on the treasury. The majordomo, being an employee of the government, obeyed the order as a rule, whenever the articles called for existed at his mission." See also James, *In and Out of the Old Missions,* 97–98.

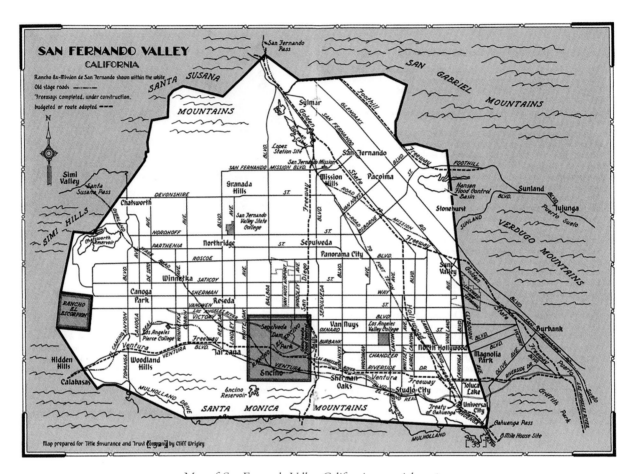

Map of San Fernando Valley, California, copyright 1961.
Artist Cliff Wrigley for Title Insurance and Trust Company, Los Angeles. *CW/CHS/TICOR.*

CHAPTER 15

# LAND GRANTS
# AND NEFARIOUS SCHEMES

*This program went beyond the general opinion in California, which was that mission
lands belonged only to mission Indians. In their succeeding set of regulations for the
colonization of California by Mexicans, the commission [Commission for the Development of the Californias—headed by Manuel de Mier y Terán, minister of war,
Supreme Executive Power, Mexico City, 1824] stated that Christian Indians who
could run their own affairs were to have priority in the division of mission land and
were to receive as much as they could cultivate.*

—C. Alan Hutchinson, *Frontier Settlement in Mexican California*

NDER THE SECULARIZATION of the Mexican period, there was an egalitarian attitude toward the distribution of mission
lands. Lands that were originally to be distributed
only to mission Indians were now available to non-
native requesters, and among those who came forth
to make their claims were colonists, government
appointees, and Californios.

In 1833 Lt. Antonio del Valle requested a grant
for Rancho San Francisco, the former outpost of
the mission, but his claim was denied. He made
another attempt in 1839. This time Gov. Juan Bautista
Alvarado (1836–1842) granted the petition, despite
the protest filed on behalf of the missionaries and
Indians in the region by mission prefect Fray Narciso Durán.[1] The land grant, approved on January
22, 1839, was the first and became known as El
Estancia de San Francisco de Xavier. It was the sec-

ond-largest area of land carved out of ex-mission
property and consisted of 48,612 acres.[2]

Del Valle took possession of the ranch, to which
he moved with cattle and sheep, and built an adobe
house at the foothills on the southeastern edge of
the Santa Clarita Valley. For a time, he and his family feared taking up residence there because of hostilities with the Indians, who were angered by his
prior treatment of them regarding property stolen
from the mission and his confiscation of their land.[3]
William E. P. Hartnell, who was appointed mission

---

[1] Perkins, "Rancho San Francisco," 107.

[2] Ibid., 105; Perez, *Land Grants in Alta California*, 89, which shows
that the grant for Rancho San Francisco awarded to del
Valle was of the amount cited. The acreage was larger than
usually allowed, as grants to all national lands were restricted by the Mexican government to eleven square leagues, or
about 47,480 acres. [This included 1 square league (1 *sitio
de ganado mayor*, abbr. 1 *sitio*) to be irrigable, 4 *sitios* for farming, and 6 *sitios* for pasturage]; W. W. Robinson, *The Story of
San Fernando*, 15.  [3] Engelhardt, *San Fernando Rey*, 57–59.

Oil painting of General Andrés Pico by unknown painter, ca. 1847. This painting was in the Marie W. Harrington Collection and now belongs to the Archival Center, which had it restored. The painting now resides in the Governor's Room at the west end of the convento. *Ken Pauley photograph, 1979. KEP/ACSFM.*

was nullified after examination showed the overlap on the Rancho San Francisco grant.[5]

Ignacio did much building on the property: a corral near Camulos; the twenty-room Camulos adobe home, with wide verandas surrounding a central patio, in 1861; and in 1867 the first commercial winery in the state. El Rancho Camulos was the official home of the del Valle family until Ignacio mortgaged it to Henry Mayo Newhall in 1879. The last del Valle left the Camulos premises in 1924.[6]

El Rancho Tujunga, east of the mission, was the third largest land grant in the valley after Rancho Ex-Mission de San Fernando (1846) and Rancho San Francisco de Xavier (1839). The steps the claimants took to acquire the ranch have been recorded.[7] Pedro López, a Mission San Fernando mayordomo, and his brother Francisco, who was the mayordomo at Rancho San Francisco and, incidentally, the individual credited with discovering gold at Placerita in 1842, filed for and successfully obtained Rancho Tujunga between November 1840 and February 1841. Later, the U.S. District Court confirmed ownership to the grant's patentees (i.e., securers), David W.

visitador general by Gov. Juan Bautista Alvarado, was sent to the ex-missions to investigate the state of emancipation of the population. He was at Mission San Fernando in June 1839 and wrote in his diary about the Indian community's complaints, especially about their concern that their land was taken from them and that they would grow hungry from then on if their land was not returned to them.[4]

Antonio del Valle did not enjoy his property for long. In 1841 he died, leaving the property to his son Ignacio. In 1843, the title of Camulos, located on the western end of the ranch, was temporarily clouded by a grant to Pedro Carrillo, but the grant

---

[4] William E. P. Hartnell, *The Diary and Copybook of William E. P. Hartnell—Visitador General of the Missions of Alta California in 1839 and 1840,* 41–48.

---

[5] Perkins, "Rancho San Francisco," 110; Whitley, *Archaeological Survey,* Historical Background, Chapter 2.4.

[6] Ruth W. Newhall, "El Rancho San Francisco," in *The Newhall Ranch: The Story of the Newhall Land and Farming Co.* (San Marino, Calif.: The Huntington Library, 1958), 35–48, esp. 45 (hereafter cited as "Rancho San Francisco").

Alexander *et al.*, on October 10, 1874, at which time the ranch's size was recorded at 6,661 acres.[8]

❋      ❋      ❋

Once emancipated, Indians who had obtained Mexican citizenship could singly or in partnerships petition for and acquire land grants for properties parceled from ex-mission land.[9] In 1843 several applied for land grants. Samuel, a Tataviam Indian, petitioned for and was granted land northwest of the mission. It measured 1,000 varas squared, or approximately 173 acres. Pedro Joaquín and thirty-eight others petitioned for and were granted a large plot, one league square (approximately 4,316 acres), located south of the tract granted to Samuel.[10]

The partnership of Tiburcio Cayo (Roque), Román, and Francisco Papabubaba petitioned for and was granted Rancho Encino, also measuring one league square.[11] José Miguel Triunfo petitioned for a small parcel called Rancho Cahuenga, situated northeast of the mission. It was one-quarter league squared or one-eighth *sitio*, approximately 540 acres. The grantee date was May 5, 1843. At the U.S. Land Commission hearings on August 2, 1872, it was appraised at only 388.34 acres, with the patentee again being David W. Alexander.[12]

Besides the Indians, other citizens could apply for land. Among them was Californio Vicente de la Osa, an attorney, who received a 4,064-acre grant in the southeastern region of the valley for his Rancho Providencia on March 23, 1843.[13]

In 1845, three Indians known as Urbano Chari, José Odón, and Manuel submitted a petition and obtained Rancho El Escorpión at the western end of the San Fernando Valley. Their small plot measured slightly over one-half league square, or 1,110 acres. Many years later, on December 11, 1876, the trio became their own patentees after the Board of the U.S. Land Commission confirmed the validity of their land grant.[14]

Mexican governor Manuel Micheltorena (1842–45) approved at least three of the above grants but also issued a decree in March 1843 that ordered the return of the missions to Franciscan control. That action and others he performed were found so repugnant to the Californios that they rose in rebellion and forced Governor Micheltorena to leave the territory on February 22, 1845.[15]

During his tenure as governor, Pío Pico (1845–46) began to dispose of mission properties in earnest. At Mission San Fernando he first leased, without a grant deed or title, the entire holdings in the valley, which amounted to 121,542⅓ acres, to his brother Andrés and Juan Manso, for nine years at $1,120 per year. He eventually appropriated the remaining parcels belonging to Samuel and Pedro Joaquín and aggregated them into the larger Rancho Ex-Mission de San Fernando, which at this time was, by far, the largest tract of land affiliated with the ex-mission. It was the largest area for any single grant in California.[16]

In a sleight of hand, Governor Pico sold the ex-

---

[7]  Viola Carlson, "Rancho Tujunga, A Mexican Land Grant of 1840," in *Rancho Days in Southern California: An Anthology with New Perspectives*, Kenneth Pauley, ed., Brand Book 20 (Studio City, Calif.: Westerners, Los Angeles Corral, 1997), 62–79 (hereafter cited as "Rancho Tujunga").

[8]  Perez, *Land Grants in Alta California*, 102.

[9]  Johnson, "The Indians of Mission San Fernando," 259.

[10]  Ibid., 260.

[11]  Ibid.; Perez, *Land Grants in Alta California*, 65, where during U. S. Land Commission hearings, January 8, 1873, Rancho Encino was determined to be about 4,461 acres.

[12]  Perez, *Land Grants in Alta California*, 57; Johnson, "The Indians of Mission San Fernando," 260.

[13]  Perez, *Land Grants in Alta California*, 83.

[14]  Ibid., 66; Johnson, "The Indians of Mission San Fernando," 260.

[15]  Chapman, *Spanish Period*, 483; James, *In and Out of the Old Missions*, 247–48.

[16]  Engelhardt, *San Fernando Rey*, 65, 67n, where it was recorded that on December 5, 1845, "Pío Pico leased the Mission to his brother and Juan Manso, but not for the benefit of the Indians."

(*above*) Adobe home of Geronimo Lopez and family. The home became famous as the Lopez Station from 1861 to 1865. The Butterfield stageline was stationed here. San Fernando's first post office was established here in 1869. The land is now under the Van Norman Reservoir, whose water serves the city of Los Angeles. Unknown photographer, ca. 1880s. *LAA.*

(*opposite*) The Lopez Adobe is located today in the city of San Fernando. *LAA.*

mission rancho that he was leasing to his brother and Juan Manso to Eulógio de Célis, a native of Spain.[17] The sale was consummated under Mexican authority on June 17, 1846, for the amount of $14,000, the governor receiving funds for it in advance. The proceeds went to neither the Church nor the Indians, but to Pío Pico himself for Mexico's imminent war effort against the United States. Two thousand acres of the property, just west of the mission buildings, were set aside for his brother Andrés, and the tract was called Pico Reserve (or Reservation). Shortly after receiving this fraternal favor, Gen. Andrés Pico sold the Pico Reserve to de Célis and used the proceeds for his war chest.[18]

Under the provisions of the sale, the Church and its appurtenances were reserved and de Célis agreed to care for the old Indians still in residence and

respect their right, during their lifetime, to plant crops. He was also to provide food, clothing, and housing for the last resident Franciscan missionary at Mission San Fernando, Fr. Blas Ordaz.[19] Considering Andrés Pico a friend (it was known that they accompanied each other on antelope hunting trips to the nearby Elizabeth Lake country), de Célis honored Pico's lease to reside at the mission. Pico, to fulfill his part of the contract, was to continue operating the lands as a cattle ranch.[20]

[17] Robinson, *The Story of San Fernando*, 12, 15; Engelhardt, *San Fernando Rey*, 65–67.

[18] Daughters of the American Revolution, *The Valley of San Fernando*, 31.

[19] Weber, *The Mission in the Valley*, 29; Robinson, *The Story of San Fernando*, 12.

[20] Weber, *The Mission in the Valley*, 29–30.

After the American conquest of California, the U.S. Land Commission was established in 1851 to ascertain the validity of land titles granted during the Spanish and Mexican regimes. During this decade and the next, the U.S. government ordered the return of some mission buildings and lands to the Catholic Church and assigned Bishop José Sadoc Alemany of Monterey to act as the Church's trustee.[21]

The Land Commission put former governor Pío Pico on the witness stand to answer questions related to the sale of mission lands. He made the following justification:

> I made the grant under and by virtue of my authority as governor and for the purpose of providing means to carry on the war. . . . I had authority to make the grant by virtue of instructions from the Minister of War and Marine of Mexico.[22]

In October 1852, Eulógio de Célis filed his claim with the board of land commissioners to uphold his petition to all the leagues of the valley land that were deeded him by Pío Pico. The board confirmed his claim but it was not during his lifetime that the United States District Court upheld the board's findings and issued the patent. The land survey showed that Rancho Ex-Mission de San Fernando's acreage was the largest of any single grant in California.[23]

Meanwhile, Andrés continued to reside at the former mission and use its buildings as his home, or at least as his stock ranch and summer vacation home.

[H]e entertained lavishly and was host to many distinguished people. He had been popular with the Californios, whose cause he so bravely defended, and was equally popular with the incoming Americans. He is said to have charmed his guests with his singing of Spanish songs. On Sundays he put on bullfights in the plaza before the Mission Church. He liked the company of artists such as Vischer and James Walker to whom the Mission buildings and Valley scenes offered romantic subject.[24]

When Andrés Pico's lease expired in 1854, he paid de Célis' lawyer, Edward Vischer, $15,000 for an undivided half-interest in the ex-mission rancho. On May 21, 1862, Andrés conveyed his interest to his brother Pío, who in turn, on July 2, 1869, sold it to the San Fernando Farm Homestead Association for $115,000 and used the money to build a hotel adjoining the Los Angeles Plaza.[25]

Before his title to the property could be confirmed, de Célis returned to his home in Bilbao, Spain, where he died in 1869. The final patent was

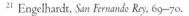

[21] Engelhardt, *San Fernando Rey*, 69–70.

[22] Robinson, *The Story of San Fernando*, 12.

[23] Ibid., 17.

[24] Ibid., 15.

[25] Ibid., 21.

not issued to the de Célis estate until January 8, 1873. The estate was placed under the superintendence of Edward Vischer, who was his attorney but is better known today as an accomplished artist. De Célis' widow and children returned to California, and the couple's eldest son, Eulógio F. de Célis, was appointed administrator of the estate; the real property amounted to 116,858.43 acres, which was 5,500 acres smaller than the original grant, due to claims confirmed to other rancho petitioners in the valley.[26]

By the proclamation of May 31, 1862, President Abraham Lincoln confirmed church title to 170.20 acres of ex-Mission San Fernando property. Holdings included the buildings, cemetery, orchards, and roughly 100 acres of surrounding land.[27] The small rancho grants issued to mission Indians were also confirmed, except for the one to the Indian Samuel, who, in fact, had never filed a formal claim and had sold part of his holdings to Gerónimo López, son-in-law of the former mayordomo Don Pedro López.

The Butterfield Overland Mail Stage company, commonly called the Butterfield Stage line, and sometimes Express, was established in 1857 and ran from Los Angeles to San Francisco through Cahuenga Pass, Frémont Pass, and Lyon Pass.[28] On land that remained legally a portion of Rancho Ex-Mission San Fernando, Gerónimo López built a large house, known popularly as the López Station. There, he maintained a Butterfield stagecoach station on the route of the line that ran between 1861 to 1874. At this location, the valley's first post office was established in 1869. The entire area, including the station, became covered with water after the Van Norman Reservoir was constructed in 1913.[29]

In his book *Missions of Upper California—1872*, Edward Vischer wrote extensive commentary to accompa-

---

[26] Ibid., 15–16.

[27] Ibid.; Engelhardt, *San Fernando Rey*, 70–82.

[28] Daughters of the American Revolution, *The Valley of San Fernando*, 37.

[29] Weber, *Memories of an Old Mission*, 22–23; Robinson, *The Story of San Fernando*, 19.

(*above*) Home of Andrés Pico (Pico Adobe) at Mission San Fernando, ca. 1915. *CHS/TICOR (7432).*

(*right*) General Andrés Pico, possibly a daguerrotype, ca. 1847.

(*opposite*) Pico Adobe, Andrés Pico's home and today the headquarters of the San Fernando Valley Historical Society, is located a few blocks south of the convento. The painter is Claude A. Wisman, an artist and Los Angeles police officer, who was rehabilitating from a gunshot wound at the time. His artwork and many other important images of San Fernando Valley history are found at the Pico Adobe. Unknown photographer, 1927. *LAA.*

ny his sketches of the California missions and the people associated with them. His work is subtitled "A Supplement to Vischer's Pictorial of California" and was dedicated to his patrons. Vischer wrote in detail, and repeated likely exaggerated claims of extreme old age of his subjects, who were said to be 115 and 130 years old. He also sketched Andrés Pico at Mission San Fernando in 1865.

The most remarkable instances of Indian longevity are two couples of extreme old age, which were shown to us at San Fernando and are represented in the corresponding sketch—they were probably

the oldest remnants of their race in all Southern California, even if, as not unlikely, the statement should be somewhat exaggerated—Ildefonso (called Alifonso) who even at the arrival of the first missionaries was a grandfather through four grown up sons, whose age was given 130 years by computation, and Agapito, 115, the first adult Indian, also a grand-

SOUTHERN MISSION ORCHARD.    GENERAL DON ANDRES PICO OF LOS ANGELES, 1865.    VAQUEROS LASSOING CATTLE.

CORRIDOR of the FARM-BUILDING.    A CALIFORNIAN MAGNATE IN HIS HOME.    EX-MISSION of SAN FERNANDO.

Gen'l D. ANDRES PICO, with his adoptive daughter, visiting the quarters of the aged S'. Fernando INDIANS.    V.FISCHER, 1865.

CHAPEL and PRINCIPAL BUILDINGS of the EX-MISSION SAN FERNANDO.

father then, baptized in San Fernando (as seen by the baptismal register) and both living with their first wives of an age corresponding to their custom of early marriage. Ildefonso bent by old age and reduced to nearly a skeleton, yet showed indications of fine proportions (he must have measured six foot in his prime). . . . [He is] apparently indifferent to his surroundings yet very nervous at the even momentary absence of his old dame, of whom he seemed extremely jealous. The other old couple seemed to enjoy their matrimonial bliss in undisturbed serenity, happy in each other's presence and contented through their innate cheerful disposition.

Don Andrés, now General *Don* Andrés Pico, resident owner of the Fernando estate, a brother to Ex-Governor Don Pío Pico, at the time of his country's peril was foremost to oppose the American occupation as long as there was any hope of successful resistance. The Stars and Stripes once established, he proved a faithful guardian of the new order of things. Released from all binding obligations which few, if any, respected after the change, his humane impulses prompted him to provide for the wants of these poor broken servants of the Mission, and he has done so through years of drought and starvation as well as in years of plenty; a little feeble help in the orchards, besides their humble blessings is all the return he can receive. . . .

In our sketch, looking toward the eastern [it is clear from the sketch that Vischer really meant the Santa Monica Mountains to the south] mountain ridges, we show the Mission buildings at some distance, while the middle ground exhibits some vaqueros testing the qualities of new broken horses. The foreground, as of right, is dedicated to our gallant host accompanied by a little niece, visiting the wigwams of his superannuated Indians. After a cordial entertainment at San Fernando, our kind host insisted upon taking us in his buggy to the distant way-station [López Station] of the overland stage route, on the slope of the Cuesta de Santa Susana, where a most delightful spot, at his compadre's [Gerónimo López's] "el Basco," afforded us [a] good night's quarter.[30]

❁     ❁     ❁

As time went on, more properties changed hands. By January 1873, Vicente de la Osa acquired Rancho Encino, the property granted to Román, Francisco, and Rogue. Miguel Leonis, the French Basque rancher who became the son-in-law of Odón, acquired rights to Rancho Escorpión.

The division of the valley came after negotiations between the San Fernando Farm Homestead Association and the heirs of de Célis. Approximately 60,000 acres in the southern half went to the association and 56,000 acres in the northern half went to the heirs. In 1874, the heirs sold their portion to two former state senators from northern California, George K. Porter and Charles Maclay.[31]

Subdivision and development of the valley began. The extensive vineyards, olive groves, and orchards on ex-mission lands gave way to barley, wheat, and corn fields and sheep and pig farming. Agriculture later disappeared and succumbed to urbanization—with the indigenous population virtually disappearing in the process.

(*opposite page*) Watercolors by Edward Vischer, ca. 1865. (*top*) "Corridor of the Farm-Building, A California Magnate In His Home, Ex-Mission of San Fernando, Southern Mission Orchard, General Don Andrés Pico of Los Angeles, 1865, Vaqueros Lassoing Cattle." (*bottom*) "Chapel and Principal Buildings of the Ex-Mission San Fernando—and a smaller caption—Indians, Mission Indians of California—Alifonso, Agapito." The painting depicts Gen. Don Andrés Pico, with his adoptive daughters, visiting the quarters of the aged San Fernando Indians. The oldest surviving mission Indians of California are said to be (by computation): Alifonso 130, Agapito 115, and their first wives about 100 years old. *EV/JBG.*

---

[30] Edward Vischer, *Drawings of the California Missions, 1861–1878*, Plates 32 and 33.

[31] Robinson, *The Story of San Fernando*, 24.

View of west wing ruins and church in 1922. *ACSFM*.

# CHAPTER 16

# RUINS AND RESTORATION

*Ruins change so fast that one cannot keep pace: they disintegrate, they go to earth, they are tidied up, excavated, cleared of vegetation, built over, restored, prostrate columns set on end and fitted with their own or other capitals. . . . One must select for contemplation some phase in a ruin's devious career, it matters little which, and consider the human reaction to this; or merely enjoy one's own.*

—Rose Macauley, *Pleasure of Ruins*

THE SANTA BARBARA EARTHQUAKE of December 21, 1812, was the second significant natural disaster to strike the region following the establishment of the mission, bringing death and destruction to the missions of Southern California. It followed the disastrous San Juan Capistrano earthquake, which occurred two weeks earlier. Its epicenter was not known for certain but was believed to be located offshore in the Channel Islands. Estimated to be about 7.0 on the Richter scale, it caused severe damage from Santa Barbara to San Fernando, a distance of over one hundred miles. The earthquake reduced to rubble some of the missions farther west but, for the most part, spared Mission San Fernando, which required only the addition of thirty new beams to support the church wall.[1]

In the ensuing years, the mission began to fall into ruins, hastened by the relentless forces of nature and the benign neglect of man. Normal weathering eroded the buildings. Rain and wind caused damage to the roof and walls of all the buildings, especially those in the quadrangle. Lack of repair to the church roof allowed the adobe walls and their protective layers of limestone to deteriorate. Once the roof tiles were gone, the adobe began to crack and dissolve in portions. The roof of the sacristy, baptistry, and belfry all began to collapse in the late 1860s. The adobe walls of the belfry developed large cracks, weakened, and collapsed in the late 1880s and 1890s, totally disintegrating in the 1920s.

In October 1890 the smokehouse dormer atop the convento collapsed. By the middle of the decade, missing tiles allowed many holes to form on the convento roof. Around 1895 a section of the convento wall above the large rear (north) archway just east of the smokehouse crumbled.

Charles F. Lummis, historian and founder-director of the Southwest Museum, spearheaded the California Landmarks Club (CLC), which banded

---

[1] Bancroft, *History of California*, 2: 358. The December 8, 1812, earthquake was estimated to be a 7.5 on the Richter scale. Probably occurring on the San Andreas Fault with a theorized epicenter near Wrightwood, this quake is remembered as the Mission San Juan Capistrano temblor in which forty Native Americans were killed during Mass when the domed stone church collapsed on them.

Crumbled church wall, quadrangle columns, and bricks removed from
in front of the west quadrangle, ca. 1915. *ACSFM.*

CLC roof beginning to weather; concrete pillars shoring the church walls
and repairs being made to the sacristy, ca. 1917. *ACSFM.*

Remains of the quadrangle's west wing, 1923. *ACSFM.*

together in 1895 to preserve historic sites in the southland. The CLC started with the southern missions, scheduling Mission San Fernando for 1897.[2] In October 1896, prior to any work being performed, Lummis began his photographic journal of Mission San Fernando and chronicled the progress of the preservation project into the 1920s.

In the late spring of 1897, modest restoration work began on the church and convento simultaneously. Four thousand tiles, needed for the convento, were recovered from surrounding ranches by the CLC during scavenging tours. Adobe and burnt brick were also needed to repair the walls and dormer of the convento. The huge arch next to the dormer on the north side was made with a smaller opening, as Landmarks Club members believed it was inherently unstable because of its size. The dormer, too, was restored and the north wall was patched.

The CLC replaced the wooden beams and covered the church with sheet-roofing. By September 8, the CLC had new roofs placed over both the church and convento, temporarily stabilizing the walls to prevent further erosion. Restoration was completed just in time for the mission's centennial celebration, which took place on the following day, Thursday, September 9, 1897.[3] Next, the Most Reverend Eulógio Gregorio Gillow y Zavalza (1841–1922), the exiled archbishop of Oaxaca, began some restoration work on the convento. In 1913, when he was exiled to the United States, he went to live in San Antonio, Texas. From there he wrote to the bishop of Monterey-Los Angeles, prefacing his letter with remarks about Fray Junípero Serra's Oaxaca-California connection in order to emphasize his (Zavalza's) own. He proposed that the convento at San Fernando be restored and used for a school to train teenage boys and older men in agricultural pursuits. In his letter, he also proposed

---

[2]  Mark Thompson, *American Character: The Curious Life of Charles Fletcher Lummis* (New York: Time Warner Trade Company, 2001), 185–86.

[3]  See sidebar, next page.

the establishment of a printing office to produce leaflets and books in defense of the besieged Church of Mexico. His last proposal was to oversee the construction of a railroad going from San Diego to peninsular California, which was intended to improve communications and bring catechismal instructions to the inhabitants there.

The archbishop was able to raise seed money and $500 from the Catholic Church Extension Society to start his restoration project. He restored several rooms in the convento, but there is no record of which ones. There are indications that he was expected to pay a quarterly rent for the facilities but defaulted on his payments. Possibly because of financial difficulties, he returned to Oaxaca in 1921, where he died the next year. It is unknown how long work on the convento continued.[4]

The next effort took place in 1916, under the auspices of the Landmarks Club and a special committee headed by Lucretia del Valle, the well-known

leading lady of John Steven McGroarty's "Mission Play." She organized a candle sale and a Candle Day to raise money for strengthening the walls and replacing a portion of the roof, which had been repaired once before by the CLS, but had, by now, become dilapidated again. Memorial candles sold would bear the name of the donor and were to be lit at the services held on the night of August 6.

Candle Day and the 147th anniversary of Portolá's discovery of the San Fernando Valley were a unique celebration—to raise funds for repairs. Over six thousand people attended the festivities. Enough money was collected to not only add a new roof, but also begin repairs to the church walls.[5] In 1917, Hernando G. Villa painted a pastel of the west wing of the quadrangle, with a tent to the left of the church. This painting is interesting in that it shows

---

[4] Weber, *Memories of an Old Mission,* 47–48.

[5] Weber, *The Mission in the Valley,* 92–93. This painting (page 305) was made by Hernando G. Villa (1881–1952) on February 18, 1917. John & Marian Bowater Collection, now at the Andrés Pico Adobe in Mission Hills. Courtesy of the San Fernando Valley Historical Society (SFVHS).

---

## THURSDAY, SEPTEMBER 9, 1897—CENTENNIAL CELEBRATION
## CHARLES F. LUMMIS DIARY

Charles F. Lummis often wrote in a combination of English and broken Spanish. The English equivalents are provided here.

I wake up at 7:30 [A.M.], I shave, work with San Fernando [preparation to go to the mission to photograph the centennial celebration]. I go to town [Los Angeles] alone and there is no letter. I pay Preston $70.25 for Harmer up to September 12th. I return home. Ground glass broke and I go down and get another. Eve [wife] and I leave with the two children at 1:45 [P.M.]. There is a great crowd and much work in regard to the tickets—I sell 65 tickets there. We leave at 3:15 [P.M.] with three coaches and we add two in River Station. We arrive at San Fernando at 4:10 [P.M.]. Rev. Wilbur and other reception committee members receive us and treat us to the body of rey [i.e., either received Holy

Communion (?), or were shown around the San Fernando (Rey) grounds (?)]. I remain 1 hour at the station, taking care of the people's transport—I arrive at last love [Mission San Fernando, at which Lummis had just led in the restoration of the church's and convento's roofs] at 5:15 [P.M.]. I take three pictures. I eat lunch at the portal [under the convento's arched portico]. I chat with Bishop Montgomery, Colonel Otis, [about] Mrs. Otis' poem. Three cheers for San Fernando and the people.—We returned all right, the train jogging along at 8:14 [P.M.] arriving at home at 8:40 [P.M.]. I eat lunch. 3 photos.*

---

* Lummis diary provided courtesy of the Southwest Museum, Los Angeles.

(*above*) Church and remaining adobe walls of the quadrangle during Dr. Mark R. Harrington's restoration, ca. 1940. From Marie Walsh Harrington Collection (now Archival Center). *MWH/ACSFM.*

(*right*) Photo by Hugh Pascal Webb taken February 25, 1939. Most of the work on the roof and adobe walls of the church was completed under Dr. Mark R. Harrington's restoration project. Exceptions were the bell-tower and sacristy, which were not completed until 1944–46, after World War II. From the Marie Walsh Harrington Collection (now Archival Center). *HPW/ACSFM.*

restoration work in progress, with money collected from the 1916 Candle Day fundraiser.

The Oblates of Mary Immaculate Order was put in charge of religious administration at the mission in 1923. Acting as the Oblate Superior over Mission San Fernando, Father Charles Siemes, the first rector and pastor at Saint Ferdinand's Church in the city of San Fernando, began minor restoration efforts. Father Siemes and two assistants had the convento's columns renovated and the rear wall strengthened with a new foundation and five large steel anchors. The former mayordomo's house, now the janitor's lodging, was rebuilt with a one-slope roof, giving it the appearance of a chicken coop. At this time the walls of the church were also strengthened with heavy steel braces and concrete columns.[6]

By 1927 funds for restoration came from a loan

---

[6]  Ibid., 106–07.

(*left*) This photo by Wayne C. "Dick" Whittington, ca. 1945, shows electric lines drawn to the church on poles. Fresh adobe walled up a portion of the church near the center. The last ruins of the sacristy can be seen. *WDW/ACSFM.*

(*below*) The west wing of quadrangle ruins and recently restored church, ca. 1945. *LAA.*

280

taken out by the Oblate Fathers.[7] The Oblates proceeded to replace the worn patchwork on the church roof with a new roof made of tile. Lummis documented the extensive preparations to cure adobe and manufacture other materials used in construction during this restoration.

A second Candle Day in 1937 was held to raise funds for continuing preservation work on the church roof and walls. Tiles and adobe blocks were fashioned out of scraps of materials collected from the site.[8]

Architectural drawings were made in 1936 by the Historic American Buildings Survey (HABS), Works Progress Administration, under the direction of the U.S. Department of the Interior, National Park Service, Branch of Plans and Design. (See pages 186–89.) Artist-architect Gregory Holt created a series of tinted drawings for the Federal Arts Project supporting restoration efforts. After the drawings were completed, two important figures arrived on the scene—one a cleric, the other a curator.

Father Charles Burns arrived in 1938 and injected new energy into restoration plans. This young priest had a keen interest in the history, preservation, and restoration of the mission. He generated public interest by staging a large outdoor field Mass in the east garden to commemorate the 141st anniversary of the mission's founding. Thousands of interested visitors participated in the day-long program that included a fiesta and barbecue. The event was a catalyst in the formation of a fund-raising group headed by Thomas Binda, a local banker, who raised $25,000 to restore the church roof and several other buildings, including the belfry, arches of the convento, and the rebuilt mayordomo's house, some of which still stand.[9]

Dr. Mark R. Harrington, curator of the Southwest Museum, was the other force in Mission San Fernando's restoration. He and Father Burns founded the Friends of the Mission, which raised funds for restoration during the late 1930s and early 1940s. Their first task was to restore the church and rooms in the convento. Father Burns obtained a loan for this work, which was to be repaid by admission fees to the mission and donations from special interest groups and individuals.[10]

On behalf of The Friends of the Mission, Dr. Harrington prepared a three-year plan for restoration of the mission:[11]

First year: Repairs to the walls of old church, the roofs of the church and convento, and grounds beautification.

Second year: Interior of old church to be completed; old workshops and old bell tower and sacristy restored.

Third year: Convento and old workshops restored.

According to plan, in the first year, the walls of the church were strengthened with forty thousand adobe bricks, made at a cost of $2,400. The church was re-roofed for the third time and with new roof tiles. The woodwork for the interior of the church was restored under the direction of William Irontail, a noted builder and son of a Sioux Indian chief. A truncated, triangular façade was constructed in the place where the belfry once stood and was attached to the church to give lateral support to its south and west walls, in case of an earthquake.

On September 7, 1941, the restored third church was rededicated after being closed for sixty-seven years. Over five thousand persons attended the morning Mass.[12]

Three months later, the United States entered

---

[7] Engelhardt, *San Fernando Rey*, 132–34.

[8] Ibid.

[9] Weber, *The Mission in the Valley*, 106–07.

[10] Ibid.

[11] Authors interview with Marie T. (Walsh) Harrington in 1979.

[12] Weber, *The Mission in the Valley*, 110–11.

Texas in 1944 and was unable to see the project through to its completion. Work on the bell tower and sacristy persevered, however. The entire project could not be accomplished in Dr. Harrington's optimistic timetable due to interruption by war, but work was finally completed satisfactorily in 1946.

Later restoration work on the church and convento was funded by the Friends of the Mission. During the years 1949 and 1950, work on the west and south wings of the quadrangle, supervised by Arthur Ballin, was funded by grants from the William Randolph Hearst Foundation.[13]

From the 1950s onward, life and activities at Mission San Fernando were rather routine. A few face-lifts and roof repairs were made to the convento in 1963. Life was peaceful and quiet until Tuesday, February 9, 1971, at 6:02 A.M., when the disastrous Sylmar earthquake struck southern

World War II. The nation turned its efforts to war production. All major work on the mission was brought to a halt. Some minor remodeling work, however, continued: a temporary apartment for Dr. Harrington and his first wife, Endeka, was made in the attic of the convento, and minor alterations were made for plumbing, which were subsequently removed because they were historically incorrect.

Unfortunately, Father Burns was transferred to

California.[14] Mission San Fernando had survived the large earthquakes of 1812, 1852, and 1906, which inflicted far more damage on other Alta California missions and rancho structures. This time, though, Mission San Fernando was not so fortunate. The temblor was devastating. It caused extensive damage to both the church and convento. The interior

[13] Weber, *Memories of an Old Mission*, 86–88.
[14] Weber, *The Mission in the Valley*, 126–28.

(*opposite, top*) Church's west wall and bell tower about 1900. Large cracks in both have widened. Note the Porter Land and Water Company farm equipment and a makeshift door in the church, ca. 1898. *ACSFM.*

(*opposite, bottom*) The west wall section of the church, between the window and door, has now crumbled, ca. 1915. *KEP.*

(*right, top*) From the north orchard, looking toward the church and baptistry and adobe wall, 1924. *CHS/TICOR (4488).*

(*right, bottom*) Remnants of the adobe wall that once surrounded the north orchard are covered with tile to protect what little remains. Ken Pauley photo, 1979. *KEP.*

of the church was buried under plaster. Portions of the choir wall collapsed. The floor buckled in several places.

When Church authorities estimated the damage, they voiced grave doubts as to whether the buildings could be restored. Only the steel-reinforced workshops and living quarters of the west wing, restored two decades earlier, remained intact. Both the church and convento sustained heavy damage. Demolition was considered for both buildings but the decision was made to spare the convento, which was "yellow-tagged," meaning that it was repairable. The church, however, was "red-tagged," which signified that it was condemned and would have to be demolished.

For the convento, care was taken to replace only the most weakened parts with modern materials. Several interior and exterior walls were replaced and pillared with wooden reinforcements and concrete blocks. The floors, ceilings, and walls were all refinished. Repair work on the convento was completed in 1973, with the emphasis on stability rather than historical preservation.

Private donations and other funds from the Archdiocese of Los Angeles aided the reconstruction of the church and the exhumation and reburial of four resident friars (Friars Tómas Eleuterio Esténaga and José de Miguel were known to be buried under the church floor, and Friars José Antonio Urrestí and Martin de Landaeta in unmarked graves).[15] In 1973 the remaining walls of the old church were leveled, in preparation for reconstruction of a likeness of the famous third church. The walls were so well constructed that large machinery used to scrape the site

---

[15] Nunis, "The Franciscan Friars," 243.

had to strain for an extended time and several wreckers' balls were ruined in repeated attempts to reduce the edifice to rubble.

Prior to demolition, great care was taken that the church would be accurately reconstructed and its contents preserved. Church dimensions, architectural details, and decorations were meticulously recorded. Mission artifacts, damaged or not, were temporarily stored at the nearby seminary. Fred Rolla and other specialists were enlisted to restore damaged statues, furniture, and Indian artifacts.

Dedication of the fourth chapel took place on November 4, 1974, presided over by His Eminence, Cardinal Timothy Manning, and attended by a throng of worshipers.[16]

—————

[16] Ibid., 131–33.

(*opposite, top*) Scaffolding along the southern wall of the church permits restorers to shore up the wall with adobe bricks that were made on site, ca. 1938. *ACSFM.*

(*opposite, bottom*) In early 1917, restoration of the church. Workmen reinforce the south wall with concrete-embedded columns. *ACSFM.*

(*right*) Steel reinforcing columns are added to strengthen previously placed concrete pillars on the church's north wall, ca. 1923. *UCLA.*

Twenty-three years after the Sylmar earthquake, another devastating temblor occurred, on Monday, January 17, 1994, at 4:31 A.M., with its epicenter about one mile south of Northridge. The church had only minor damage inflicted on it since it had been strengthened in 1973 to comply with new building codes for earthquakes. The convento sustained extensive damage but remained standing because of previous retrofitting after the Sylmar earthquake. Once again, Msgr. Weber insisted that the building be yellow-tagged so that it could be retrofitted rather than demolished and reconstructed.

Dislodged plaster on the walls and ceiling of the convento exposed all walls. For art historian Dr. Norman Neuerburg, the earthquake was a serendip-

itous event which allowed him to inspect bared archaeological evidence and determine the building's various phases of construction. His findings were published posthumously.[17]

The California Water Proofing and Restoration Company (WPRC), with O'Leary & Teresawa architectural consultants, performed earthquake stabilization and preservation work. After this extensive work was completed in 1997, the Archdiocese of Los Angeles contracted with WPRC to build a replica of the small corporal or "guard's" bell tower, which once graced the west end of the convento.

---

[17] Neuerburg, "Biography of a Building," 291–310.

The photos on this page were produced by Merge Studios in 1953–54 for the Department of Water and Power (#1885-53 and -54). (*left*) The west garden and reconstructed west wing are shown. (*bottom*) A seminary was built approximately where the east wing once stood. Today the building is a high school. *MS/ACSFM.*

The gradual decay and destruction of the mayordomo's house is shown in photos from about 1890 (C. C. Pierce) into the early 1920s (C. F. Lummis).

(*above*) Buckboard at the east end of convento.
View by C. C. Pierce, ca. 1890. *CCP/CHS/TICOR (11461).*

(*opposite, top*) A close-up view of the mayordomo's house, at the start of its collapse, ca. 1889. *ACSFM.*

(*opposite, middle*) *342. East End of San Fernando Mission*—A colloidal on cardboard (*carte-de-visite*) made by Frank L. Park. Photo ca. 1898. *FLP/SWM-P1900.*

(*opposite, bottom*) East end of the convento and the mayordomo's house show advancing roof decay. The front adobe wall has started collapsing. By C. C. Pierce, ca. 1904. *CCP/CHS/TICOR (2268).*

(*opposite, top*) The mayordomo's house at the east end of the convento crumbles. Photograph by W. C. Dickerson, ca. 1912. *WCD/SWM-N1480.*

(*opposite, bottom*) The roof of the mayordomo's house has crumbled and the adobe walls are now exposed to the elements. Unknown photographer, ca. 1915. *KEP.*

(*right*) Major reconstruction of the mayordomo's house used as the mission's gift shop in the 1960s. Photo by K. Kaminsky. *ACSFM.*

(*below*) Mayordomo house and convento after Sylmar earthquake restoration work in 1974. Ken Pauley photograph, 1977.

(*opposite, top*) Material is collected at the east wing of the quadrangle to construct adobe blocks for the church, ca. 1938. *ACSFM.*

(*opposite, bottom*) Adobe blocks, formed in molds, are left to dry, then stacked. Restorers then use them on the south wall of the church, ca. 1938. *ACSFM.*

(*this page, top*) Father Charles Burns employs "adobe men." Under P. Rosales's direction, they produced a huge number of sun-dried adobe blocks for church construction, ca. 1938. *ACSFM.*

(*this page, bottom*) Scaffolding and adobe bricks piled at base are used to shore up a portion of the church's south wall, 1939. *ACSFM.*

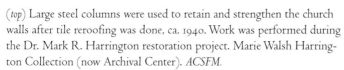

(*top*) Large steel columns were used to retain and strengthen the church walls after tile reroofing was done, ca. 1940. Work was performed during the Dr. Mark R. Harrington restoration project. Marie Walsh Harrington Collection (now Archival Center). *ACSFM.*

Arthur Ballin is seen working on a portion of the adobe wall that once enclosed the north orchard (*right*) and on a newly constructed wooden gate at the southern entrance to mission grounds (*left*), ca. 1950. *ACSFM.*

The convento is reroofed in October 1963. *ACSFM.*

The ruins of the sacristy, old corbels, and the adjacent wall to the church, 1931.
Marie Walsh Harrington Collection (now Archival Center). *MWH/ACSFM.*

This is the same general view and angle as seen above, 2003. *KEP.*

(*left*) Looking south through the doorway of the roofless sacristy, 1931. The circular fountain may be seen in the distance. From Marie Walsh Harrington Collection (now Archival Center). *MWH/ACSFM.* (*right*) A similar view, years later, ca. 1940. *LAA.*

298

(*pages 286–87 and 298–301*) For the period March 1949 to October 1954, a photohistory of reconstruction of the quadrangle's west wing was captured by two sources. This sequence of photographs was taken by Jaspar G. Schad in 1949. *JGS/ACSFM.*

300

(*opposite, top*) The new buildings after completion of the west wing.
Photographed by Douglas Scott Bliven, ca. 1960. *DSB/ACSFM.*

(*opposite, bottom*) The newly completed west wing of the quadrangle
and reroofed convento, ca. 1960. Photograph by Douglas Scott Bliven.
*DSB/ACSFM.*

(*above*) The west garden in the early 1970s. *ACSFM.*

(*right*) Wooden statue at San Fernando Mission. Photograph by F. H. Maude & Company, ca. 1895. *FHM/ACSFM.*

(*below*) Window shutter with peephole. Federal Arts Project, 2404 West 7th Street, Los Angeles, California. 1938. (a-1) So. Cal.—*4017(1)-AR-8. ACSFM.*

(*above*) Geoffrey Holt drawing of restored design at exterior main door and exterior portico leading into the sala in the convento. Index of American Design: Federal Arts Project, 1939. *GH/SWM-P19054.*

(*left*) Door leading into convento from the portico. By Geoffrey Holt during the Federal Arts Project, ca. 1940. *GH/ACSFM.*

Pastel painting of the church undergoing restoration after a Candle Day fundraiser.
Note the tent next to the church probably was used to house tools and equipment. The artist was
Hernando G. Villa (1881–1952), who made this rendition on February 17, 1917. From the John & Marian
Bowater Collection at the Andrés Pico Adobe, courtesy of the San Fernando Valley Historical Society. *H. G. Villa/SFVHS.*

(*above*) Damage to the north wall of the convento, inflicted by the Northridge temblor on January 17, 1994. *ACSFM.*

Various roof, wall and flooring reinforcements to the second floor of the convento made by the California Water Proofing and Restoration Company, O'Leary & Teresawa Architect consultants (1996–97), 2000. Ken Pauley photographs. (*bottom row, center*) Ken Pauley takes measurements on the convento's second floor at the west end. Troy Greenwood photograph, 2000. *KEP.*

(*above*) Severe damage to church's southern wall from the 1971 Sylmar quake. *ACSFM.*

(*right*) Extensive earthquake damage in the sacristy behind the church nave. Photo by Keystone Photo Services, Inc., 1971. *KP/ACSFM (LA129-78).*

(*above*) Interior decorated walls in the convento show earthquake damage, 1971. *ACSFM.*

(*left*) Door and wall inside room in the convento. *ACSFM.*

Remains of one of the mission's friars ares found on
the gospel side of pulpit. Archaeological excavations were
performed prior to razing and reconstructing the fourth chapel.
Photo was made on April 30, 1973, the day that demolition
began on the third church. *ACSFM.*

310

FOUR VIEWS OF CHURCH DEMOLITION
(*this page and opposite*) After the 1971 Sylmar
earthquake, demolition began on April 30, 1973,
with the use of heavy equipment. *ACSFM*.

View of west garden before Archival Center construction began shows
the workshops, bell tower, and chapel. Postcard by Ken Pauley, 1977. *KEP.*

# CHAPTER 17

# THE MISSION IN MODERN TIMES

*In many ways, the role that Mission San Fernando occupies in the busy world of the 1990s differs sharply from that of the 1790s. No longer perched on what was then the "rim of Christendom," the outpost bearing the spiritual patronage of a sainted king of Spain has no resident missionary, offers no catechism classes for native Americans, and provides no opportunity for technical or agricultural development.*
—Msgr. Francis J. Weber,
"San Fernando . . . Its Role in the New Millennium"

OVER TWO HUNDRED YEARS AGO, Mission San Fernando, Rey de España, was one of twenty-one settlements in Alta California, the northern frontier of Spanish expansion. The mission began humbly, peaked at age twenty-three, and then began to decline to a ruinous state at age sixty-five. Extinction of all of its structures was avoided when the Catholic Church reclaimed title to its properties and 170 acres of land in 1862. Historically-minded individuals and groups began making efforts to preserve and restore its structures at its hundredth birthday in 1897.

For the time being—and barring a disaster from which there is no recovery—the mission has completed reconstruction and restoration of many of its structures. In this century, it has turned its efforts to beautification and routine maintenance of the buildings and grounds.

The role that Mission San Fernando plays today is far different from the one it played in the past. No longer is the mission an outpost of Spanish colonization and expansion. No longer is it a center of agriculture with its attendant occupations and commerce. No longer are the indigenous peoples under the wardship of Franciscans.

Mission San Fernando, though still mindful of its religious purpose and steeped in the past, keeps an eye on the future. It has endeavored to promote scholarly research and to preserve and display the history of the mission to the public. The Archival Center and the Mission Museum were established to accomplish these goals.

The Archival Center has promoted itself as a force in teaching and learning in the twenty-first century. On September 13, 1981, Cardinal Timothy Manning of the Archdiocese of Los Angeles dedicated the Archival Center, located in the west garden of the mission.[1] Under the direction of Msgr. Fran-

---

[1]  Msgr. Francis J. Weber, *Memories of an Old Country Priest Mission* (Mission Hills, Calif.: Saint Francis Historical Society, 2000), 280–81; Liturgy of Dedication and Convocation on Mission History: September 13, 1981, for the Archives Building of the Archdiocese of Los Angeles at Mission San Fernando, program (Mission Hills, Calif.: Mission San Fernando, 1981), 8 pp.

(*this page and opposite, top*) Earthquake damage to the library in the convento, 1971. Keystone Photographs (LA128-35-N2). *ACSFM.*

(*opposite, bottom*) Bibliotheca Montereyensis— Angelorum Dioeceseos, located in the repaired convento, after the 1971 earthquake. Ken Pauley photograph, 1979. *KEP.*

cis J. Weber, the center continues to collect and preserve historical documents and records, making them available to scholars for the study and interpretation of Catholic and California history.[2]

As the quantity of knowledge increases exponentially over shorter periods of time, the need for the Archival Center is apparent. A wide assortment of books, pictures, and documents is found in the center. To expand its holdings, the center desires to acquire pertinent retired materials from other libraries, new American Catholica, bibliography, and archivology.

Mission San Fernando also houses an important mission library collection, the *Bibliotheca Montereyensis—Angelorum Dioeceseos*, by Francisco García Diego y Moreno. Today the collection contains about seven hundred titles, although there were more when it was first formed. It found a home in a special library room in the convento in 1969. Dating back to 1842, it was gathered into a library, moved from place to place over the years, and almost went into obscurity.[3]

The earthquakes of 1971 and 1994 hit the convento hard, but extensive retrofitting of the building has kept the library intact. Photographs show the library before and just after the temblors.[4]

A future attraction at Mission San Fernando will be the expanding and ever-changing Historical Museum, which will blend permanent museum exhibits with private collections. Located in rooms in the west wing of the quadrangle, the museum has display cases of art, native craftwork, artifacts, and documents from early mission days.

Thousands of visitors (there were 35,000 in 2001), including the obligatory California fourth-grade students, travel to Mission San Fernando to see a historical site and church, a living mission with roots in a by-gone age. Today one can attend Mass, sit in

2   Weber, *Memories of an Old Country Priest,* 283–93.

3   Weber, *The Mission in the Valley,* 122–25.

4   Ibid., 124; Francis J. Weber, "San Fernando, Rey de España: Its Role in the New Millennium," *Southern California Quarterly* 79, 3 (Los Angeles: HSSC, 1997): 284–86.

comfortable pews in the church, and listen to per-fectly reproduced electronic bell melodies. Under sunny southern California skies, one may stroll through the well-manicured gardens, ornamented by strutting peacocks. One can only imagine attend-ing services in the humble church edifice of a much earlier era and hearing the bronze bells toll, amidst the sights, sounds, and smells of bucolic sur-roundings.

Images captured by artists' pen, brush, or camera lens have added another dimension to the experi-ence of the visitor or reader. They show the flow of life and speak of the lives of past inhabitants. They show the birth, breakdown, and near death of an institution. Out of the crumbled adobe and splinters came rebuilding. It is a testament to the resilience and resolve of humankind not to only pre-serve but also to regenerate.

(*above*) Cardinal Timothy Manning, flanked by Auxiliary Bishops John Ward and William Johnson, offers Mass to commemorate the fourth church, which replaced the one destroyed by the 1971 Sylmar earthquake. Photo by Ken Pauley, November 4, 1974. *KEP/ACSFM.*

(*left*) Baptistry and bougainvillea on north side of the church, 1979. Ken Pauley photograph. *KEP.*

(*above*) Newly-completed Archival Center in the west garden. Photo by Ken Pauley, 1982. *KEP.*

(*right*) View of library in the Archival Center. Photo by Ken Pauley, 1986. *KEP/ACSFM.*

(*below*) Document storage and work station in the Archival Center. *ACSFM.*

(*above, left*) Msgr. Francis J. Weber, Cardinal Timothy Manning and Fr. Virgilio Biasiol, O.F.M., pose outside in the west garden.

(*above*) Cardinal Timothy Manning and Msgr. Francis J. Weber stroll along the walkway between the Archival Center and the west wing of the quadrangle (now the mission museum).

(*left*) Sir Daniel J. Donahue, patron of the San Fernando Mission Archival Center, speaks at the dedication on September 13, 1981.

(*left*) On the bright sunny day of the opening of the Archival Center, invited speakers and honored guests celebrate:
(*left to right*) Dr. Martin Ridge, The Huntington Library; Dr. W. N. Davis, Jr., archivist, State of California; Sister Magdalen Coughlin, C.S.J.; Cardinal Timothy Manning, Archdiocese of Los Angeles; Dr. Doyce B. Nunis, Jr., Distinguished Professor Emeritus of History, University of Southern California; Sir Daniel J. Donahue, representing the Dan Murphy Foundation; and Msgr. Francis J. Weber, director of the Archival Center, Mission San Fernando, Mission Hills, California.
*All photos, KEP.*

Ceramic plates and ashtray showing Mission San Fernando.
*From the Michael Patris Collection.*

(*above*) Fray Junípero Serra Memorial Chapel, 1984. *KEP.*

(*right*) Invitation to the dedication of the Fray Junípero Serra Memorial Chapel at San Fernando Mission, Mission Hills. California Services were conducted by His Eminence, Cardinal Timothy Manning, archbishop of Los Angeles, 1984. The invitation and art work on it were created by Dr. Norman Neuerburg. *NN/ACSFM.*

(*opposite, top*) On August 23, 1985, Msgr. Francis J. Weber holds an enlarged version of the new 44-cent Junípero Serra stamp that was issued by the U.S. Postal Service one day previous. Photo by Brian Gadbery of the *Los Angeles Times. Gadbery/ACSFM.*

(*opposite, bottom*) California Mission Studies Association charter members Dr. Norman Neuerburg and Edna Kimbro discuss mission matters in the parking lot of Mission San Fernando at the CMSA conference, 1988. Ken Pauley photograph. *KEP.*

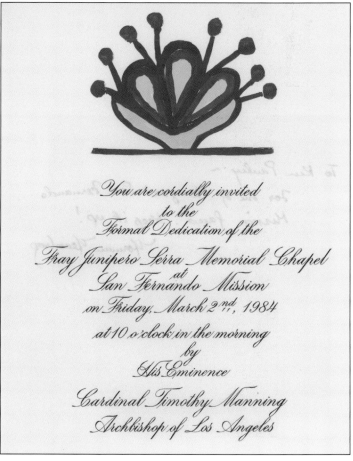

*You are cordially invited
to the
Formal Dedication of the
Fray Junipero Serra Memorial Chapel
at
San Fernando Mission
on Friday, March 2nd, 1984
at 10 o'clock in the morning
by
His Eminence
Cardinal Timothy Manning
Archbishop of Los Angeles*

# APPENDIXES

Oil painting of Saint Ferdinand III. *KEP.*

## APPENDIX A

# FERDINAND III— KING OF SPAIN—THE SAINT

Ferdinand III, king of Spain in the thirteenth century, was the patron of the seventeenth mission in Alta California. His contemporaries were the well-known saints and heroic figures St. Francis of Assisi, St. Dominic of Spain, St. Thomas, St. Bonaventure, St. Elisabeth of Hungary, St. Clara of Assisi, and St. Louis, king of France.

Saint Ferdinand of Spain, the third king of that name, was the son of Alfonso IX, king of Leon, and Doña Berengaria, daughter of Alfonso III, king of Castile. Her sister was Blanche, who became the mother of St. Louis IX, king of France. Ferdinand was born near Salamanca in 1198.

Ferdinand's mother, Queen Berengaria, became the legal heir to the throne of Castile since her father, King Alfonso III of Castile, and his successor—her brother—King Henry I, had died in 1214 and 1217, respectively. She, however, gave up her rights to the throne in favor of her son Ferdinand, who, at the age of eighteen, became Ferdinand III, king of Castile.

Ferdinand's father, Alfonso IX, reigned over Leon, but his son's promotion and now prominence, raised ire in his covetous father. Although relations between them were not harmonious, they nevertheless formed an alliance against the Moors, Muslims who invaded Spain in the eighth century.

Ferdinand was known to be severe in his administration of the law but gentle and forgiving in his personal life. He had many accomplishments: He founded the University of Salamanca and rebuilt the Cathedral of Burgos; funded hospitals, bishoprics, monasteries, and churches; reformed Spanish law; and was an excellent administrator and just ruler.

Ferdinand is better known for his campaigns against the Moors, fighting not to extend his territories but to rescue Christians from subjugation by the infidels, as he called them. He engaged in almost uninterrupted wars for twenty-seven years with the Moors in Spain. When asked by his cousin St. Louis if he would join him on a joint expedition to the Holy Land, he replied: "We do not lack Infidels at home." With a huge army, he was victorious at Baeza and Andújar in Andalusia. After the death of Alfonso IX, he united forces and brought war to Cordova, capturing it in 1236. On the heels of these came victories at Jaén, Murica, Cadiz, and Seville in 1249.

Ferdinand's aim was to liberate Spain from the Moors and to propagate the Christian faith. The Moors had seized a large portion of Spain, but in the end succumbed to the massive armies of the king of Castile and Leon, which had assembled from

FERDINAND III.
Roy d'Espagne
d'Apres Kilyan.

Paris chez Duflos le Jeune, Rue St Victor

A.P.D.R.

(*left*) FERDINAND III—Roy d'Espagne d'Apres Kilyan—Paris chez Duflos le Jeune, Rue St Victor, A.P.D.R. A painting courtesy of James B. Gulbranson. *JBG.*

(*below*) Line drawing of Saint Ferdinand—Ferdinand III, King of Castile and Leon. Inspired by a painting by Murillo. *CHS/TICOR.*

Frieze on a wall in Spain with the inscription "Esta yglesia de Sn Fernando esta unida ala de Sn Juan de Letran de Roma y participa de sus yndulgencias." *KEP.*

Aragon, Navarre, Catalonia, and even from the Muslim kingdom of Granada. All sent him reinforcements. After fierce combat, his coalition overcame Moorish resistance and Ferdinand led his troops into Seville in 1248.

Ferdinand III died on May 30, 1252, while planning to pursue the Muslims into Africa with a flotilla assembled at Biscay. He had a great funeral and pilgrimage, which was participated in by Jews, Muslims, and Christians. He was buried in the cathedral of Seville in the habit of the secular Franciscan Order.

Religious strife and conflict persisted in Spain, however, for another 250 years, with the Jewish and Muslim expulsion completed by 1492 under Ferdinand (The Catholic) and Isabella's reign.

King Ferdinand was beatified on May 31, 1655, by Pope Alexander VII. For his role in defeating the Moors in the south of Spain, he was canonized by Pope Clement X in 1671.

❖     ❖     ❖

Sources: Charles E. Chapman, *A History of Spain* (New York: The Macmillan Company, 1918), 76–77; Jean Descola, trans. from French by Elaine P. Halperin, *A History of Spain* (New York: Alfred A. Knopf, 1963), 151–54; Louis Bertrand and Charles Petrie, *The History of Spain*, 2nd ed. (London: Eyre & Spottiswoode, 1956), 133–35.

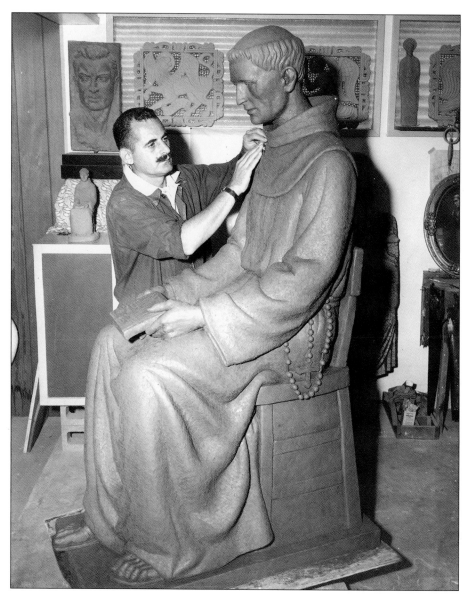

Sculptor Stephen Zakian applies the finishing touches to his statue of
Fray Fermín Francisco de Lasuén, 1955. *SZ/SCP (A-19041).*

# SECOND MISSION *PRESIDENTE* FRAY FERMÍN FRANCISCO DE LASUÉN

THE FOUNDER of Mission San Fernando, Rey de España, was born of Basque descent at Vitoria, in the province of Alava, Cantabria, Spain, on June 7, 1736, to Lorenzo de Lasuén and María Francisca de Arasqueta. At the age of fifteen, Lasuén the son received the Franciscan habit at the Convento de San Francisco, Vitoria, in March 1751 and began studies for the priesthood at Vitoria and later at Aranzazu. Lasuén was recruited by the convento's emissary, Pedro Perez de Mezquía, to work in the Nueva España missions in 1758. Leaving Cádiz on the vessel *El Jason*, he arrived in Vera Cruz, Mexico, in 1760 and entered San Fernando College, Mexico City, where he was ordained to the priesthood in 1761. Fr. Lasuén's native tongue was Basque, and he often complained of his imperfect Spanish. His letters, however, contradict his personal assessment, as his diaries, official reports, and ecclesiastical correspondence were often eloquent.

In 1762 Fr. Lasuén was sent to the Sierra Gorda missions of Querétaro, Mexico, and ministered there until 1767, when he was sent to Lower California to assist mission *presidente* Junípero Serra in taking over the Baja missions, formerly administered by the Jesuits, who had just been expelled from all Spanish dominions. There are no records of his Serra

Gorda labors or adventures, but he left there with Fr. Juan Crespí and arrived in Tepic, where he stayed at the Jaliscan friary of Santa Cruz de Zacate until his departure for Lower California. Under sail from San Blas on the *Concepción*, he arrived in Loreto, Lower California, on April 1, 1768.

Fr. Lasuén went to Misión San Francisco de Borja in the northern peninsula, where he built structures (there were none when he arrived) and faithfully served until 1769. He then traveled to Velicatá (the Franciscan Misión San Fernando established there by Fr. Serra on May 14, 1769) in order to minister to the Portolá expedition encamped there while on their entrada to the north. He returned to Borja and served until 1773, when administrative control was released to the Dominicans, the Franciscans having moved onward to Upper California. Fr. Lasuén awaited Fray Francisco Palóu and Sergeant José Francisco Ortega at Borja. All three departed on the second expedition to San Diego, arriving there on August 30, 1773.

Fr. Palóu, acting as interim president during Serra's absence in Mexico, assigned Fr. Lasuén to Mission San Gabriel, where he remained until 1775. In June of that year he traveled with a pack train to Monterey, escaping an Indian attack along the

(*left*) Sculptor Stephen Zakian makes some adjustments to his statue of Fray Fermín Francisco de Lasuén, while Rev. William Trower holds a painting for the artist to compare, ca. 1955. Photograph courtesy of the Archival Center, San Francisco Mission. *SZ/ACSFM [SCP (A-19040)]*.

(*below*) The life-size statue of Fray Lasuén is ensconced in the west garden at Mission San Fernando, ca. 1957. *ACSFM*.

Santa Barbara Channel that resulted in the death of six Indians in their entourage. They arrived in Monterey on June 25, and Fr. Lasuén began ministering to Capt. Fernando Rivera y Moncada, his soldiers and their families at the presidio.

In 1775, Fr. Serra and Captain Rivera, deciding to establish Mission San Juan Capistrano, sent Fr. Lasuén from Monterey to San Diego. Fr. Lasuén and Fr. Gregorio Amurrió traveled to the spot where the mission was to be founded. Lt. (formerly Sgt.) José Ortega and soldiers arriving from San Diego met the missionaries, who on October 30 raised a cross, hung a bell, and said Mass. Indians to the south caused construction at the new mission to be halted because of their burning of Mission San Diego and the murder of Fray Luís Jayme. Ortega and his men hurried back to San Diego and the missionaries followed. Fr. Lasuén stayed at San Diego without employment until Serra re-established peace at San Diego in the summer, and then re-founded Mission San Juan Capistrano in November 1776.

Lasuén next served short terms at Mission San Gabriel, which he disliked very much, as noted in *Franciscan Missionaries in Hispanic California*, and San Luis Obispo, but Serra redirected Lasuén to serve at Mission San Diego, which he also greatly detested, according to Geiger. He served until October 11, 1785, when he received notification that he had been elevated to the presidency, succeeding Fray Junípero Serra, who had died on August 28, 1784. San Fernando College confirmed Fr. Lasuén's presidency earlier on February 6, 1785, and Fr. Palóu again acted as interim *presidente*, this time in the north in 1785.

It is said that despite Fr. Lasuén's early dissatisfactions, moodiness, discontentment, and eagerness for retirement, out of obedience he persevered in Alta California. As time passed, he proved to be an admirable and capable administrator and spiritual leader. He served an additional eighteen years and founded nine missions, as Serra did, but his mate-

rial and spiritual achievements were substantially larger than those of his predecessor. His mission buildings and expansion projects, including Mission San Fernando, remain to a large extent as we know them today.

From winter 1786 to summer 1797, second mission *presidente* Fr. Lasuén founded seven missions: Santa Barbara (December 4, 1786), La Purísima de Concepción (December 8, 1787), Santa Cruz (August 28, 1791), Soledad (October 9, 1791), San José (June 11, 1797), San Juan Bautista (June 24, 1797), and San Miguel (July 25, 1797). These were founded for the purpose of closing the gaps between existing Alta California missions in the north.

Two gaps remained to be closed in the south, one between San Buenaventura and San Gabriel, and the other between San Juan Capistrano and San Diego. One was filled by Mission San Fernando, Rey de España, founded on September 8, 1797. The other was San Luis Rey Mission, Fr. Lasuén's ninth and last, founded on June 13, 1798.

Fr. Lasuén died at La Misión San Carlos Borromeo de Carmelo (Carmel), on June 26, 1803, and was buried in a stone vault of the sanctuary, closest to the main altar on the gospel side. His remains were discovered with others under heavy debris in 1856. He was exhumed

The fiberglass statue of Fray Fermín Francisco de Lasuén is situated high above Main Street in downtown Ventura. *KEP.*

twice, in 1882 and 1943, and his grave is marked with a stone slab bearing his name.

There are two known statues of Fr. Lasuén in the California Southland. One is a concrete statue that was made by Stephen Zakian in 1955, which stands today in the west garden of Mission San Fernando.

The other statue, a larger-than-life representation made of fiberglass in 1960, stood for almost two decades in front of the administration building at Fermín Lasuén High School, located about a mile from Point Fermín on the Palos Verdes peninsula. The statue remained at the San Pedro, California, high school until its closure at the end of the 1971 academic year. In 1979, the buildings became a senior citizens' home operated by the Little Sisters of the Poor. Before the school's conversion, Cardinal Timothy Manning suggested that the statue be given to the Buenaventura Mission. Around April 1979 it was taken to Ventura and placed atop a pedestal attached to an exterior wall of the hotel adjacent to the Buenaventura Mission. Today this grey-colored statue of Fr. Fermín Francisco de Lasuén gazes down on Main Street in downtown Ventura.

Sources: Francis F. Guest, O.F.M., *Fermín Francisco de Lasuén (1736–1803): A Biography* (Washington, D.C.: Academy of American Franciscan History, 1973); Maynard Geiger, O.F.M., *Franciscan Missionaries in Hispanic California, 1769–1848* (San Marino, Calif.: The Huntington Library, 1969), 136–42.

# APPENDIX C
# FRIARS AND OFFICIATING PRIESTS RESIDENT AT THE MISSION

| Priests | Lifespan | Years at Old Mission San Fernando Rey |
|---|---|---|
| Fray Fermín Francisco de Lasuén | 1736–1803 | Founder, Sept. 8, 1797 |
| Fray Francisco Dumetz | 1734–1811 | 1797–1806 |
| Fray José Antonio de Uría | 1769–1815 | 1806–1808 |
| Fray Pedro Múñoz | 1773–1818 | 1807–1817 |
| Fray José Antonio Urrestí | 1775–1812 | 1808–1812 |
| Fray Joaquín Pascual Nuez | 1781–1821 | 1812–1814 |
| Fray Vicente Pascual Oliva | 1780–1848 | 1814–1815 |
| Fray Marcos Antonio Vitoria[1] | 1760–1836 | 1817–1820 |
| Fray Francisco F. Román de Ulibarri | 1773–1821 | 1819–1820 |
| Fray Francisco Gonzáles de Ibarra[2] | 1782–1842 | 1820–1835 |
| Fray Pedro Cabot | 1777–1836 | 1835–1836 |
| Fray Tomás Eleuterio Esténaga | 1790–1847 | 1836–1837 |
| Fray Blas Ordaz[3] | 1792–1850 | 1837–1847 |
| Reverend José M. Rosales | 1816–1885 | 1848–1849 |
| Reverend Sebastian Bongioanni, sscc | —— | 1849–1850 |
| Reverend Amable Petithomme, sscc | 1796–1860 | 1851–1852[4] |
| Reverend James Burns | 1869–1905 | 1902–1903 |
| Reverend Alexander LeBellegay | 1855–1941 | 1903–1906 |
| Reverend James O'Neill | 1875–1944 | 1906–1907 |
| Reverend Felix Zumarrage, cfm | —— | 1908–1912 |
| Reverend Gerald I. Bergan | 1853–1924 | 1912–1918 |
| Reverend Joseph B. Roure | 1882–1933 | 1918–1922[5] |
| Reverend William Trower | 1911–1995 | 1953–1957 |
| Monsignor Kevin Keane | 1920–1993 | 1957–1961 |
| Reverend James Hanson | 1919–1975 | 1961–1966 |
| Monsignor Carl Gerken | 1921–1982 | 1966–1970 |
| Monsignor Eugene Frilot | 1929– | 1970–1974 |
| Monsignor John Reilly | 1922–1998 | 1974–1979 |
| Monsignor Joseph Cokus | 1933– | 1979–1981 |
| Monsignor Francis J. Weber | 1933– | 1981–[6] |

[1]  Also known as Marcos Antonio Saizar de Vitoria y Odri-
    ozola.

[2]  Also known as Ibarra.

[3]  Fr. Blas Ordaz was the last resident Franciscan priest at Mis-
    sion San Fernando.

[4]  There were no resident priests at Mission San Fernando
    between 1853 and 1902. Occasionally priests attached to the
    Plaza Church of *Nuestra Señora de los Angeles* would come out
    to the mission and officiate.

[5]  The Oblates of Mary Immaculate were assigned to Mis-
    sion San Fernando in 1923. The first to serve under the
    Oblates was Father Charles Siemes. Most notable for his
    restoration efforts was Father Charles Burns (1938–1944).
    Brother James Hart (1874–1959) also served with distinc-
    tion at the mission from 1934 to 1954.

[6]  There were many more resident friars and priests supporting
    ecclesiastic duties than shown here. Only those officiating
    (i.e., in charge) are listed. For a thorough biography of Mis-
    sion San Fernando friars, see Doyce B. Nunis, Jr., "The
    Franciscan Friars of Mission San Fernando, 1797–1847,"
    in *Southern California Quarterly* 79, 3 (Los Angeles: HSSC, 1997):
    217–48.

# GLOSSARY

| | |
|---|---|
| *adelantado* | governor of a frontier province |
| *alta* | above or upper, as in Alta California (U.S. California above approximately the 32.5° parallel) |
| *arriero* | muleteer |
| *asesor* | counselor or legal advisor to the provisional government (as used in text) |
| *asistencia* | sub-mission with resident converted Indians, but no resident missionary or priest |
| *atole* | drink prepared with corn meal gruel |
| *ayuntamiento* | city or borough council |
| *bando* | law or edict from supreme government in Spain |
| *baja* | below or lower, as in Baja California (Mexican California below approximately the 32.5° parallel) |
| *campanil* | bell tower or belfry (also *campanario*) |
| *capilla* | chapel or small church for place of worship |
| *carne seca* | dried beef, jerky |
| *carreta* | cart or wagon, usually a two-wheel ox-drawn cart |
| *cédula* | royal letter, document, or decree |
| *chapulín* (pl *chapulines*) | locust(s) or large grasshopper(s) |
| *chía* | a seed used by the Indians for food and a beverage made from the bush *via columbariae.* |
| *ciénega* | swamp or marsh |
| *convento* | convent or monastery, Fathers' dwelling or Long building (as used in text) |
| *Cortes* | Parliament or Supreme Court in Spain |
| *cuartel* | soldiers' living quarters |
| *cura* | vicar or substitute parish priest |
| *curato* | full-fledged parish |
| *diputación* | Monterey's delegation or Assembly Council |
| *doctrina* | Indian community converted to Christianity but lacking a parish; a semi-parish |
| *encino* | live oak tree (*Quercus agrifolia*) found in the San Fernando Valley |
| *enramadita* | little arbor |
| *entrada* | entry or entrance (Portolá's expedition into Alta California in 1769, as used in text) |
| *españolado* | Spanish-like or pertaining to the customs of Spain |
| *estancia* | cattle ranch, rancho for a mission |
| *fanega* | volumetric measure of capacity equaling about 1.6 U.S. dry bushels |
| *gente de razón* | people of reason—i.e. those who were not Indians, but were primarily Spanish and of mixed blood |
| *granjero* | farmer |
| *habas* | broad beans |
| *iglesia* | church |
| *informe* | report or account (by government as used in text) |

| | |
|---|---|
| *instrucción* (pl *instrucciones*) | written order by local authorities |
| *interrogatorio* | questionnaire, esp. the 1812 series of questions sent to the missionaries regarding cultural life |
| *jabonería* | soap factory or tallow vat |
| *jácal* (pl *jacales*) | hut, shed, or wigwam |
| *legua* | league, a length measuring 5,000 varas, 4,180 meters, or approximately 2.59 English miles |
| *manit* | Gabrielino Indian word for the hallucinatory jimsonweed drug (*Datura wrightii*) |
| *mano* | hand stone for grinding seeds |
| *mayordomo* | steward or administrator, majordomo in English |
| *metate* | grinding stone with concave upper surface |
| *mortero* | mortar bowl for grinding solids |
| *neófito* | neophyte, novice, or beginner |
| *oruga* | caterpillar |
| *peón* | Indian gambling game |
| *permisión* (pl *permisiones*) | permission or authorization, esp. in regard to Spanish land grants |
| *peso de cuero* | leather dollar, i.e., cow hide |
| *pregunta* | question, esp. the request from the official government interrogatorio |
| *ranchería* | collection or a settlement of Indian houses |
| *respuesta* | answer, esp. the response to the official government interrogatorio |
| *sala* | living or drawing room, parlor or large salon |
| *sinodático* | annual donation made to the bishop by priests attending the synods (*sínodos*) |
| *sínodo* | synod, an ecclesiastical governing or advisory council |
| *sitio* | abbreviated reference to *sitio de ganado de mayor*, or one square league (approx. 4,316 acres) |
| *soldado de cuero* | leather-jacketed Spanish soldier |
| *taparabo* | loincloth |
| *toloache* | hallucinatory drug *Datura wrightii* used in the Chinigchinich cult (also jimsonweed) |
| *zaguán* | passageway, portico, or large doorway |
| *zanja* | ditch, trench, or culvert |

❈     ❈     ❈

Reference: *Simon and Schuster's International Dictionary—English/Spanish: Spanish/English*, Tans de Gámez, ed. (New York: Simon and Schuster, 1973).

# ABBREVIATIONS

ABBREVIATIONS in the captions, notes, and bibliography indicate the institutions and individuals who provided photographs, artwork, and other source material used in *An Illustrated History*. Abbreviations also indicate the artists and photographers, and, when information is known, a short biographical sketch is provided. Abbreviations in the captions cross-reference an image by an artist or photographer with the source. Italicized numbers after the biographical sketches or sources are the pages where the images appear for that abbreviation. The words "Courtesy of" are implied in the captions, except in special cases where the source requires credit in a specific format.

**ACSFM**   Archive Center San Fernando Mission, Mission San Fernando, 15151 San Fernando Mission Road, Mission Hills, California 91345. *3, 6, 30, 47, 48, 49, 65, 69, 70, 72, 98, 110, 115, 117, 122, 127, 128, 129, 136, 138, 142, 145, 147, 148, 150, 153, 156, 158, 159, 185, 205, 213, 214, 217, 222, 223, 226, 232, 233, 234, 235, 236, 245, 246, 248, 266, 274, 276, 277, 279, 280, 282, 284, 286, 287, 289, 291, 292, 293, 294, 295, 296, 297, 298, 299, 300, 301, 302, 303, 304, 307, 308, 309, 310, 311, 314, 315, 316, 317, 320, 321, 330.*

**ACV**   Adam Clark Vroman (1856–1916), photographer. Vroman was born on April 15, 1856, in La Salle, Illinois. He started working for the railroad in 1874. For his wife's health they moved to Pasadena, California, in 1892, but there she survived only until 1894. Afterwards, he entered into partnership with J. S. Glasscock and opened a book and photographic supply store. The store has prospered for many years, and Vroman's Bookstore still operates in Pasadena today. Vroman died July 24, 1916, in Altadena, California. Clarity in detail and the sharpness of his Mission San Fernando images attest to this photographer's artistic and technical skills. *92, 98, 161, 176, 181, 193, 194.*

**AD**   Andrew Dagosta (1923– ), painter and watercolorist, was born in Omaha, Nebraska, in 1923. He studied art at Omaha Tech and after graduation served in the 12th Air Force in Italy during World War II. In 1946

he went to Glendale, California, and attended the Hollywood Art Center. He has owned a commercial art studio in Pasadena since 1948. Andy is a founding member of the American Indians and Cowboy Artists (AICA) and the Collegium of Western Art and is a member of the Los Angeles Corral of The Westerners. He and his art were reviewed in *Desert Magazine* in October 1975; among his many awards, Dagosta captured first place at the 1970 Death Valley Open Arts Show. *99, 191.*

**AK**   Anthony Kroll, engraver, produced many engravings for the mission, including labels, wall images, and motifs for Msgr. Francis J. Weber's books on the California missions, and Mission San Fernando's gold embossed logo that is used on stationery and other promotional materials. The Mission San Fernando engraving was made in 1979. (*in photo above:* Anthony Kroll demonstrates usage of a hand-operated printing press at the Archival Center dedication on September 13, 1981. *KEP.*) *3.*

**BA**   Ben (Benjamin) Abril (1923–1995), artist in oils, acrylics, and watercolors, was born in Los Angeles in 1923. After a two-year stay in England with the U.S. Air Force, Abril decided to become an artist. He studied at the School of Allied Arts, Glendale College, and at the Los Angeles Art Center. From 1966 to 1977, he was architectural coordinator for Los Angeles County. He produced many representations of the Bunker Hill area, thirty-six of which are in the collection of the Natural History Museum in Los Angeles County. Abril illustrated children's books for Follett Publishing and also worked as a scenic artist for the film industry. Some of his paintings are in the U.S. Navy collection. The king of Spain has a painting of the San Luis Rey Mission, and the Vatican now has an oil painting of Sallie James Farnham's Serra statue in Brand Park, which was made especially for Pope John Paul II (1987). Ben Abril died in Los Angeles, California, on June 7, 1995.

Ben Abril Collection, mid-twentieth century. Two photographic albums, photographs..6 linear feet (Boxes: ov, half-letter). Photographs of paintings by Ben Abril depict historic buildings and scenes in Los Angeles. Also some publicity (newspaper clippings) connected with his paintings, some of which are in the Museum collections. Also loose b/w and color photos of the artist at work. Found at the Seaver Center for Western History Research, Natural History Museum of Los Angeles County. *228.*

**CCP**   Charles C. Pierce (1861–1946), photographer and photo collector, was born in Massachusetts on November 25, 1861. Arriving in southern California in 1886, he established himself as a professional photographer and collector with an intense interest in the growth of rural Los Angeles. This interest led to his extensive photo documentation of changing residential and business neighborhoods. He purchased other important early photographic collections, notably the substantial George Wharton James collection of Indian images. Pierce often removed the trademarks and made his own negatives from the prints. He sold his entire collection of more than 22,000 photographs and negatives to the Title Insurance & Trust Company in 1941. His collection was bequeathed to the California Historical Society's History Center, Los Angeles, in 1977. Photographs..2 linear feet (Boxes: letter, 5″ × 7″). Photographs of Los Angeles and Southern California found at the Seaver Center for Western History Research, Natural History Museum of Los Angeles County. *18, 19, 79, 87, 94, 107, 117, 134, 144, 152, 170, 171, 175, 181, 211, 223, 288, 289.*

**CEW**   Carleton E. Watkins (1829–1916), photographer, was born on November 11, 1829, in New York State. He came to California in 1851 and studied photography with R. H. Vance in San Jose, California. He actively photographed his subjects up and down the Pacific Coast. He lost his studio and negatives to Isaiah W. Taber in 1876 during an economic downturn. He resolutely set out to make a New Series of California scenes, including the missions of California. Fate was not kind to Watkins, however, as most of this work was lost in the 1906 San Francisco earthquake and fire. Fortunately, four New Series photographs for Mission San Fernando were spared. He died at the Napa State Hospital in 1916. Collection, ca. 1880. New Series—Mission San Fernando, photographs..4 linear feet (Boxes: ov.) found at the Seaver Center for Western History Research, Natural History Museum of Los Angeles County. *100, 106, 118, 131.*

**CFL**   Charles Fletcher Lummis (1859–1928), folklorist and photographer, was born March 13, 1859, in Lynn, Massachusetts. C. F. Lummis is one of the most colorful and influential figures in California history. He was a linguist, folklorist, city librarian, author, ethnographer, and probably best known as a first-rate photographer and California mission restorer. He trekked from Cincinnati, Ohio, on foot across the United States, arriving in Los Angeles on February 1, 1885. Here he contacted Col. Harrison Gray Otis, publisher of the *Los Angeles Times*, to produce a weekly dispatch about events on the walk, which led to his being made city editor of the *Times*. Later, he founded the *Out West* magazine (1886), which became the *Land of Sunshine* (1902). Next, he spearheaded in 1895 the California Landmarks Club (CLC), whose charter was the restoration of missions San Luis Rey (and its asistencia San Antonio de Pala), San Juan Capistrano, and San Fernando. He built his own home at El Alisal with rocks obtained from the nearby Arroyo Seco and commenced work on the Southwest Museum in 1907. From 1896 to the early 1920s he extensively photographed Mission San Fernando. (*in photo above*: Charles Fletcher Lummis in his corduroys, wearing a medal conferred to him by the king of Spain.) *66, 67, 122, 133, 145, 146, 164, 165, 166, 168, 176, 182, 183, 211, 212, 213, 242.*

**CHS**   California Historical Society Collection, currently housed at the University of Southern California. *14, 18, 19, 32, 52, 56, 57, 63, 65, 79, 82, 86, 87, 90, 94, 95, 107, 114, 116, 117, 118, 119, 120, 130, 132, 134, 144, 146, 150, 152, 161, 167, 170, 173, 175, 181, 182, 193, 205, 206, 211, 221, 223, 232, 233, 242, 243, 247, 264, 271, 288, 289, 326.*

**CK**   Charles Koppel (fl. 1853–1865), survey artist and painter, was born in Germany. When Congress authorized a survey of possible railroad routes connecting the Mississippi River to the Pacific coast, Koppel was engaged as the official artist and civil engineer for the California portion of the expedition. The party sailed from New York to San Francisco, arriving in 1853. The survey began in Benicia, just east of San Pablo Bay (near San Francisco), and ended in San Diego. The reports filled twelve volumes and credit Koppel with twenty-one full-page lithographs and twenty-six wood cuts. He is best known for his 1853 view of Los Angeles, which was published in vol. 5, part 1, of the Survey Report. Koppel prepared a sketch of an Indian woman harvesting the fruit of prickly pear at Mission San Fernando. This was made into an engraving by J. W. Orr in Schenectady, New York, in 1853. In 1978, Russell Ruiz used this motif in his oil painting of the San Fernando mission grounds. The only other known work by Charles Koppel is a portrait in oil of his friend Jefferson Davis, who supervised the railroad survey. The portrait was lithographed in 1865. *54.*

**CMSA**    California Mission Studies Association, P.O. Box 3357, Bakersfield, California 93385.

**CW**    Cliff Wrigley, mapmaker, designed and drafted San Fernando Valley maps for the Title Insurance and Trust Company, 1965. *264.*

**DAR**    Daughters of the American Revolution. The DAR was founded in 1890; its headquarters are 1176 "D" St., NW Washington, D.C. 20006. The DAR is a volunteer women's service organization dedicated to promoting patriotism, preserving American history, and securing America's future through better education for children.

As one of the most inclusive genealogical societies in the country, the DAR boasts 170,000 members in 3,000 chapters across the United States and internationally. Any woman eighteen years or older—regardless of race, religion, or ethnic background—who can prove lineal descent from a patriot of the American Revolution is eligible for membership. DAR members of the San Fernando Valley Chapter published a comprehensive history, *The Valley of San Fernando*, in 1924.

**DSB**    Douglas Scott Bliven, photographer. Honored with the Master of Photography and Photographic Craftsman awards from The Professional Photographers of America Institute, Bliven made two beautiful photographs of the restored west wing and garden, ca. 1960. *302.*

**ED**    Edwin Deakin (1838–1923), landscape, architecture, and still life painter, was born in Sheffield, England, on May 21, 1838. Little is known of his education or art training. He is said to have been a self-taught artist. He came to America in 1856 and settled in Chicago where his professional career began in 1869 with portraits of northern Civil War heroes. In 1870, after he moved to San Francisco and set up his art studio, he became a solid member in the local art scene. He rapidly gained a fine reputation as a painter while exhibiting regularly with the San Francisco Art Association (SFAA) and the Mechanics' Institute Fairs. He joined the

Bohemian Club and became a close associate of Samuel Brookes, with whom he shared a studio. Having developed an early enthusiasm for ruins and historic architecture, Deakin in later years turned to painting these subjects in a style that was termed "romantic, picturesque, and nostalgic" by Paul Mills, curator, Oakland Art museum (see Ruth I. Mahood, *A Gallery of California Mission Paintings by Edwin Deakin*). Most of his paintings are characterized by the skillful rendering of architectural surfaces. Deakin is most famous for his series of twenty-one mission paintings. Off and on between 1870 and 1899, he produced no less than three complete sets of the twenty-one California missions. Two sets in oils are in large format and are nearly identical. One of these, obtained about 1930, is now in the Los Angeles County Museum of Natural History, and the other was brought to light by Howard Willoughby out of the Deakin Estate and now resides at Mission Santa Barbara. A third set, in smaller format and in brilliant watercolors, was produced. From 1887 to 1890 he painted in Europe and exhibited at the Paris Salon. From that time until his death on May 11, 1923, he lived in Berkeley, California, on a large tract of land on which he had built a mission-style studio. *162.*

**EV**    Edward Vischer (1808–1878), artist, publisher, merchant, and real-estate agent, was active in San Fernando from 1852 to 1878. He was born in Regensburg, Bavaria, on April 6, 1808. He received a formal training and became a clerk with an Indian trading company. In 1827 he was sent to Mexico, Central and South America, and finally to California. While in California at the time of secularization, he witnessed the changes coming to the missions, especially to Mission Dolores in San Francisco in 1841. After working most of his life in the shipping services business, Vischer, buoyed by success from some early sketches, turned to artistic endeavors. He created two magnificent colored drawings of Mission San Fernando during his trips to the California missions between 1863 and 1873. Although Vischer was not a photographer, some photographs by Henry T. Payne and William M. Godfrey were erroneously attributed to him, and vice versa. It was common in the early days of photography for real and pseudo-photographers to purchase collections and re-identify them for personal gain. *272.*

**FAP**    Index of American Design: Federal Arts Project (1936–38).

**FHM**    Frederick Hamer Maude (1858–1959), doctor and photographer, was born in Little Mollington, Cheshire, England, in 1858 to a prosperous and distinguished family. Dr. Maude received a medical degree from the University of Aberdeen in 1883, but left the profession in 1883 and arrived in Ventura, California, via Canada, around 1890. He moved to Los Angeles and bought Charles B. Waite's photographic business in 1895, changing its name to F. H. Maude & Co. An accomplished photographer as far back as medical school, Maude made an extensive collection of Southwest scenes including Yosemite, the Grand Canyon, deserts, Zuni and Hopi Indians, and the California missions. Maude worked with George Wharton James, perhaps as a partner. He died at the Los Angeles County Hospital on October 4, 1959, a month short of his 101st birthday.

F. H. Maude Original Print Collection, ca.1890–1920. Photographs..4 linear feet (Boxes: letter). Includes Mt. Lowe, Los Angeles, Redlands, Catalina Island, agricultural scenes, and Missions Santa Barbara and San Fernando. For original Maude negatives, see P-2.2. For an album of Maude prints of Southwest Indians, see P-100. For an album of Maude prints of California Missions, see P-132. Photograph Album of California Missions, circa 1890s. Album..2 linear feet (Boxes: flat letter) Thirty-three photographs of California missions including San Diego, San Luis Rey, San Juan Capistrano, San Gabriel, San Fernando, Santa Barbara, and Carmel. Some of the prints have Maude's name on them. For original Maude photographs, see P-99.

Photographic resources, indicated by P-#s shown above, may be found at the Seaver Center for Western History Research, Natural History Museum of Los Angeles County. *29, 119, 120, 222, 304.*

**FLP**　Frank L. Park, photographer, operated at his Frank L. Park & Company in Los Angeles, with a studio at 211 West First Street (1898), at 609 East Sixth Street (1899–1900), and at 37 South Raymond Avenue, Pasadena (1900). His last studio was at 120½ South Spring Street, Los Angeles (1902–03).

Frank L. Park Collection, c. 1900. Photographs..2 linear feet (box: half-letter), found at the Seaver Center for Western History Research, Natural History Museum of Los Angeles County. *289.*

**FP**　Francis Parker, photographer, established his first studio at 523 Kearny Street, San Francisco, in 1871 and later at 740 5th Street, Los Angeles, Downey Block, and was partner in Parker & Hasselman in 1878–80. Parker also operated as Tuttle & Parker, a studio in San Diego in the 1880s, and as Parker & Parker & Company, Parker & Judd, and Parker & Son, West Side 5th Street between F and G Streets, starting in 1895. *127.*

**FQN**　Frank Q. Newton, Jr. (1921–2004), instrument maker and photographer, was born in Illinois in 1921.

He arrived in the San Gabriel Valley with his family after graduating from high school in 1939. In 1941 Newton worked on airplane flight test equipment and developed a strong interest in western history and photography. From his western U.S. travels, he accumulated an archive of thousands of large- and 35mm-format images. Frank took the photograph of Dr. Norman Neuerburg seen in the Dedication. *6.*

**GEM**　G. E. Moore, photographer, was active in Lakeport, 1887–93. *86.*

**GGJ**　G. G. Johnson, photographer, made a classic photograph of an elderly Indian woman and her daughter at their adobe home near Mission San Fernando. *52.*

**GH**　Geoffrey Holt (1883–1977), landscape, still life and architectural detail artist, was born in England in 1883. He lived in Minneapolis during WWI as a designer with the John S. Bradstreet Co. (furniture and interiors). By 1921 he was living in San Francisco, and in the 1930s moved to Los Angeles. He painted landscapes in oils and watercolors in the realistic manner of the English School. For Mission San Fernando, Holt made many mission drawings of walls, doors, and windows for the Index of American Design Federal Arts Project, 1939–41. He received a Special Mention Award at the Minnesota State Fair in 1915. He later moved to Long Beach, where he lived until his death in 1977. Two of his California mission paintings, ca. 1910, are in the collection of the Society of California Pioneers, and a Grand Canyon landscape is in the Santa Fe Railway Collection. *304.*

**GHZ**　George Hazard, view photographer, was active in southern California ca. 1908. Hazard negatives are in a collection owned by Ernest Marquez, Canoga Park. This collection of negatives is mostly of Santa Monica Canyon, Malibu, Palos Verdes, and Los Angeles, but also includes the Yorba Adobe in Orange County. Hazard negatives were typically inscribed in ink, in Hazard's recognizable handwriting. For the images he made of Mission San Fernando, his descriptions were oftentimes inaccurate and inappropriate. *136, 136, 155, 233, 244.*

**GWJ**　George Wharton James (1858–1923), author, lecturer, and photographer, was born in Gainsborough, England, on September 27, 1858. He made his home in Pasadena and was active in promoting and writing about the West and Southwest. He was noted for his photographs of California Indians (the collection that Charles C. Pierce acquired) and missions. He was a part of the Arroyo committee with colleagues C. F. Lummis, James Blanchard, Charles C. Pierce, Frederick H. Maude, and others. *80, 118, 193.*

**HAP** Harold A. Parker (1878–1930), commercial photographer, filmmaker, and adventurer. He was fourteen years old when his family moved from Iowa to Pasadena in 1892. The next year he was enrolled at Throop Polytechnic Institute (the forerunner of Caltech), where he demonstrated an aptitude for things mechanical. A course in photography led to his experimentating with the medium. In 1900 he went into business; in 1904 he opened his studio in a pair of rooms at 54 East Colorado Boulevard and was soon supplying images to a wide variety of clients. Parker also dabbled in films, providing still footage for the Nevada Motion Picture Company, but his Pasadena-based operation unfortunately burned down in 1917. Parker's adventurous spirit was detailed in local news accounts. Whether he was floating over the San Gabriel Mountains in a hot air balloon or hovering over the Huntington Hotel as a passenger on the inaugural flight of Roy Knabenshue's famous dirigible, Parker went to extraordinary lengths to get the best shot. In addition to making the earliest aerial photographs of Pasadena's local environs—the orange groves, the open fields and residences—he also made extraordinary panoramic views of the mountains near Lake Tahoe. Harold Parker's prodigious career was cut short by his untimely death in 1930 at the age of fifty-two. Parker's remaining negative archive was donated by Parker's son, Donald, to the Huntington Library in 1999. *81.*

**HCF** Henry Chapman Ford (1828–1894), painter, sketcher, and etcher, was born in Livonia, New York, on August 6, 1828. Ford studied art in Paris and Florence (1857–60), then served in the Civil War, during which time he provided sketches for the pictorial press. Due to a physical disability, he served only one year in the war and, upon discharge, moved to Chicago, where he became the city's first professional landscape painter. While in Chicago, he helped found the Academy of Design and served as its president for several years. Most of his early work was destroyed when the academy burned down in 1871. Due to failing health, he was forced to seek a milder climate. In 1875 he moved to California with his wife Helen and settled in Santa Barbara, where he spent the rest of his life. His horse-and-buggy trips to the twenty-one California mission sites, gave him inspiration to create a portfolio of watercolors, oils, and etchings that are important historically. In 1883, he published *Etchings of the Franciscan Missions of California* and in 1893 exhibited this work at the Chicago World's Fair. His paintings and etchings of the missions were responsible for the revival of interest in California's Spanish heritage and indirectly for the restoration of the missions. When he was not sketching and painting in his travels, he taught art in Santa Barbara until his death on February 27, 1894. *104, 113, 115, 191.*

**HF** Hervé Friend, photo-engraver and mission photographer, was active from the 1860s (he was listed in Gloucester, Massachusetts, in the business directory of 1865) to the 1890s in Los Angeles. He established himself at 314 West First Street, Los Angeles, as "H. Friend—photo engraver," ca. 1895. He did some work for *The Land of Sunshine* magazine and knew Charles F. Lummis, George W. James, and others. *173.*

**HFR** Henry France Rile Collection, early twentieth century. Photographs, negatives..1 linear foot (Boxes: 5″×7″, half-letter). Views include southern California, particularly Santa Monica, taken by Rile. Collection is at the Seaver Center for Western History Research, Natural History Museum of Los Angeles County. *174.*

**HFW** Henry F. Whithey, mission photographer, ca. 1936. *145, 190.*

**HHF** Henry ("Harry") Fenn (1845–1911), scenic topographical painter, illustrator, and etcher, was born in Richmond, Surrey, England, on September 14, 1845. He was trained as a wood engraver before coming to the U.S. in 1855. After studying art in Italy, he became one of the nation's leading book illustrators and traveled widely in Europe and the U.S. Illustrations of his watercolors of California appeared in William Cullen Bryant's *Picturesque America* (1872), *Picturesque California* (1888), and *Century Magazine* (1891). Fenn was one of the founders of the American Watercolor Society, Society of Illustrators, and Salmagundi Club. Maintaining a studio in New York City, Fenn was a long-time resident of Montclair, New Jersey, and exhibited at the National Academy of Design and the American Water Color Society. One of his most well-known works was "View of the Colt Residence," which featured the home of the famous arms manufacturer, Samuel Colt. He died at Montclair, New Jersey, on April 21, 1911. *247.*

**HL** The Huntington Library, 1151 Oxford Road, San Marino, California 91108. *62, 67, 126, 131, 134, 173, 175, 198, 217, 219, 289.*

**HM** Henry Miller, topographical artist. Miller sketched California towns and missions in 1856–57. These sketches were reproduced in *Account of a Tour of the California Missions, 1856* (Grabhorn Press, 1952), and in *Thirteen California Towns from the Original Drawings* (Book Club of California, 1947). While the proportions in his sketches were often inaccurate, his drawing and shading were well executed. His works are rare and of great historical importance. *74.*

**HPW** Hugh Pascal Webb (1876–1960), photographer, was born in Mentmore, Buckingham, England, June 2, 1879. He was married to Edith Buckland Webb, and was noted for photographs he made for his wife's classic book *Indian Life at the Old Missions* (1952). He died in Los Angeles, California, on August 8, 1960. *279.*

**HSSC** Historical Society of Southern California, 200 East Avenue 43, Los Angeles, California 90031.

**HTP** Henry T. Payne (ca. 1845–?), photographer, lived on 6th Street in Los Angeles, California, in June 1880. He specialized in stereographs under the name "H.T. Payne, Semi-Tropical California Views." He was probably the first to go outside of Los Angeles to photograph the suburbs, Santa Monica being his favorite locale. He showed his slides at the Philadelphia Exposition of 1876, thereby advertising southern California to the rest of the country. *130, 150, 216, 232.*

**IWT** Isaiah West Taber (1830–1912), daguerreotypist, ambrotypist, photographer, sketch artist, and dentist, was born in New Bedford or Fairhaven, Massachusetts, on August 17, 1830. He went to sea at the age of fifteen and spent several years working on whaling ships in the North Pacific. In 1850 he came to California, where he spent four years working first as a miner, then as a farmer. In 1854 Taber returned to New Bedford, where he studied dentistry and began a dental practice. His interest in amateur photography eventually turned into a career. He settled in Syracuse, New York, where he opened his first studio. In 1864 he returned to California persuaded by photographers Henry W. Bradley and William H. Rulofson, for whom he worked until at least 1869. In 1871 Taber established the "Taber Gallery" at No. 12 Montgomery Street in 1871. His highly successful business was well-known for portraiture and a vast stock of California and Western views (many of which were the unacknowledged works of other photographers). Taber had the good fortune, during the winter of 1875–76, to acquire the entire Carleton E. Watkins Collection, which was lost in a foreclosure that included all of *Watkins' Pacific Coast View* negatives, and his photographic equipment. Taber, with the help of financier John Jay Cook, took over the Watkins Yosemite Art Gallery in 1876. Taber enjoyed much success in California and abroad: he was awarded the photographic concession of the Midwinter Fair of 1893–94 in San Francisco; he was sent to London in 1897 to photograph the pageant of the Queen Victoria Jubilee; and he was commissioned to photograph King Edward VII. In 1906 the San Francisco earthquake and fire destroyed his entire collection of glass plates, view negatives, and portraits on glass. Fortunately, several important mission photo-graphs survived. Taber did not rebuild his business and died of heart failure on February 22, 1912. *85, 116, 131.*

**JBB** James B. Blanchard, stereographer and photographer. He was listed in the sophisticated Callerman catalogues as active in the 1890s–1910s. He was in partnership with Konold (Los Angeles, 1902, at 513 North Main and 213½ North Spring) and Charles C. Pierce, at various times in his career. *67.*

**JBG** James B. Gulbranson, photo collection. P.O. Box 8055, Van Nuys, California 91409-8055. *54, 85, 99, 113, 149, 185, 189, 191, 241, 272, 326.*

**JGS** Jasper G. Schad (1932–), Dean Emeritus of Libraries at Wichita State University and photographer. He was previously at California State University, Northridge, California, where he taught U.S. History. In mid- to late 1949, Dr. Schad made an extensive set of mission photographs during reconstruction of the west wing of the quadrangle at Mission San Fernando. The reconstruction work was funded by the William Randolph Hearst Foundation. He is currently working on a social history of art in southern California from 1915 to 1930. *286, 287, 298, 301.*

**JRP** John R. Putnam and W. S. Valentine Studio, stereo photographers. The studio was active in Los Angeles, ca. 1898–1912. John R. and Arion Putnam, commercial photographers, were also partners with a studio at 79 Temple Block, junction of North Spring and Main, Los Angeles, 1895–1902.

**JV** Jim Valtos (1934–), artist, furnished fine-line ink drawings of Mission San Fernando, 1979. He studied at the Art Center of Los Angeles and worked professionally at Litton Industries and RCA. *83, 108, 140, 141.*

**KEP** Kenneth E. Pauley (1938–), aerospace engineer, mission photographer, author, and editor, produced the *California Missions Calendar* with Ernest Marquez (AllState Savings & Loan, 1978); postcards for the Mission San Fernando gift shop (1977–1979); miniature book *The California Missions—Then and Now* (1985) with coauthor Ernest Marquez; editor for Brand Book No. 20, *Rancho Days in Southern California—An Anthology with New Perspectives*, Los Angeles Corral of The Westerners (1997); author of the four-part series *Weights and Measurements in California's Mission Period* for the California Mission Studies Association. *2, 6, 17, 20, 29, 44, 58, 70, 71, 79, 83, 84, 88, 89, 95, 97, 99, 100, 102, 103, 108, 114, 125, 127, 133, 136, 140, 141, 153, 155, 159, 161, 169, 177, 178, 179, 180, 183, 186, 187, 190, 192, 204, 208, 210, 215, 216, 224, 225, 227, 230, 235, 236, 237, 238, 239, 240, 244, 248, 249, 266, 282, 283, 290, 291, 296, 304, 306, 307, 312, 315, 316, 317, 318, 320, 321, 324, 327, 337, 338, 343.*

**KK**   K. Kaminsky, photographer, 1961, who took the photographs of Stephen Zakian and the Reverend William Trower, while the sculptor was constructing the concrete statue of Fray Fermín Francisco de Lasuén in 1955. *217, 291.*

**KPS**   Keystone Photo Service, Inc., Los Angeles photo studio. Photographs made at Mission San Fernando were taken by Keystone after the Sylmar earthquake in 1971 (unknown photographer).

Keystone Photo Service, Inc. Photograph Albums of Scenes of Southern California, ca. 1920. Ten (10) vols. (in 7 boxes); 34 × 55 cm, shows animals in southern California. Found at the Seaver Center for Western History Research, Natural History Museum of Los Angeles County. *128, 129, 248, 307, 315.*

**LAA**   Lopez Adobe Archives, 1100 Pico Street, City of San Fernando, California 91340. Photographic collection is held in trust by the San Fernando City Historical Commission, 117 MacNeil Street, San Fernando, California 91340. *38, 39, 73, 87, 88, 151, 157, 160, 174, 183, 184, 196, 205, 212, 213, 218, 220, 225, 229, 233, 268, 269, 270, 280, 297.*

**LACMNH**   Los Angeles County Museum of Natural History, History Collections, 900 Exposition Blvd., Los Angeles, California, 90007. Edwin Deakin oil painting, courtesy of LACMNH. *162.*

**LAPL**   Photo Collection/Los Angeles Public Library, 630 W. Fifth Street, Los Angeles, California 90071. *73, 112, 114, 123, 222.*

**LBR**   Lawrence B. Robinson Collection, Los Angeles, California. Henry Chapman Ford oil painting of Mission San Fernando was provided courtesy of Dr. and Mrs. Lawrence B. Robinson. *104.*

**LU**   Larry Underhill (1952–), commercial photographer, was born in Burbank, California. He attended the Art Center College of Design, Pasadena, receiving his Bachelor of Fine Arts in photography in 1976. He began work at Garrett AiResearch in February 1977, where he worked as a staff photographer until 1999. He photographed two historical views at the Bicentennial Celebration for Mission San Fernando, in front of the convento. The event took place on Saturday, September 8, 1997, two days before the actual date. The San Fernando Police bicyclists were helpful in blocking off San Fernando Mission Road, thereby enabling the photographer to make these images. *169, 192.*

**MRH**   Mark R. Harrington (1882–1971), curator of the Southwest Museum, restorer of Mission San Fer-

nando in the 1930s and 1940s, historian, writer, photographer, and husband of Marie Harrington, née Walsh, author of *The Mission Bells of California.*

**MS**   Merge Studios, photo studio. Studio photographers prepared two photographs of Mission San Fernando for the Department of Water and Power (#1885–53 and –54). The first was the west wing of the quadrangle after the 1938–1954 work had been completed; the second was the seminary, which was built approximately where the east wing originally stood. *286, 287.*

**MWH**   Marie Harrington, née Walsh (1907–1986), wife of Dr. Mark R. Harrington, bell expert and collector, Mission Hills, California. Her collection is now at the Archive Center San Fernando Mission (ACSFM), Mission Hills, California. *245, 246, 249, 279, 294, 296, 297.*

**NN**   Norman Neuerburg (1926–1997), mission art historian, art professor, collector. Photo collection is now at the Santa Barbara Mission Archive-Library (SBMAL), Santa Barbara, California. *320.*

**RN**   Rexford Newcomb, professor of the History of Architecture, University of Illinois, architectural draftsman, map artist (Mission San Fernando church), and author of *The Old Mission Churches and Historic Houses of California*, 1925. *148, 216.*

**RR**   Russell A. Ruiz (1925–1988), sketcher, fine-line ink artist, and painter, was born in California on September 3, 1925. He was a graduate of Brooks Institute of Photography. While serving overseas in the Navy, he became afflicted with muscular dystrophy and was brought back to the United States in 1949. In military service he prepared numerous sketches of strategic Navy sites in isometric view, where his only inputs were aerial plan view photographs. In 1977 this author consigned his artist-friend to paint and ink sketch three views of 1830s Mission San Fernando. One oil painting and two fine-line ink sketches were completed in 1978. Russell lived in Santa Barbara, California, with his wife, Alice, and son, Russell Clay, until his death on June 25, 1988. (*in photo above*: Russell Ruiz in 1979. Russell made an oil painting and three fine-line sketches of the mission complex and Santa Barbara ranchería "Mispu" for the authors in 1978. *KEP*.) *44, 95, 97.*

**SBHS**   Santa Barbara Historical Society, 136 East De La Guerra, Santa Barbara, California 93101. *124.*

**SBMAL**    Santa Barbara Mission Archive-Library, Old Mission Santa Barbara, 2201 Laguna Street, Santa Barbara, California 93105. *46, 98, 191.*

**SBMNH**    Santa Barbara Museum of Natural History, 2559 Puesta del Sol Road, Santa Barbara, California 93105.

**SBTHP**    Santa Barbara Trust for Historic Preservation, 123 East Canon Perdido Street, P.O. Box 388, Santa Barbara, California 93102-0388.

**SCP**    SC Photos—University Photographer, University of Southern California, Los Angeles. *328, 330.*

**SCVHS**    Santa Clarita Valley Historical Society, P.O. Box 221925, Newhall, California 91322-1925.

**SCWHR**    Seaver Center for Western History Research, Natural History Museum of Los Angeles County, 900 Exposition Boulevard, Los Angeles, California 90007. *92, 121, 176, 181, 193, 194, 216.*

**SFVHS**    San Fernando Valley Historical Society, Andrés Pico Adobe—Box 7039, 10940 Sepulveda Boulevard, Mission Hills, California 91346. *6, 189, 191, 252, 268, 305.*

**SMRC**    South Western Mission Research Center, *SMRC—Newsletter,* Arizona State Museum, The University of Arizona, Tucson, Arizona 85721-0026; P.O. Box 213, Tumacácori, Arizona 85640.

**SPNBP**    Security Pacific National Bank Photographic Collection, Los Angeles, California (now at the Los Angeles Public Library). *73, 112, 114, 123, 222.*

**SWM**    Southwest Museum, Braun Research Library, P.O. Box 41558, Los Angeles, California 90041-0558. *18, 26, 27, 28, 59, 65, 66, 67, 68, 80, 81, 86, 112, 116, 118, 119, 121, 122, 130, 133, 142, 145, 146, 154, 161, 164, 165, 166, 168, 170, 171, 172, 173, 176, 177, 179, 182, 183, 193, 206, 211, 218, 219, 222, 242, 243, 246, 290, 304.*

**SZ**    Stephen Zakian (1918–1969), sculptor who lived in Inglewood, California. Zakian created a concrete statue of Fr. Fermín de Lasuén in 1955. In 1964 Zakian executed the bronze bust of dentist Dr. Waldon I. Ferrier, which was formally presented to the School of Dentistry, University of Washington, in May. Zakian died in Los Angeles on January 1, 1969. *328, 330.*

**TG**    Troy Greenwood (1953–), draftsperson and artist. Troy made beautiful reproductions of architectural drawings of Mission San Fernando, which were originally made for the Historic American Building Survey and prepared by the U.S. Department of the Interior Office of National Parks, Buildings and Preservation Branch of Plans and Design, Survey No. 37-5, 1936. The original architectural drawings were used with the Index of American Design Federal Arts Project by Dr. Mark R. Harrington and Father Charles Burns, ca. 1936–41. *61, 76, 77, 78, 186, 187, 306.*

**TICOR**    Title Insurance and Trust Company— Research Photo Collection, Los Angeles, California. Collection is now at CHS, housed at the University of Southern California. *14, 18, 19, 32, 52, 56, 57, 63, 65, 79, 82, 83, 86, 87, 90, 94, 95, 107, 114, 116, 117, 118, 119, 120, 130, 132, 134, 144, 146, 150, 152, 161, 167, 170, 173, 175, 181, 182, 193, 205, 206, 211, 221, 223, 232, 233, 242, 243, 247, 264, 271, 288, 289, 326.*

**TJT**    Thomas J. Taylor, artist who worked on the Index of American Design: Federal Arts Project. *246.*

**UCB**    University of California, Berkeley, The Bancroft Library, Berkeley, California, 94720-6000. *56, 74, 85, 116, 131, 247.*

**UCLA**    University of California, Los Angeles, Department of Special Collections, Charles E. Young Research Library, Box 951575, Los Angeles, California 90095-1575. *64, 72, 96, 100, 106, 118, 124, 130, 137, 143, 158, 174, 195, 219, 223, 285.*

**USC**    Regional History Collection of the Doheny Memorial Library, housed at the University of Southern California/ARC, Los Angeles, California 90089-0182. *56, 57, 83.*

**WA**    William Adam (1846–1931), painter, born in Tweedmouth, England, on August 29, 1846. Adam studied under Delecluse in Paris, with Brydall and Greenless in Glasgow, and had some training in Buenos Aires before emigrating to Boston, Massachussetts, in the latter part of the nineteenth century. He moved to California in 1894 and settled in Pacific Grove on the Monterey Peninsula. Known as "Professor" Adam, he gave art lessons in his rose-covered cottage at 450 Central Avenue. He specialized in views of the Monterey area, such as sand dunes and cottage and garden scenes, etc. Not much is known of his mission paintings except for his ca. 1919 oil rendition of the convento at Mission San Fernando showing the two doors at the west end, blocked in after at least fifty years of use. Adam died in Pacific Grove on October 17, 1931. *121.*

**WCD**    Warren C. Dickerson (1853–1936), commercial photographer, worked for postcard companies and did photography around the country. About one-third of his negatives are images of California and are in the

Seaver Center's collection. The center has postcard albums and negatives. Warren C. Dickerson (1853–1936) Collection, ca.1890s–1920. Postcard albums, negatives..55.2 linear feet (Boxes: 5″ × 7″, ov.). Included are several postcard albums arranged geographically by state and locality. Found at the Seaver Center for Western History Research, Natural History Museum of Los Angeles County. Many of Dickerson's negatives and prints, especially those of Mission San Fernando, are also housed at the Southwest Museum. *68, 145, 154, 177, 179, 218, 219, 243, 290.*

**WDW** Wayne C. "Dick" Whittington (1896–1985), photographer, was born in California on March 13, 1896. He founded "Dick" Whittington Studio in 1924. He cleverly named his studio after the fourteenth-century Lord Mayor of London with the legendary cat. For two decades the studio was southern California's leading commercial photographic studio. Whittington photographed nearly every major business and manufacturer in the area. Among the long list of his firm's clients were Ford Motor Co., Gilmore Oil, See's Candies, Maddux Airlines, The Broadway Department Stores, and developers Marlowe-Burns. The studio photographed Los Angeles as it grew, including some historic landmarks, such as the Mission at San Fernando, ca. 1940. Whittington died in Los Angeles, California, on March 22, 1985. *280.*

**WGP** William M. Graham Photos. Graham, a photographer, was a partner in Graham & Morrill Photography, Los Angeles, California (1897–98). He moved his studio from 119 South Spring Street (1897) to 125½ Spring Street (1898), where he became the sole proprietor, operating as the Graham Photo Company (1899–1905). *126, 134, 175, 217, 219, 289.*

**WHF** William H. Fletcher, view photographer, arrived in Los Angeles in 1885 from Vermont. At least three *cartes-de-visite* of Mission San Fernando are known to be made by Fletcher. *88.*

**WMG** William Mollock Godfrey (ca. 1825–1900), daguerreotypist, photographer, and dentist, was probably born near Minisink, New York, around 1825. Godfrey studied dentistry and briefly practiced as a dentist in Ann Arbor until 1850. He learned the techniques of daguerreotype in Michigan. In early spring 1850, Godfrey joined a wagon train and arrived in Hangtown (now Placerville), California, in the fall. Unsuccessful at placer mining, he turned to photography. He leased and then purchased a daguerreotype camera, traveling up

and down the state taking photographs. He briefly settled in Los Angeles, where he took many stereographic views of Los Angeles and southern California in the 1860s and 1870s. While he was in Los Angeles, he was associated at various times with photographers Stephen A. Rendall and Henry T. Payne (the Sunbeam Gallery). He produced an extraordinary number of photographs of Los Angeles, Santa Monica, Wilmington Harbor (now San Pedro), San Diego, and the missions (including Mission San Fernando). He established a business for photographic services in Watsonville for a short time. He then returned to Los Angeles. In 1865 he moved to San Bernardino, where he began a short-lived gallery with M. A. Franklin. He returned to dentistry shortly thereafter and was married in 1866, remaining in San Bernardino. In 1869 he moved to 2nd and San Pedro Streets in Los Angeles and became a photo-journalist. On a trip to San Diego, he took pictures of New Town and at least one mission. In 1870 he photographed the first locomotive of the Los Angeles and San Pedro Railroad and made photos for the U.S. Army Corps of Engineers on contract. Godfrey opened a "New and Elegant Photographic Gallery" (The Sunbeam Gallery) in the Temple Block, Los Angeles, and traveled to local Southland ranchos to take pictures. In late 1872 he went into partnership with Dudley P. Flanders, Los Angeles, but in 1875 he returned to San Bernardino. He lived until on or about November 4, 1900, when he died from injuries suffered in a fall. He is buried at the Pioneer Cemetery in San Bernardino. See **HTP** (Henry T. Payne). *150, 216.*

**WPB** William Phipps Blake (1825–1910), sketch artist and illustrator, was born in New York City on June 21, 1825. Educated as a mineralogist and chemist, he served as geologist for the U.S. Railroad Survey team in southern California, which was headed by Lt. Robert Stockton Williamson, from 1853 to 1856. His reporting included sketches and woodcut illustrations of the California deserts, Sierra Nevada mountains, scenes of the city of San Diego and its bay, and several southern California missions. Blake's sketch of the San Fernando Valley was made into a tinted lithograph and is found in the *Geological Report on the Exploration in California for Railroad Routes*, Plate VI. From 1895 to 1905 Blake became professor of mineralogy and geology at the School of Mines, University of Arizona. Later he taught at the University of California, Berkeley, until shortly before his death on May 22, 1910. *99.*

# BIBLIOGRAPHY

### Books

Bancroft, Hubert Howe. *History of California*, 7 vols. San Francisco: A.L. Bancroft and Company, Publisher, 1884.

Bearchell, Charles A., and Larry D. Fried. *The San Fernando Valley—Then and Now*. San Fernando, Calif: Windsor Publications, Inc., 1988.

Beebe, Rose Marie, and Robert Senkewicz, eds. *Lands of Promise and Despair: Chronicles of Early California, 1535–1846*. Santa Clara, Calif: Santa Clara University; Berkeley, Calif: Heyday Books, 2001.

Berger, John A. *The Franciscan Missions of California*. New York: G.P. Putnam's Sons, 1941.

Bolton, Herbert Eugene. *Fray Juan Crespi: Missionary Explorer on the Pacific Coast 1769–1774*. Berkeley, Calif: University of California Press, 1927.

Boscana, Gerónimo. *Chinigchinich, Historical Account of the Belief, Usage, Customs and Extravagancies of the Indians of this Mission of San Juan Capistrano Called the Acagchemen Tribe*. Trans. Alfred Robinson, anno. John P. Harrington. Banning, Calif: Malki Museum Press, 1978.

Britton, N. L., and J. N. Rose, *The Cactaceae: Descriptions and Illustrations of Plants of the Cactus Family*, 4 vols. in 2. New York: Dover Publications, 1963.

Bryant, Edwin. *What I Saw in California*. New York: D. Appleton & Company, 1848.

Castile, George Pierre. *North American Indians: An Introduction to the Chichimeca*. New York: McGraw Hill Book Company, 1979.

Chapman, Charles E. *A History of California—The Spanish Period*. New York: The Macmillan Company, 1926.

Cleland, Robert Glass. *Cattle on a Thousand Hills*. San Marino, Calif: The Huntington Library, 1975.

Clinch, Bryan J. *California and its Missions*, 2 vols. San Francisco: The Whitaker and Ray Company, 1904.

Collins, John A. *San Fernando Rey—The Mission in the Valley*. San Fernando, Calif: San Fernando Printing Co., 1923.

Cook, Sherburne F. *The Conflict Between the California Indians and White Civilization*. Berkeley, Calif: University of California Press, 1976.

Costo, Rupert and Jeannette, eds. *The Missions of California: A Legacy of Genocide*. San Francisco: Indian Historian Press, 1987.

Coues, Elliott. *On the Trail of a Spanish Pioneer: The Diary and Itinerary of Francisco Garcés, 1775–76*. 2 vols. New York: Francis P. Harper, 1900.

Crespí, Juan. *A Description of Distant Roads: Original Journals of the First Expedition into California, 1769–1770*. Trans. and ed. Alan K. Brown. Calexico, Calif: San Diego State University Press, 2001.

Crosby, Harry W. *Gateway to Alta California: An Expedition to San Diego, 1769*. San Diego, Calif: Sunbelt Publications, 2003.

Daughters of the American Revolution. *The Valley of San Fernando*. San Fernando Valley Chapter. San Fernando, Calif: DAR, 1924.

Elder, Paul. *The Old Spanish Missions of California*. San Francisco: Paul Elder & Co., 1915.

Egenhoff, Elizabeth L., ed. *Fabricas*. Sacramento: California State Printing Office, 1952.

Engelhardt, Zephyrin, O.F.M. *Missions and Missionaries of California*, 4 vols. San Francisco: James H. Barry Co., 1912.

———. *Mission San Diego*. San Francisco: James H. Barry Co., 1920.

———. *San Fernando Rey—The Mission of the Valley*. Chicago: Franciscan Herald Press, 1927.

———. *Mission San Gabriel*. San Gabriel, Calif: Mission San Gabriel, 1927.

———. *San Luis Rey Mission—The King of the Missions*. San Francisco: James H. Barry Co., 1921.

———. *San Gabriel Mission—and the Beginnings of Los Angeles*. San Gabriel, Calif: Mission San Gabriel, 1927.

Fages, Pedro. *A Historical, Political and Natural Description of California by Pedro Fages, Soldier of Spain*. Trans. Herbert

Ingram Priestley. Berkeley: University of California Press, 1937.

Fields, Maria Antonia. *Chimes of Mission Bells—An Historical Sketch of California and Her Missions.* San Francisco: The Philopolis Press, 1914.

Forbes, Mrs. A. S. C. *California Missions and Landmarks—El Camino Real.* Los Angeles: copyrighted by A. S. C. Forbes, 1915.

Ford, Henry Chapman. *Etchings of California.* Santa Barbara, Calif: Edward Selden Spaulding, 1961

Geary, Gerald J. "The Secularization of the California Missions (1810–1846)." Ph.D. diss., Washington D.C: Catholic University of America, 1934.

Geiger, Maynard, O.F.M., *Franciscan Missionaries in Hispanic California, 1769–1848.* San Marino, Calif: The Huntington Library, 1979.

Geiger, Maynard, O.F.M., and Clement W. Meighan. *As the Padres Saw Them: The California Indian Life and Customs as Reported by the Franciscan Missionaries, 1813–1815.* Santa Barbara, Calif: SBMAL, 1976.

Gibson, Robert O. *Indians of North America—The Chumash.* New York: Chelsea House Publishers, 1991.

Guest, Francis F., O.F.M. *Fermín Francisco de Lasuén (1736–1803): A Biography.* Washington, D.C: Academy of American Franciscan History, 1973.

Gutiérrez, Ramón A., and Richard J. Orsi, eds. "Contested Eden: California Before the Gold Rush." Special issue of *The Magazine of the California Historical Society* 76, 2–3 (Berkeley: University of California Press, 1997).

Haas, Lisbeth. *Conquests and Historical Identities in California, 1769–1936.* Berkeley: University of California Press, 1995.

Hartnell, William E. P. *The Diary and Copybook of William E. P. Hartnell—Visitador General of the Missions of Alta California in 1839 and 1840.* Trans. Starr Pait Gurcke, ed. Glenn J. Farris. Spokane, Wash: The Arthur H. Clark Company; Santa Clara, Calif: CMSA, 2004.

Heizer, Robert F., ed. *The Destruction of California Indians.* Santa Barbara, Calif: Peregrine Smith, Inc., 1974.

———, and M. A. Whipple. *The California Indians—A Source Book.* Berkeley and Los Angeles: University of California Press, 1951.

Hittell, Theodore. *History of California,* 4 vols. San Francisco: N. J. Stone & Co., 1897.

Holway, Mary Gordon. *Art of the Old World and New Spain and the Mission Days in California.* San Francisco: A. M. Robertson, 1922.

Hughes, Edan Milton. *Artists in California 1786–1940,* 2 vols. 3rd edition. Sacramento, Calif: Crocker Art Museum, 2002.

Hutchinson, C. Alan. *Frontier Settlement in Mexican California: The Hijar-Padrés Colony and Its Origins.* New Haven, Conn: Yale University Press, 1969.

Jackson, Helen Hunt. *Ramona—A Story.* Boston, Mass: Cambridge University Press, John Wilson and Son, 1894.

Jackson, Robert H., and Edward Castillo. *Indians, Franciscans, and Spanish Colonization: The Impact of the Mission System on California Indians.* Albuquerque: University of New Mexico Press, 1995.

Jackson, Robert H. *Indian Population Decline: The Missions of Northwestern New Spain, 1687–1840.* Albuquerque: University of New Mexico Press, 1994.

James, George Wharton. *In and Out of the Old Missions of California.* Boston and Cambridge, Mass: The University Press, 1905.

Jorgensen, Lawrence C., ed. *The San Fernando Valley — Past and Present.* Los Angeles: Pacific Rim Research, 1982.

Keefer, Frank M. *History of San Fernando.* Glendale, Calif: Stevenson Printing Co., 1944.

Kenneally, Finbar, trans. and ed. *Writings of Fermín Francisco de Lasuén,* 2 vols. Washington, D.C: Academy of American Franciscan History, 1965.

Kroeber, Alfred L. *Handbook of the Indians of California.* Smithsonian Institution Bureau of American Ethnology Bulletin 78. Washington, D.C: Government Printing Office, 1925.

La Pérouse, Jean François Galaup de. "The First French Expedition to California." In *Early California Travels Series,* 25. Trans. and ed. Charles N. Rudkin. Los Angeles: Glen Dawson, 1959.

Lauritzen, Jonreed. *The Cross and the Sword.* Garden City, New York: Doubleday & Company, Inc., 1965.

Mahood, Ruth. *Photographer of the Southwest—Adam Clark Vroman, 1856–1916.* Los Angeles: The Ward Ritchie Press, 1961.

———, ed. *Gallery of California Mission Paintings by Edwin Deakin,* Bulletin 3. Los Angeles: L.A. County Museum of Natural History, 1966.

Macauley, Rose. *Pleasure of Ruins.* New York: Barnes & Noble, Inc., 1953.

Manly, William Lewis. *Death Valley in '49: An Important Chapter of California Pioneer History.* Bishop, Calif: Chalfant Press, Inc., 1977. Originally published as *Death Valley in '49.* San Jose, Calif: The Pacific Tree and Vine Co., 1894.

Margolin, Malcolm. *Monterey in 1786: Life in a California Mission—The Journals of Jean François de La Pérouse.* Berkeley, Calif: Heyday Books, 1989.

McCawley, William. *The First Angelinos: The Gabrielino Indians of Los Angeles*. Banning, Calif: Malki Museum Press/Ballena Press Cooperative Publication, 1996.

McGarry, Daniel D. *Educational Methods of the Franciscans in California*, vol. 7, no. 30. Washington, D.C: The Academy of American Friars, 1950.

McGroarty, John Steven. *Mission Memories*. Los Angeles: Neuner Corp., 1929.

Meyer, Michael C., William L. Sherman and Susan M. Deeds. *The Course of Mexican History*. 6th edition. New York: Oxford University Press, 1999.

Miller, Henry. *Account of a Tour of the California Missions, 1856—The Journal and Drawings of Henry Miller*. San Francisco: The Book Club of California, 1952.

Murguía, Alejandro. *The Medicine of Memory: A Mexica Clan in California*. Austin: University of Texas Press, 2002.

Newcomb, Rexford. *The Old Mission Churches and Historic Houses of California—Their History, Architecture, Art and Lore*. Philadelphia, Penn: J. B. Lippincott & Co., 1925.

Newmark, Harris. *Sixty Years in Southern California*. New York: Knickerbocker Press, 1926.

Nostrand, Jeanne Van. Biography of the artist. *Edward Vischer, Drawings of the California Mission, 1861–1878*. Intro. by Thomas Albright. San Francisco: The Book Club of California, 1982. Originally published as *Missions of Upper California, 1872. Notes on the California Missions, a Supplement to Vischer's Pictorial of California, Dedicated to its Patrons*. San Francisco: Winterburn & Co., Printers and Electrotypers, 1872.

Nunis, Doyce B., Jr., ed. *Southern California's Spanish Heritage—An Anthology*. Los Angeles: HSSC, 1992.

Oak, Henry L. *A Visit to the Missions of Southern California in February and March 1874*. Frederick Webb Hodge Anniversary Publication Fund, vol. 11. Highland Park, Calif: Southwest Museum, 1981.

Older, Mrs. Fremont. *California Missions and Their Romances*. New York: Coward-McCann, 1938.

Pitts, Leonard. *The Decline of the Californios*. Berkeley: University of California Press, 1970.

Perez, Crisostomo N. *Land Grants in Alta California*. Rancho Cordova, Calif: Landmark Enterprises, 1996.

Pohlmann, John O. "California's Mission Myth." Ph.D. diss., University of California at Los Angeles, 1974.

Ralston, Jackson H. "Pious Fund of the Californias." In *Foreign Relations of the United States—1902: United States vs. Mexico* (Washington, D.C: Government Printing Office, 1903).

Reynolds, Gerald (Jerry). *Santa Clarita: Valley of the Golden Dream*. Granada Hills, Calif: World Communications, Inc., 1992.

Robinson, Alfred. *Life in California*. New York: Wiley & Putnam, 1846.

Rolle, Andrew. *California, A History*, 4th edition. Arlington Heights, Ill: Harlan Davidson, Inc., 1987.

Sandos, James A. *Converting California: Indians and Franciscans in the Mission, 1769–1836*. New Haven, Conn., and London: Yale University Press, 2004.

Saunders, Charles Francis, and J. Smeaton Chase. *The California Padres and Their Missions*. Boston and New York: Houghton-Mifflin Co., 1915.

Schuetz-Miller, Mardith K. *Building and Builders in Hispanic California, 1769–1850*. Tucson, Ariz: SMRC/Santa Barbara, Calif: SBTHP, 1994.

Simpson, Lesley Byrd. *The Encomienda in New Spain*. Berkeley: University of California Press, 1950.

Smith, Donald E. and Frederick J. Teggart, eds. "Diary of Gaspar de Portolá during the California Expedition of 1769–1770." *Publication of the Academy of Pacific Coast History*, vol. 1, no. 3. Berkeley: University of California Press, 1911.

Smith, Francis Rand. *The Architectural History of Mission San Carlos Borromeo*. Berkeley, Calif: California Historical Survey Commission, 1921.

Sunset Books. *The California Missions: A Pictorial History*. Menlo Park, Calif: Lane Magazine and Book Company, 1974.

Teggart, Frederick J., ed. "The Portolá Expedition of 1769–1770: Diary of Miguel Costansó." *Publication of the Academy of Pacific Coast History*, vol. 2, no. 4. Berkeley: University of California Press, 1911.

Thomas, David Hurst, ed. *Columbia Consequences*, 3 vols. Washington, D.C: Smithsonian Institution Press, 1989–1991.

Thompson, Mark. *American Character: The Curious Life of Charles Fletcher Lummis*. New York: Time Warner Trade Publishing, 2001.

Vischer, Edward. *Drawings of the California Missions, 1861–1878*. San Francisco: The Book Club of California, 1982.

Vroman, Adam Clark. *Dwellers at the Source*. New York: Grossman, 1973.

Walsh, Marie T. *The Mission Bells of California*. San Francisco: Harr Wagner Publishers, 1934.

Webb, Edith Buckland. *Indian Life at the Old Missions*. Los Angeles: Warren F. Lewis, 1952.

Weber, David J. *The Spanish Frontier in North America*. New Haven, Conn: Yale University Press, 1992.

Weber, Francis J. *El Caminito Real—A Documentary History of California's Estancias*. Hong Kong: Yee Tin Tong Printing Press, Ltd., 1988.

————. *El Caminito Real—A Documentary History of California's Asistencias*. Hong Kong: Yee Tin Tong Printing Press, Ltd., 1988.

————. *El Caminito Real—A Documentary History of California's Presidio Chapels*. Hong Kong: Yee Tin Tong Printing Press, Ltd., 1988.

————. *Memories of an Old Country Priest Mission*. Mission Hills, Calif: Saint Francis Historical Society, 2000.

————. *Memories of an Old Mission—San Fernando, Rey de España*. Mission Hills, Calif: Saint Francis Historical Society, 1997.

————. *San Fernando Mission: An Historical Perspective*. Los Angeles: Westernlore Press, 1968.

————. *The Mission in the Valley*. Hong Kong: Libra Press Ltd., 1975

Weinstein, Robert A. and Larry Booth. *Collection, Use, and Care of Historical Photographs*. Nashville, Tenn: American Association for State and Local History, 1977.

Williamson, Robert Stockton. *Report of Explorations in California for Railroad Routes, Explorations and Surveys for a Railroad Route to the Pacific*, vol. 5. Washington, D.C: Government Printing Office, 1853.


## BOOKLETS AND PAMPHLETS

*California Missions*. Riverside, Calif: Glenwood Mission Inn, 1912.

*The Early Pacific Coast Photographs of Carleton Watkins*. Berkeley: University of California Press, Water Resources Archives, 8, 1960.

Harrington, Marie W. *Mission San Fernando: A Guide*. Mission Hills, Calif: San Fernando Valley Historical Society, 1974.

————. *San Fernando Mission*. Thousand Oaks, Calif: Gregor Mendel Botanic Foundation, vol. 1, no. 2, 1974.

Harrington, Mark R. *The Story of San Fernando Mission*. Mission Hills: San Fernando Mission Curio Shop, 1954.

Robinson, W. W. *Fabulous San Fernando Valley*. Los Angeles: Western Federal Savings and Loan Association, n.d.

————. *San Fernando Valley: A Calendar of Events*. Los Angeles: Title Insurance & Trust Co., 1951.

————. *The Spanish and Mexican Ranchos of San Fernando Valley*. Highland Park, Calif: Southwest Museum Leaflet 31, 1966.

————. *The Story of San Fernando Valley*. Los Angeles: Title Insurance & Trust Co., 1964.

Weber, Francis J. *The Ezcaray Altar Pieces at San Fernando Mission*. Mission Hills, Calif: San Fernando Mission, 1997.


## ARTICLES, MAGAZINES, AND PERIODICALS

"Ancient Chapel Given to Mission." *Los Angeles Herald Express*, January 28, 1944.

"Ancient Library Comes to Mission." *Los Angeles Times*, May 26, 1968.

Baker, Charles C. "Mexican Land Grants in California." *Southern California Quarterly* 9, no. 3 (1914): 237.

Barger, William J. "Furs, Hides, and a Little Larceny." *Southern California Quarterly* 85, 4 (winter 2003): 382–412.

Bean, Lowell J., and Charles R. Smith. "Gabrielino." In *Handbook of North American Indians—Volume 8 California*. Washington, D.C: The Smithsonian Institution (1978): 538–49.

California Archives. *State Papers, Missions*, 6: 175.

"Candle Day Service." *Los Angeles Times*, November 7, 1938.

"Candle Rites." *San Fernando Examiner Sun*, November 1, 1937.

"Candle Rites." *San Fernando Sun*, November 2, 1937.

"Carillon." *Santa Monica Outlook*, December 19, 1931.

Carlson, Viola. "Rancho Tujunga, a Mexican Land Grant of 1840." In *Rancho Days in Southern California: An Anthology with New Perspectives*. Ed. Kenneth Pauley. Brand Book No. 20 Los Angeles: The Westerners—Los Angeles Corral, 1997, 62–79.

"Chapel Bulldozed." *Los Angeles Times*, April 4, 1974.

"Chapel Demolition Started." *Van Nuys News*, April 24, 1973.

"Club Saves San Fernando Mission." *San Fernando Valley Times*, May 30, 1964.

"Completion of Repairs Celebrated at Mission." *Los Angeles Times*, November 7, 1974.

"Club Saves San Fernando Mission." *San Fernando Valley Times*, May 30, 1964.

"Completion of Repairs Celebrated at Mission." *Los Angeles Times*, November 7, 1974.

"Dedication of Restored Monastery Rooms." *San Fernando Sun*, September 27, 1940.

"Dwell Again and Rebuild." *Los Angeles Daily Times*, February 20, 1906.

"Early Days in Los Angeles." *Los Angeles Herald Express*, October 27, 1887.

"Earthquake." *Van Nuys News*, February 20, 1971.

"Field Mass Benefit." *Los Angeles Times*, September 12, 1938.

"Governor's Room Restored." *Los Angeles Times*, June 10, 1943.

Guest, Francis F., O.F.M. "An Examination of the Thesis of S. F. Cook on the Forced Conversion of Indians in the California Missions." *Southern California Quarterly* 61 (spring 1979): 1–77.

———. "An Inquiry Into the Role of the Dicipline in California Mission Life." *Southern California Quarterly* 71 (spring 1989): 1–68.

———. "Cultural Perspectives on California Mission Life." *Southern California Quarterly* 65 (spring 1983): 1–65.

Hass, Lisbeth. "Emancipation and the Meaning of Freedom in Mexican California." *Boletín: The Journal of the California Mission Studies Association* 20, no. 1 (2003): 11–22.

Hamilton, Andy. "Are Our Missions Haunted?" *Los Angeles Times*, 28 March 1937.

Harrington, Marie T. "Site of Water Source Dedicated." *Intake Magazine*. Los Angeles: Department of Water and Power 43, no. 1 (1966): 4.

———. "Early Water Supply." *California Herald*, March 1966.

———. "California's Pioneer Oil Well." *Desert Magazine* (October 1978): 38–40.

Harrington, Mark R. "San Fernando Bells Ring Again." Southwest Museum *Masterkey* 2, no. 2 (1946): 64–6.

"Historic Chapel Falls to Wrecker's Shovel." *Los Angeles Times*, April 24, 1973.

Hoover, Ken. "New Father Looks Down on Ventura." *Ventura Star-Free Press*, April 21, 1979.

"Hotel Planned for Mission Grounds." *San Fernando Sun*, December 14 and 27, 1945.

"Indian Dormitory." *Van Nuys News*, January 1, 1971.

Ivey, James E. "Secularization in California and Texas." *Boletín: The Journal of the California Mission Studies Association*, 20, no. 1 (2003): 23–36.

Jacobs, Julie. "Convento To Be Repaired." *Van Nuys News*, 9 April 1971.

James, George Wharton. "Mission Style in Modern Architecture." *Indoors & Outdoors Magazine* 4, no. 6 (1907): 271–75.

Johnson, John R. "The Indians of Mission San Fernando." *San Fernando Rey de Espana 1797–1997: A Bicentennial Tribute. Southern California Quarterly* 79, no. 3 (1997): 249–90.

Layne, J. Gregg. "The First Census of the Los Angeles District—Año 1836." In *Southern California Quarterly* 57, 3 (1936): 193.

Lothrop, Gloria Ricci. "A Pictorial History of Mission San Fernando." In *San Fernando Rey de Espana 1797–1997: A Bicentennial Tribute. Southern California Quarterly* 79, 3 (1997):311–27.

Lovejoy, Ora A. "A Study of Place Names." *Southern California Quarterly* 11, no. 1 (1918): 48.

Lummis, Charles R. "Thus Far and Much Farther: Summary of Landmarks Club Work." *Out West* 19, no. 1 (1903): 7–24.

"Major Restoration Planned for San Fernando Mission." *Los Angeles Examiner*, February 9, 1949.

Merriam, C. Hart. "Village Names in Twelve California Mission Records," in *University of California Archaeological Survey Reports* 74 Berkeley, Calif: University of California Press, 1968, 93–102.

Miller, J. Marshall. "Frémont Memorial Park—Four Early Surveys." *Southern California Quarterly* 15, no. 2 (1932): 280–1.

Mills, Elizabeth T. "Old Indian Paintings at Los Angeles." *Overland Monthly* 36, no. 3 (1901): 766.

"Mission San Fernando." San Francisco *Daily Alta California* (June 26, 1865): p. 1, column 6.

Neuerburg, Norman. "Biography of a Building: New Insights into the Construction of the Fathers' Dwelling, An Archaeological and Historical Resume." *San Fernando Rey de Espana 1797–1997: A Bicentennial Tribute. Southern California Quarterly* 79, no. 3 (1997): 291–310.

———. "The Indian Via Crucis from Mission San Fernando: An Historical Exposition." *Southern California Quarterly* 79, no. 3 (1997): 329–82.

———. "Paintings in the California Missions." *American Art Review* 4, no. 1 (1977).

———. "Henry Chapman Ford, Painter of Early California." *Ventura County Historical Society Quarterly* 41, no. 4 and 42, no. 1 (1966).

Newhall, Ruth W. "El Rancho San Francisco." In *The Newhall Ranch: The Story of the Newhall Land and Farming Co.* (San Marino, Calif: The Huntington Library, 1958).

Nunis, Doyce B., Jr. "The Franciscan Friars of Mission San Fernando, 1797–1847." *San Fernando Rey de Espana 1797–1997: A Bicentennial Tribute. Southern California Quarterly* 79, no. 3 (1997): 217–48.

"New Life for Old Mission." *North Hollywood Valley Times*, July 15, 1941.

"Ownership of Mission Paintings." *Los Angeles Times*, February 2, 1969.

Parks, Marion. "In Pursuit of Vanished Days." *Southern California Quarterly* 14, no. 2 (1929): 193.

Perkins, Arthur B. "Rancho San Francisco: A Study of a California Land Grant." *Southern California Quarterly* 32, no. 2 (1957): 97–125.

"Photos Depict Restoration of Famed Mission." *Valley Times*, March 4, 1960.

Polley, Frank J. "Americans at the Battle of Cahuenga." *Southern California Quarterly* 13, no. 2 (1894): 47.

"Reclaim Mission from Ruins, San Fernando Being Restored." *Los Angeles Examiner*, March 11, 1917.

"Rededication of Fourth Church." *The Tidings*, November 4, 1974.

"Relics of Ancient Water System Stand Near Mission Wells." *Intake Magazine* 26, 5 (1949): 9, 18.

"Religious Pageantry Will Draw Thousands to Mission Sunday." *San Fernando Sun*, September 5, 1941.

"Reopening of Church." *San Fernando Sun*, September 25, 1941.

"Restoration of Mission Building Begins." *Los Angeles Times*, October 2, 1963.

"Restoration Work Begins." *Van Nuys News*, October 2, 1963.

Rust, Horatio. "Rogerio's Theological Seminary." *Out West* Magazine 21, no. 3 (1904): 243–48.

Sandos, James A. "Christianization Among the Chumash: An Ethnohistoric Approach." *American Indian Quarterly* 15 (1991): 65–89.

———. "Converting California: Indians and Franciscans in the Mission, 1769–1836." *Boletín: The Journal of the California Mission Studies Association* 20, no. 1 (2003): 5–10.

———. "Levantamiento!: The 1824 Chumash Uprising Reconsidered." *Southern California Quarterly* 67, no. 2 (summer 1985): 311–29.

"San Fernando to be 1842 Library Home." *Los Angeles Times*, May 26, 1968.

Servín, Manuel P. "The Secularization of the California Missions: A Reappraisal." *Southern California Quarterly*, 47, no. 2 (1965): 133–49.

"17th Century Chapel at Mission." *Los Angeles Times*, January 29, 1944.

"S. F. Mission Recovers from '71 Quake Scars." *San Fernando Sun*, January 17, 1973.

"Spanish Chapel at Mission." *San Fernando Sun*, February 25, 1944.

"300 at Valley Mission Fete." *Los Angeles Examiner*, April 14, 1952.

"Tours Rescheduled." *Van Nuys News*, August 1, 1973.

"Tower Restoration." *Los Angeles Herald Express*, January 20, 1945.

Trout, Narda. "Restoration Agreement." *Los Angeles Times*, September 17, 1972.

"The Valley in Progress." *San Fernando Sun*, October 16, 1966.

"The Valley's Yesterdays." *Los Angeles Times*, October 21, 1962.

Villegas, Isabelle. "San Fernando Mission, 1797–1825." Southwest Museum *Masterkey*, 20, no. 1 (1946).

Walker, Edwin F. "A Metate Site at San Fernando." In *Five Prehistoric Archeological Sites in Los Angeles County, California*, vol. 6 Los Angeles: Southwest Museum, 1951, 15–26.

Walsh, Marie T. "California's Saints for Whom the Missions Are Named." *Los Angeles Times*, 24 January 1932.

Weber, Francis J. "Appear to Lean—Adobe Sides Taper at San Fernando." *San Fernando Valley Times*, April 18, 1964.

———. "Breath of Olden Days." *San Fernando Valley Times*, April 13, 1964.

———. "Club Saves San Fernando Mission." *San Fernando Valley Times*, May 30, 1964.

———. "Historic Mission Bell: Mystery Shrouds Its Past." *San Fernando Valley Times*, May 9, 1964.

———. "Indian Customs, Vices Told." *San Fernando Valley Times*, March 28, 1964.

———. "The Mission Ranchos." In *Rancho Days in Southern California: An Anthology with New Perspectives*. Ed. Kenneth Pauley. Brand Book No. 20. Los Angeles: The Westerners—Los Angeles Corral, 1997: 44–61.

———. "Mission San Fernando Buildings Restored." *San Fernando Valley Times*, June 6, 1964.

———. "Mission San Fernando Secular Chaos." *San Fernando Valley Times*, June 13, 1964.

———. "Mission Stations Unique in Indian Art." *The Tidings*, April 8, 1966.

———. "Old Records Are Treasured *San Fernando Valley Times*, May 23, 1964.

———. "San Fernando—How Mission Grew from 1797–1822." *San Fernando Valley Times*, April 6, 1964.

———. "San Fernando Mission." *San Fernando Valley Times*, March 21 1964.

———. "Mission Convento is Outstanding Architecturally." *San Fernando Valley Times*, May 2, 1964.

———. "San Fernando Mission—How Friars Taught Indians." *San Fernando Valley Times*, May 2, 1964.

———. "San Fernando, Rey de Espana: Its Role in the New Millennium." *San Fernando Rey de Espana 1797–1997: A Bicentennial Tribute. Southern California Quarterly* 79, no. 3 (1997): 284–86.

———. "The Stations of the Cross at San Fernando Mission." In Southwest Museum *Masterkey* 19, no. 1 (1965).

———. "San Fernando, Rey de España: Its Role in the

New Millennium." *Southern California Quarterly* 79, no. 3 (1997): 383–404.

Whitley, David. "Intensive Phase I Archaeological Survey of the West Ranch Area, Newhall Ranch, Los Angeles County." Excerpt from Ethnographic Background. Archaeological Information Center. Fullerton, Calif: California State University, 1994.

Wood, Raymund. "Juan Crespí: Southern California's First Chronicler." In *Spanish California's Spanish Heritage*. Ed. Doyce B. Nunis, Jr. Los Angeles: HSSC, 1992, 33–75.

# INDEX